Spirits and Trance in Brazil

Bloomsbury Advances in Religious Studies

James Cox, Steven Sutcliffe and Will Sweetman

This ground-breaking series presents innovative research in theory and method in the study of religion, paying special attention to disciplinary formation in Religious Studies. Volumes published under its auspices demonstrate new approaches to the way religious traditions are presented and analysed. Each study will demonstrate its theoretical insights by applying them to particular empirical case studies in order to foster integration of data and theory in the historical and cultural study of 'religion'.

Appropriation of Native American Spirituality, Suzanne Owen

Becoming Buddhist, Glenys Eddy

Community and Worldview among Paraiyars of South India, Anderson H. M. Jeremiah

Conceptions of the Afterlife in Early Civilizations, Gregory Shushan

Contemporary Western Ethnography and the Definition of Religion, Martin D. Stringer

Cultural Blending in Korean Death Rites, Chang-Won Park

Globalization of Hesychasm and the Jesus Prayer, Christopher D. L. Johnson

Innateness of Myth, RitskeRensma

Levinas, Messianism and Parody, Terence Holden

New Paradigm of Spirituality and Religion, Mary Catherine Burgess

Post-Materialist Religion, Mika T. Lassander

Redefining Shamanisms, David Gordon Wilson

Reform, Identity and Narratives of Belonging, Arkotong Longkumer

Religion and the Discourse on Modernity, Paul-François Tremlett

Religion as a Conversation Starter, Ina Merdjanova and Patrice Brodeur

Religion, Material Culture and Archaeology, Julian Droogan

Spirit Possession and Trance, edited by Bettina E. Schmidt and Lucy Huskinson

Spiritual Tourism, Alex Norman

Theology and Religious Studies in Higher Education, edited by D. L. Bird and Simon G. Smith

The Problem with Interreligious Dialogue, Muthuraj Swamy

Religion and the Inculturation of Human Rights in Ghana, Abamfo Ofori Atiemo

UFOs, Conspiracy Theories and the New Age: Millennial Conspiracism, David G. Robertson

Spirits and Trance in Brazil

An anthropology of religious experience

Bettina E. Schmidt

University of Wales Trinity Saint David

Bloomsbury Academic
An imprint of Bloomsbury Publishing Plc

B L O O M S B U R Y
LONDON · OXFORD · NEW YORK · NEW DELHI · SYDNEY

Bloomsbury Academic

An imprint of Bloomsbury Publishing Plc

50 Bedford Square	1385 Broadway
London	New York
WC1B 3DPNY	10018
UK	USA

www.bloomsbury.com

BLOOMSBURY and the Diana logo are trademarks of Bloomsbury Publishing Plc

First published 2016

Bettina E. Schmidt, 2016

Bettina E. Schmidt has asserted her right under the Copyright, Designs and Patents Act, 1988, to be identified as Author of this work.

British Library Cataloguing-in-Publication Data

A catalogue record for this book is available from the British Library.

ISBN:HB : 978-1-4742-5567-7
ePDF : 978-1-4742-5568-4
ePub : 978-1-4742-5569-1

Library of Congress Cataloging-in-Publication Data

A catalog record for this book is available from the Library of Congress.

Series: Bloomsbury Advances in Religious Studies

Typeset by Newgen Knowledge Works (P) Ltd., Chennai, India.
Printed and bound in Great Britain

Dedicated to my sister Daniela

Contents

Illustrations

Acknowledgements

Research is always a collaborative work, in particular for an anthropologist. This book would have been impossible to write without the endless support of my Brazilian colleagues and friends. I am immensely grateful in particular to Professor Frank Usarski at the Pontifícia Universidade Católica de São Paulo and Professor Vagner Gonçalves da Silva at the Universidade de São Paulo.

The Department of Postgraduate Studies in Study of Religions at the Pontifícia Universidade Católica de São Paulo was my host during my sabbatical and offered me not only a place to work but also a home away from home. Several of their postgraduate students introduced me to their religious communities, which were often the subject of their own theses. They became invaluable gatekeepers for my research as they opened access to religious communities. Some of them even became friends.

I am also extremely grateful for the generosity of all who participated in my research, who answered patiently my questions and tolerated my accent, who allowed me to attend their ceremonies and explained to me what I observed, who spoke with me about beliefs and practices and all the other things that came up, and who welcomed me into their midst. Thank you for trusting me with your stories.

The Changing Face of Ecstatic Religions in Brazil

Introduction

Sometimes I feel as if my arms fall asleep, or my legs, and sometimes I even feel as if I'm having a heart attack. With each orixá [African deity] I have a different feeling. Sometimes it begins with dancing, quite violent, but I'm still conscious. Nevertheless, I can control myself, or stop dancing, and I intend to stop dancing and stand, but when I least expect it, I lose control again. In my first session, I wanted to stop dancing . . . But I could not stop and began dancing with the other leg.

(Interview on 14 April 2010 in São Paulo)

The sensation is the same, the sensation of having lost contact with the world. For example, every time I go into the state, it is as if I am leaning over a building of more than twenty floors, looking down. At any given time somebody might arrive and push me down. There is panic. It is always this way. As I am in a high place, very high, looking down, and then I turn round and see that somebody is coming in my direction and pushing me with their hands.

(Interview on 21 May 2010 in São Paulo)

I felt the voice leaving my body, but unlike other people who do not have consciousness, I found that only a fraction of me was not conscious . . . I felt that the person spoke in my head, I heard and spoke. At times I was afraid

of not speaking correctly, or that the person speaking was me. As it passed
I thought ah, was it only in my imagination? . . . But as time passed, I had
ideas that I never had before. And this was the biggest sensation. I felt an
embrace. I had no more doubts.

(Interview on 27 May 2010 in São Paulo)

These three excerpts from interviews I recorded in Brazil in 2010 recount private recollections of experiences usually classified under the label spirit possession. They illustrate the diversity of the memories people have of them and their different ways of making sense of them. Throughout the last decades, anthropologists have collected numerous accounts of indigenous explanations of spirit possession and its siblings trance and mediumship from all over the world, and many have argued for and against the validity of these perceptions. Though it is possible to describe the phenomenon and even to classify such experiences according to their function for the individual or the collective, it seems impossible to go beyond the indigenous understanding since it rests upon the recognition of the spirit world as real, whether it is regarded as desirable or an affliction in need of a cure. Edith Turner comments,

> Anthropologists have long been interested in what [practitioners] believe
> about spirits and the ritual events which surround spirit encounters. But
> it is the [practitioner] reports of experiences with spirits that are regarded
> as appropriate anthropological material, not the experiences themselves
> . . . Scholars of religion tend to explain accounts of spirit encounters in
> terms of metaphor. The issue of whether or not spirits actually exist has not
> been faced. (Turner 1994: 71)

For the person going through it, the experience confirms the existence of spirits and deities without any doubt (Crapanzano 2005: 8693). After the first shock of the initial experience is overcome, people learn to explain the experience in a specific conceptual framework which the individual understands and is familiar with. The Jungian psychotherapist José Jorge de Morais Zacharias, whom I interviewed about his involvement in Afro–Brazilian religions, explained this process as follows: 'If a person experiences something unusual and is not given an explanation [by his or her surroundings], it will cause anxiety and disorder, even mental instability. It is only when a culturally embedded explanation is delivered that the experience becomes meaningful and structured.'[1] However, as I discovered in Brazil, there are several different cultural explanations within one culture. My interviewees distinguish clearly between different experiences that, from an outside perspective, could all be classified under the label 'ecstatic religion', despite the fact that people often move between traditions and are familiar with more than one framework. As Michael Lambek rightly points out, the interpretation of spirit possession in its cultural context 'allows us to avoid the opposite fallacy . . . of seeing trance behaviour as purely instrumental strategy, a product of individual self-interest' (Lambek 1989: 37). Throughout this book I argue in favour of local accounts and include excerpts from narratives to highlight the importance of 'provincializing the experience'. Inspired by Lambek's article on provincializing God (2008), I argue for an understanding of spirit possession as *deictic* term, hence to provincialize the experience by embracing locally specific features. Deixis is a linguistic term that highlights the problem that the meaning of certain words depends on a given context. A typical example of deictic terms are the words 'here' or 'now' because the determination of their referents depends on the context in that sentence or situation. Lambek argues that the misreading of deictic terms has led to the transformation of these terms from context-dependent concepts into stable, objectified referents. The outcome is that religious practices have been misinterpreted. He insists that 'a deictic word is one that is open and inclusive, characterized by a both/ and rather than an either/or logic', and continues that 'attention to deixis implies putting practice ahead of belief' (Lambek 2008: 137). Following his lead I argue that the conceptualization of spirit possession as a deictic term allows me to disregard contradictory explanations and also the complex but dualistic interplay between scholars and experiencers. The outcome will be a holistic understanding of spirit possession bringing together sociological, anthropological, cognitive and emic interpretations of the experience without preferring one viewpoint over another.

My starting point has to be, therefore, the Brazilian context. In Brazil, 64.6 per cent of the population identified themselves as Roman Catholic in the national census of 2010, a drop from 73.6 per cent in 2000.[2] The figure is relatively similar to the figure of people identifying themselves as Christian in the United Kingdom (a drop from 72% in 2001 to 59.3% in 2011[3]), though the actual numbers are vastly different as the population of Brazil (estimated to be 192,376,496 in 2011) is more than three times the size of the UK population. The census data does not say anything about actual religious commitment or personal belief, but this self-identification is nonetheless interesting, in particular because in my interviews I came across a fine line between two different sets of practices: on one side the ecstatic experience, usually connected to Afro–Brazilian rituals or Spiritist practices, which was the focus of my research and which was described more in cognitive terms than in religious, and on the other side the personal commitment or non-commitment to a specific religion. Sometimes interviewees referred more to the mainstream society associated in Brazil with the national patron, Nossa SenhoraAparecida (Our Lady Who Appeared), a particular appearance of the Blessed Virgin Mary, instead of referring to the tradition to which the ecstatic rituals are connected. Nonetheless, the acknowledgement of extraordinary phenomena is quite widespread in Brazil and not seen as strange at all. It is even sometimes described as an essential characteristic of Brazilian religiosity (Droogers 1987).

Abby Day was baffled with a similar situation in the United Kingdom when she investigated the beliefs of the mainstream. She states that when asked about their religion, people often present a natal membership (I am Christian because I am baptized, because I am born into a Christian family, and so on, see Day 2011: 47–62, 182). This is also the case in Brazil, where professing to be a Christian (within any confessional specification) is still part of being Brazilian. This self-identification does not take into account any knowledge about the religious belief or a more or less regular religious practice. In this sense, Christianity, and particularly Roman Catholicism with its worship of the Virgin Mary and the saints, is regarded as one of the core aspects of Brazilian culture, even the 'cultural religion' of Brazilians. This religiosity is expressed in diverse ways, however, and Christian self-identification does not prevent people from believing and practising one of the popular traditions of Brazil. It might even seem that Afro–Brazilian rituals are not seen as religious. Like Day's research outcome, in which interviewees did not classify supernatural experiences as religious (Day 2011: 112), my interviewees in Brazil also distinguished between religion and everyday practice, between Christianity on one side and the veneration of *orixás* (African deities) and communication with the spirits of the dead on the other. Consequently, it is not only possible to practise two or more traditions at the same time but also it is not even seen as a paradox. As one colleague with life-long experience of doing research in Brazil once told me, if it were possible to tick more than one box under religious affiliation in the national census in Brazil, the data would be very different indeed.[4]

My interviewees make no secret of the fact that they 'move around' from community to community and practise different traditions, often at the same time. It is not unique for someone to celebrate Easter by attending a mass in the local church but also to participate at a celebration in a Yoruba temple led by a Nigerian immigrant. Or it is not unusual to be initiated into the cult of African deities and to practise Candomblé as well as Umbanda rituals. What is the religious framework in such a case? Christianity or the Yoruba tradition? Candomblé or Umbanda? And is it even regarded as a 'religious' framework? The confrontation with altered states of consciousness (ASC) – sometimes called supernatural beings – is not always classified as religious by the subjects experiencing it. Some people perceive communication with spirits, for instance, as a technique without a religious connotation.

In his work on religious experience, David Hay decided to ignore his interviewees' refusal to categorize their experience as religious and argues that 'it would be more correct to say that it is a type of experience which is commonly given a religious interpretation' (Hay 1982: 162–3). His insistence on continuing to use the word 'religious', obscures, as Day highlights (2011: 113), the significance of the beliefs of the individuals who reported these experiences. Labelling something creates an unequal power relationship between the scholar and the person experiencing it. Ann Taves (1999) even regards the interplay between experiencing religion and explaining experience as the central methodological problem in this field. She argues that 'each of these terms carries with it presuppositions and associations that may be at odds with, and thus distort, the experience of our historical subjects' (1999: 8). Many of the labels used by academics of different disciplines (and in different historical periods) to describe and categorize the means of communication between the human and the spiritual worlds are challenged by the actors themselves since they 'obscure the subjective experience of the native actor' (Taves 1999: 9). Though her book still uses 'religious experience' in the title, she refers to the experiences most of the time as involuntary acts that include uncontrolled bodily movements, spontaneous vocalizations, unusual sensory experiences and alterations of consciousness and/or memory (1999: 3). She wants to take the religious connotation out of the equation by moving away 'from single terms to more extended descriptive statements that identify common features' and are acceptable across disciplines and by the subjects themselves (1999: 8). However, she remains 'within the already conventionally-established contours of religious studies' (Fitzgerald 2010: 297) and does not apply her concept to other experiences. Day goes further than Taves in her critique. Because her interviewees did not describe their experiences in religious terms, Day promotes an understanding of religion and the supernatural as 'subsets of a wider set of belief understood as belonging' (2011: 114). She proposes 'to dispense with binary, subsidiary categories of belief, such as "religious" or "secular", and focus instead on multidimensional, interdependent orientations' (2011: 202). Though her project focused on 'what people believed and how they discussed those beliefs' (2011: 36), she decided from the beginning to avoid asking religious questions but instead to focus on belief in a general way. Day regards belief primarily as a 'statement of self, a way of saying who they are' (2011: 43). Hence it is purely relationally produced. I follow Taves's and to a certain degree also Day's approach by avoiding single terms. I rely instead on informal narratives[5] of different experiences in order to do justice to the diversity of religious experiences. The aim is to identify in a multidimensional approach the common features with which my interviewees identify their experiences. The outcome will hopefully be a set of features that are acceptable to the interviewees as well as to other readers of my book.

In order to highlight the role of the medium (the possessed agent), some practitioners use the term 'mediumship' (*mediunidade* in Portuguese). It acknowledges that the medium is, to a certain degree, still in control and remains conscious, though being 'used' by the spirit as a medium of communication between the spiritual and the human worlds. Not only Kardecists or Spiritists use this term but also practitioners of some Afro–Brazilian traditions, such as Umbanda. Spiritists distinguish between different types of mediumship activities or abilities (e.g. hearing, seeing or feeling a spirit, automatic writing). Umbandistas usually describe the experience, visible, for instance, in the photo of two spirits incorporating Umbanda mediums (see Figure 1.1) as a kind of

Figure 1.1 Meeting of two Umbanda mediums, São Paulo

incorporation during which they maintain some form of consciousness. Hence, despite using the same term, the interpretation varies depending on the context. Sometimes interviewees also used the term 'trance' (*transe* in Portuguese) to explain their experience, though most preferred the term mediumship.

Some Brazilian scholars use mediumship as an umbrella term for the different cultural explanations of these kinds of experience. Brigida Malandrino, for instance, incorporates the main Brazilian folk traditions Umbanda, Brazilian Kardecism and Candomblé into her *continuum mediúnico* (medium continuum), despite their differences (Malandrino 2006: 92, 102). It has also become customary to categorize these traditions under the term *espiritismo*. Statements that both Brazilian *espíritas* and *evangélicas* see religion as an instrument to cope with abnormal experiences (Machado 2009: 246) are therefore somewhat unclear because they can refer to Kardecism (also called Spiritism) or to the range of religions in the 'medium continuum'. Umbanda and Candomblé offer similar functions. However, the term 'medium continuum' contains an implicit preference for one of the indigenous interpretations discussed in Brazil. Though mediumship is also used by other scholars in a broader sense,[6] it might provoke a bias towards one kind over the others if applied to all kinds of experience. The focus of medium continuum that is derived from one specific tradition is on the experiencing subject alone, but ignores the possessing agency (see Keller 2002). Another tradition, however, centres on the role of the *orixás* as the possessing agency and explains the experience more as a merger of two entities, the possessing agency and the possessed, into a new one (see Goldman 1985). As I elaborate below, this explanation differs fundamentally from the mediumship concept; hence, it should not be situated under such a label. However, when referring to the host, the 'instrumental agency' in Keller's terminology, I follow Donovan and use 'medium' for 'a person who permits a spirit to assume control of her/his body and mind for the purpose of communicating with others' (Donovan 2000: 361).

The reason Malandrino and others use terms such as mediumship is that the term 'spirit possession' has become quite contested in Brazil, not only because the term 'spirit' does not do justice to the supernatural entities of all traditions but also because the term 'possession' (*possessão* in Portuguese) has gained a negative connotation in Brazil and people want to avoid being identified with it. There is a fine line in the Brazilian discourse between the God of Christianity and the other Abrahamic religions, the deities of the African traditions and the spirits of the ancestors. God is regarded as the Almighty, omnipotent creator of all. The concept of a creator god is incorporated into the vernacular traditions, though it is unclear whether it is a Christian influence or an original African concept. However, the origin is not important, only the conceptual difference made between the creator god and the other deities in most Afro–Brazilian traditions. The deities also have omnipotent powers, but these powers are perceived as having been derived from the creator God. The deities are sometimes compared to forces of nature, while in other interpretations the focus is on their human-like characters, hence on the individuality of each of them. The spirits also have supernatural powers and influence the human fate. But they are not omnipotent. A common feature of spirits is that they are derived from living beings. With time, spirits can become regarded as an abstract category, though in most cases spirits are seen as individuals. These conceptual differences between god, deities and spirits clearly highlight that the term spirit possession does not cover the wide range of possessing agencies in Brazil. Nonetheless, the reason for the rejection goes further.

In the public perception the term possession has a negative connotation and is firmly connected to Afro–Brazilian traditions. In this way the rejection of the term goes hand in hand with the discriminative attitude against Afro–Brazilian religions in general. However, this attitude has increased in the last decades due to increasing attacks by the neo-Pentecostal churches against Afro–Brazilian traditions (see Schmidt 2014a). As I discuss below, the confrontation focuses on all spiritual agencies, which are regarded as inferior and the cause of mental, physical and spiritual problems. Although the gods of ancient Greece, Rome, Egypt, Mesopotamia and other religions are all regarded as demons, the main attacks are directed against Afro–Brazilian religions. The (indirect) outcome of the hostility is that the possession, already linked in the public perception to the African deities, is now firmly regarded by the wider public as a demonic practice. As have other Brazilian scholars, I have switched therefore to the term 'incorporation' (*incorporação* in Portuguese) when referring to the practice commonly portrayed as spirit possession. However, as I outline below, the term incorporation describes the local interpretation of the Candomblé practice only partly. The *orixás* are perceived as forces of nature that are too powerful to be incorporated in a human body. It thus is quite common to describe the event as a 'merger' of two entities, the human one with the supernatural one.

Another type of experience with the supernatural phenomena is set in a very different context – and referred to under another label. Though in the literature it is often described as possession (e.g. Alexander 1989; Almeida 2003; Bourguignon 2004; Birman 1996; Donovan 2000), people experiencing it insist on a harsh borderline between their experience and the other experiences. I refer here to the baptism in the Holy Ghost and connected phenomena within a Christian – in particular charismatic Christian – context. People in Brazil often describe what happens when the Holy Spirit descends on someone as *inspiracão* (inspiration) or *visãodivina* (divine vision). Though all these experiences can be seen as altered states of consciousness and have similar physical features such as involuntary fits, Christians firmly reject claims to any similarity with these kinds of experiences. Despite using similar terminology when describing the feeling of spiritual baptism, the Holy Ghost is perceived in a very different way, and people experiencing it insist on categorizing the experience in a fundamentally different way within the Christian context. The spiritual baptism gives them experiential access to the divine, which they perceive as morally superior to the divine of every other belief system. Consequently, they use possession or more precisely spirit possession only to describe what happens when an inferior spirit takes over the body of a person. These terms describe an experience that is regarded as inferior and has to be reversed – exorcized, to be precise – with help of the Holy Spirit.

We see here that people explain their individual experiences in quite distinct conceptual frames and with a wide range of terms, from 'mediumship' and 'trance' to 'incorporation' and 'divine vision'. This diversity makes categorizing the experiences under one label a sheer impossibility, whether it is ASC (e.g. Crapanzano 2005) or ecstatic religions (e.g. Lewis 1971). And even the label 'religious experience' is contested, at least in its narrow definition, because not all experiences I describe are identified clearly as 'religious' by the interviewees and others due to a lack of sacred texts, large buildings and hierarchical institutions. Even active members of those communities often see themselves as Christians or as Roman Catholics or even as agnostics, though they 'serve the spirits' (to hijack a term used among Vodou[7] practitioners to describe their practice) or 'communicate with the dead' on a daily basis. A glimpse at the short sample of recollections at the beginning of the book shows that only one of the samples contains a reference to a spiritual entity.

But what exactly is 'religious experience'? Both words – 'religious' and 'experience' – are difficult to define, let alone in combination. One of the challenges is that people describing these kinds of experiences often claim to be atheistic or even agnostic and not religious at all. The use of the term 'religious experience' is rooted in Western ideology, in particular in Protestant Christianity (Sharpe 2003), which distinguishes sharply between 'religious' experience and other forms of experience. The outcome is that all but a small sample of experiences are excluded from this category. At the core of the problem is the controversy about 'religion' and its presumed connection to 'belief', which is also derived from a Protestant context (see Asad 1993). Though this link has been successfully challenged (see, e.g. de Vries 2008), it still lurks in the background of any discussion. The meaning of the term religious experience depends often more on the scholar than on the subject of the experience (Proudfoot 1985). One can even trace the term spirit possession and its history back to the development of the Western category 'Religion', as Paul Christopher Johnson argues.[8]

Johnson traces the career of the term possession back to early classical and Christian discourses of demonology as well as to accounts of possession rituals among tribal people. Johnson locates spirit possession as 'a root metaphor of the Enlightenment category, Religion' and argues that, with the development of the category Religion, rituals that were denounced as 'savage', in particular possession rituals, were 'used by Protestants as a foil to rail against "popish" ceremony' (2011: 397). As a result spirit possession and other ecstatic experiences became the antithesis to the idea of civil religion in the West. By the seventeenth century, spirit possession had become a 'generic comparative class' which 'served simultaneously as a medicalization of demonology in Europe, and a demonization of ritual practices in Africa and the Americas that were previously morally neutral' (Johnson 2011: 401). Spirit possession developed, as Johnson argues, into chronotypes of savage or early humankind.[9] He writes that

> [v]ia the labour of the negative, 'spirit possession' defined the rational, autonomous, self-possessed individual imagined as the foundation of the modern state, in canonical texts from Hobbes, Jean Bodin, Locke, Charles de Brosses, Hume, Kant, and many others, as those texts constructed the free individual and citizen against a backdrop of colonial horizons and slavery. (Johnson 2011: 398)

It was therefore just a logical consequence that, when the 1891 Brazilian constitution issued the freedom of religion, Afro–Brazilian traditions with possession rituals as their core practice were excluded; instead, they were put under the Penal Code of 1890, which regulated these practices in the name of 'public health', as Johnson explains.

While in the anthropological literature on spirit possession in the last few decades the term spirit possession has usually been applied to rituals 'in which one, or a few, or even several, of the participants in a public ritual behave in ways which believers interpret as signifying that "spirits" haven taken "possession" of them' (Platvoet 2000: 80), one should not overlook the career of the term that Johnson outlines so well. One might even argue that it is too naive to regard the term spirit possession as a purely emic term which contains 'a meaning which believers themselves attached to what they believe happens during a spirit possession ritual' (Platvoet 2000: 81) because of its long and complex trajectory in the Western ideology. Like many other academic categories, spirit possession has been constructed as a denominator of human behaviour perceived as 'savage', and consequently people experiencing it were perceived as 'inferior', whether it was a specific group of people like women or homosexual men or a whole tribe. Spirit possession was never a term used by practitioners themselves, but applied by outsiders. Nonetheless, its continuing presence in the debate is certain, as Johnson also confirms. And in this sense, Platvoet's main point that we should remain agnostic and avoid any prejudgement when dealing with spirit possession has to be the starting point of anyone whose work concerns this phenomenon.

But where does this conceptual frame lead us in defining spirit possession? Janice Boddy describes spirit possession as a 'hold exerted over a human being by external force or entities more powerful than she' (Boddy 1994: 407); hence, she defines spirit possession as 'an integration of spirit and matter, force or power and corporeal reality'. This definition places the experience in the religious spectrum as it is based on a theological presumption – that is, the existence of external forces more powerful than humans. Mary Keller challenges definitions based on such a presumption and refers to Ann Grodzins Gold's definition of spirit possession as 'any complete but temporary domination of a person's body, and the blotting of that person's consciousness, by a distinct alien power or known or unknown origin' (Keller 2002: 3–4, with reference to Gold 1988: 35). Hence, instead of using a phrase such as 'entities more powerful than humans', Keller refers to 'alien power', which is not really so different. And in the end Keller, too, locates spirit possession, together with trance and mysticism, firmly in a spectrum of religious experience. In Taves's terminology, spirit possession can be defined as uncontrolled bodily movements and alterations of consciousness, lack of memory, unusual sensory experiences and so on, hence 'involuntary acts', according to Taves. If we read it out of the wider context of her argumentation, her definition seems to imply that the body responds passively to an external stimulus, while the agency of this stimulus remains invisible. To a certain degree it echoes an understanding of agency based on free will and even points to Johnson's trajectory of the category spirit possession within Western history: While 'voluntary and willed actions are the norm, . . . involuntary and unwilled actions are abnormal' (Engler 2009a: 471, referring to Strawson 1976). People experiencing spirit possession are seen as 'not fully the agents of their actions' and consequently not fully responsible for their actions because of their altered states of consciousness.[10] However, new research sheds a different light on the possessed body and its relationship to the mind, as I explain throughout this book. As will become clear below, I want to shift the discussion about spirit possession from 'belief' to 'practice', embedded in the cultural context. By treating spirit possession as a deictic term that is open and inclusive (Lambek 2008), I put the emphasis on what people do, without distinguishing between whether they regard it as divine or demonic experience, as religious or secular.

***

The book consists of five chapters. Following this introduction, I explain my research methodology and the research context. In the second chapter, I examine the social setting of the experience. One focus is on the gender division among the participants. I discuss the common perception that more women than men have experiences with involuntary acts in Brazil. I show why this preconception is being challenged as a result of social changes in Brazil. In addition I look at class and race and discuss how these factors affect the composition of the communities.

The third chapter concentrates on the debate about religious experience. I discuss the local interpretations of the experiences within the academic discourse. Referring extensively to data from my interviews, I show how the academic debate can illuminate some of the informal narratives I collected but also how academic categorizations can overshadow the complexity of the local interpretations. In addition to the experience in the Afro–Brazilian religions and Spiritism, I also consider how the phenomenon is discussed within the neo-Pentecostal churches where the same spiritual entities are exorcized.

In the fourth chapter, I move to the debate about body and mind, a relatively new but already very lively field. The focus is on new approaches about agency and embodiment, but I also reflect on the cognitive approach debate, which is put into the context of my interview data and other material from Brazil. In the fifth chapter, the conclusion, I elaborate further how the categorization of spirit possession as deictic term can further our understanding of the practice. In the end, I hope that my assessment of the experience in Brazil can shed light on the diversity of experiences that we tend to categorize as spirit possession.

A last preliminary comment: I have been as accurate as possible in translating the information from the interviewees into academic English, but I have also attempted to make the excerpts easier to read.

Research context and methodology

This study is based on material I gathered during a period of research leave that I spent in 2010 in Brazil, mainly in São Paulo. In the literature one can find references to a prominence of spirit possession in Brazil (e.g. Engler 2009b), which attracted my interest. I chose São Paulo for my research not only because it is the largest city in Brazil but also because it is home to various Afro–Brazilian religions that were originally established in different places in Brazil. Lísias Nogueira Negrão states that 14,000 Umbanda houses; 2,500 Spiritist centres; and 1,400 Candomblé terreiros are registered in São Paulo (1996: 17), though it is difficult to estimate the actual number of communities. Due to internal migration, these traditions found a home in the city of São Paulo and therefore made access to them relatively easy. A similar diversity is present also in Rio de Janeiro and other Brazilian cities, but serendipity brought me to São Paulo.

The research atmosphere I experienced in Brazil was different from that of my former studies in the Caribbean and New York where it took time to find access to vernacular religious communities. Fátima Regina Machado, for instance, writes that it is quite normal in Brazil to speak openly about so-called abnormal[11] phenomena. Though her relatively small-scale study is not representative of Brazilian society (it is based on 306 questionnaires returned to her in São Paulo), it nonetheless presents interesting indicators about the extent of the phenomena among Brazilians: 82.7 per cent of the questionnaires mentioned experiences with extrasensual and 55.9 per cent with extramotoric phenomena (Machado 2009: 232). Among students the number is even higher as a prestudy found out: 89.5 per cent of the students responding to her questionnaire indicated paranormal (psi)experiences. This number is nearly double of a similar study in the United States, where only 55 per cent of students confessed to having had any kind of psi experience (Machado 2009: 18, referring to Zangari/Machado 1996).[12] Though this study is also not representative of all Brazilian students, it confirms Engler's observation that the belief in spirit possession is widely held in Brazil (2009a: 484), and also supports my own experience of a relatively unproblematic access to people willing to tell me their stories about extraordinary experiences. Whenever I began an empirical study before Brazil, I found that people shy away from telling an outsider, in particular a foreigner, about supernatural experiences with the spirits of the deceased or deities. But I found it much easier to establish first contact in São Paulo. However, members of the priesthood were quite reluctant to commit to interviews (or perhaps too busy to respond to phone calls and e-mails), though in the end I was able to speak with people from various different traditions about their experiences.

When I left Brazil, I had attended ceremonies at various Afro–Brazilian religious communities, Spiritist centres and Pentecostal churches and had interviewed several priests and priestesses as well as other members of their communities and discussed their religious experiences of the supernatural with them. Though some parts of the ritual remained secret, I was able to attend part of the initiation ritual into Candomblé, probably the most highly regarded Afro–Brazilian religion. Even when I visited evangelical church services, I usually encountered someone speaking openly about experiences with the divine. These conversations constitute one important feature of my research method. These informal exchanges that sometimes developed into informal interviews provided me with background information about the community and its practices, as well as giving a first glance into the local interpretation of the experience, which allowed me to constantly revisit my research framework. All interviews are openended in order to allow the interviewee to direct the interview in the direction of choice. I designed some questions to prompt people to speak openly about their extraordinary experiences as well as their understanding of them. Nonetheless, I had to improvise often, and in one instance it took me nearly half of the interview time to find out how the interviewee identified his practice (he firmly rejected the word possession and most of the other terms commonly used to describe the experience in Brazilian Portuguese). However, I learnt much from this interview and it helped me adjust my research questions. I encouraged the interviewees to tell me stories about how they became involved, whether their families were involved, how they felt during the incidents, and so on as. As Day writes (2011: 43), allowing people to recount stories and then deconstructing these stories as holistic, organic belief narratives enables the interviewees to become co-agents, constructors of knowledge. They are not only informing the interviewer but also becoming collaborators.

By speaking with individuals from different communities and traditions, I was able to learn the differences between the local discourses though, in the end, my overview of the local interpretations will never be allen-compassing. Most of my interviews were conducted in São Paulo, with only a few exceptions; hence, I did not capture all forms of experience in Brazil – not even all forms present in São Paulo. I have excluded, for instance, any experiences induced by hallucinogenic drugs such as ayahuasca; therefore, I do not discuss Santo Daime (see Dawson 2007 for more information) or other newly formed communities despite their growing popularity, in particular among urbanized youth. Nonetheless, despite the randomness of the selection of the traditions, the data reflects the intensity of the discourse about possession, incorporation and trance.

In addition to the interviews and other communications, I also collected information via participant observation of ceremonies where these experiences regularly occur. Usually I tried to observe the ceremonies of the interviewees' communities, or at least those ceremonies interviewees attended. I also, therefore, include my own observations and experiences of attending ceremonies where appropriate. However, I did not follow the path that many anthropologists working on African American religions have taken. That is, I did not attempt to experience it myself. Although I was often told that it is impossible to describe it fully, and that I need to experience it, I decided to maintain my scholarly distance and remain a participant observer instead of an observing participant. Since it is very common for anthropologists studying Afro–Brazilian religions to 'become native' and initiate into a religious community (e.g. Sjørslev 1999; for a discussion, see Capone 2010), my decision puts me in opposition to many colleagues. Despite my fascination with African American deities, which emerged during my research into Afro–Caribbean religions (Schmidt 2008) and increased in São Paulo, I could not overcome my reluctance to commit myself to the many obligations. In a way my approach follows a typical anthropological method explained here by Mark Münzel:

> While I cannot accept explanation given by millions of Brazilian believers that the divinity Xango is really present, I do not want to denigrate their experience either by reducing it to psycho-social or other factors in arrogant presumptuousness. I prefer to say that I do not understand what is going on. But I am searching for a level at which I can share some common feeling with these Brazilian believers: one small area would be the admiration for the great spectacle. (Münzel 1994: 143)

Admiration and fascination do not imply that I share with the participants their underlying feeling of the *numinous* (Otto).

My decision to maintain distance might have been influenced by the perception of the Afro–Brazilian traditions as 'religious'. However, as I indicated above, not all traditions have a religious connotation for the practitioners and not everyone who attends ceremonies – or even experiences extraordinary phenomena – refers to such things as religious. This attitude is reflected in the data of the national census. Though statistical data on such a large scale as the national census says little about personal belonging, it can give certain indicators despite the fact that the declaration of religious affiliation is a self-declaration. The figures of the 2010 census with regard to religious affiliation confirm that the majority still claim to belong to a Christian church. However, the figure is smaller as the number of self-declared atheists is growing (up to 15 million, 8.0% of the population, in 2010, from 7.3% in 2000). Another interesting development is the drop in the number of Roman Catholics (to 64.6% in 2010 from 73.77% in 2000) and the rise in the number of so-called *Evangélicas* (to 22.2% in 2010 from 15.44% in 2000). In this group, 60.0 per cent self-identified as *Evangélicas de origem Pentecostal*, 18.5 per cent as *Evangélicas de missão* (e.g. Lutherans, Presbyterians, Baptists) and 21.8 per cent were non-classified (*Evangélicas não determinada*).[13]

But these figures only represent the official side of the religious composition and overshadow the vibrant existence of popular religions. In addition to their official religious affiliation, Brazilians attend ceremonies of Afro–Brazilian religious communities and Spiritist centres, while identifying themselves as Christian. The discrepancy between practice and self-identification is only a paradox from a non-Brazilian perspective. It is not a problem at all for Brazilians. Andrew Chesnut states that half of all Brazilians have visited an Umbanda centre at least once, though most of them only sporadically, particularly during a personal crisis. The number of Brazilians practising an Afro–Brazilian religion is much smaller, although Chesnut still estimates that 15–20 per cent of Brazilians (approximately 30 million) practise Umbanda or one of the other Afro–Brazilian religions (Chesnut 2003: 106–7). Chesnut calculates that the number of people practising an Afro–Brazilian religion is even as high as the number of Protestant Brazilians, and explains that the very different figure in the national census is the result of the enduring stigma attached to African-derived religions. Christian self-identification remains a strong denominator for national identity that outshines the popular religions, which are often regarded as part of the personal spirituality of an individual, but not as the foundation for religious self-identification. In this sense, Christianity, and particularly Roman Catholicism, with its worship of the Virgin Mary and the saints, is regarded as one of the core aspects of Brazilian culture, the 'cultural religion' of Brazilians.[14] Brazilian religiosity is expressed in diverse ways, however, and Christian self-identification does not prevent people from believing and practising one of the popular religious traditions of Brazil, even though it often seems that Afro–Brazilian traditions do not 'count' as religions. However, when it comes to the census, people still prefer to identify with Christianity instead of one of the popular traditions. Thus, despite a huge campaign by the Afro–Brazilian priesthood to encourage openly confessing one's belief in the tradition one practises (one of the activists in this campaign, the Candomblé priest Francisco de Osun, supports the dialogue with the Roman Catholic Church as his participation in a special mass shows, see Figure 1.2), the 2010 figure for people self-identifying with an Afro–Brazilian religion remained on the same insignificant level of 0.3 per cent in 2010.

Chesnut, however, argues that Afro–Brazilian religions can successfully compete with the charismatic movement within the Roman Catholic Church and even with the Pentecostal churches (2003: 102). He describes a period of growth for Afro–Brazilian religions during the second half of the twentieth

Figure 1.2 Catholic mass for the Black Mother with a Candomblé Priest, São Paulo

century and presents as evidence various figures of registered Umbanda and Candomblé houses. However, he also acknowledges the enormous pressure that the Afro–Brazilian religions have faced since the 1980s when the struggle of the Pentecostal churches against them took a crusading turn. Despite the growing pressure, the number of people identifying with one of the Afro–Brazilian traditions remained stable (571,329 in 2000 and 588,797 in 2010), although the number of people identifying with Spiritism increased (from 1.3% in 2000 to 2.0% in 2010, an increase of over a million people, from 1.4 million in 2000 to 2.5 million in 2010).[15] Maladrino argues that Spiritism could have been used as an umbrella category for all kinds of Afro–Brazilian traditions in order to prevent the negative perception of 'black magic' that is still connected to Afro–Brazilian religions (Malandrino 2006: 39–40). Nonetheless, when we sum up the figures for people practising Spiritism and an Afro–Brazilian religion, less than 3 per cent of Brazilians openly acknowledge their commitment to an Afro–Brazilian or Spiritist tradition. However, core aspects of the Afro–Brazilian religions, such as the legends about the *orixás* and even some artefacts, are now elevated as part of the national heritage (Sansi 2007: 2) and portrayed in countless novels, poems, songs, movies and other artistic forms. Prandi even describes the *orixás* poetically as the core of the Brazilian soul (2005: 13–14).

Although the inclusion of the *orixás* in the cultural heritage of Brazil does not suddenly transform Brazilians into devotees of Afro–Brazilian religions, it nevertheless indicates that belief in the power of the *orixás* is widespread. An important aspect of this development is that the Afro–Brazilian religions have long surpassed the Afro–Brazilian population. Chesnut states that until the 1960s the Afro–Brazilian religions, in particular Candomblé, were essentially ethnic religions of Afro–Brazilians (though not exclusively, as we can find early descriptions of white Brazilians attending ceremonies in Candomblé houses, see Sansi 2007: 1). Already in the 1960s the number of white Brazilians participating in Afro–Brazilian rituals had increased, and since then a significant number of people with non-African ethnicity have joined these religions (Chesnut 2003: 110). Even Candomblé, often described as the most African of the Afro–Brazilian religions, has many devotees of non-African ethnicity. Although it is still labelled Afro–Brazilian, because the core of the tradition is a belief in African deities, the communities today are multi-ethnic and multiracial in their composition, from lay members to the priesthood. They reflect therefore the general population of Brazil today. Most Brazilians regard themselves as white, although according to the preliminary results of the 2010 national census, the percentage is declining (from 53.74% in 2000 to 47.73 in 2010). The 2010 data reveals an increase in the number of Brazilians identifying themselves as mulatto (from 38.45% to 43.13%) and black (from 6.21% to 14.5%). Even the number of people identifying themselves as indigenous in the census has grown slightly, from 734,000 in 2000 to 817,900 in 2010.[16] However, ethnic minorities in Brazil 'have been affected by a general tendency of the society to amalgamate and assimilate all ethnic minorities'. The author continues: 'the cultural contributions of these groups have been fused into the national culture, and are recognized as an integral part of the latter' (Camara 1997: 55). Although Camara explicitly uses the term 'ethnic minorities' for the African and Amerindian populations, he is mainly concerned with the African and neglects the Amerindian population, despite acknowledging that Amerindian culture had an impact on religious and secular life in the northern regions of Brazil (1997: 130). This attitude is fairly typical throughout Brazilian society, where the continuous presence of Amerindians is generally overlooked. This is also the case within the Afro–Brazilian traditions that increasingly purify their beliefs and practices from any indigenous (in the sense of being 'Native American') influence (see Schmidt 2013a). Nonetheless, the Afro–Brazilian traditions have also embraced indigenous elements very successfully in the last centuries as well as increasingly welcoming Brazilians from various different ethnic and racial backgrounds.

Though the perception that Candomblé is the purest of all African traditions in Brazil continues to exist (see Capone 2010), it is no longer uncontested by other traditions or even verified by the composition of the congregations, at least not in São Paulo. On the other side of the spectrum one can no longer declare Spiritism and not even its more 'intellectual' variation, Kardecism, as the spiritual alternative for predominately white and middle-class Brazilians who want to avoid the prejudice against Afro–Brazilian traditions. The communities I visited were as ethnically and racially diverse as some of the Afro–Brazilian communities. On the whole I noticed a wide interest – among middle-class Brazilians in São Paulo of all ethnic and racial categories – in experimenting with different traditions in order to find a solution for a problem or help in a difficult situation. Lifelong commitment is rare despite the attempt of the leadership to encourage people who attend ceremonies and other events to make steps towards full initiation or towards developing their mediumship abilities. This constant movement in and out of the communities affects not only the composition of the congregations but also the content of their beliefs and practices. It is therefore very difficult to present a conclusive overview of all traditions I visited. The following portrayal gives only a synopsis of them. The aim is to illuminate the research environment without singling out specific communities, though in later chapters I make reference to certain communities in order to highlight aspects of the interviews.

The primary research field of Candomblé, Umbanda and Spiritism

Candomblé

The term 'Candomblé' emerged early in the nineteenth century in Bahia, the colonial capital of Brazil and a major slave trading port. Originally it was used to describe parties of slaves and freed slaves that were usually connected to drum music (Sansi 2007: 1). Sansi highlights that from the beginning Candomblé was used by people of all social groups and races. He quotes a newspaper article from 1868 saying that 'these absurd Candomblés are so rooted, that I do no longer admire seeing Black people involved, when White people are the more passionate devotees of the cause'.[17] Nonetheless, the origin of Candomblé is firmly connected to Africa; it was founded in the customs of enslaved people from West and Central Africa. In the beginning, the 'African cult' was practised in a relatively unorganized way, but in the eighteenth century an urbanized form of the 'African cult' began to be established. During the nineteenth century the first Candomblé houses were founded (Silva 2005: 43).[18] From the beginning, Candomblé was mainly an urban phenomenon where Afro–Brazilians of Yoruba descent (so-called Nagôs) were disproportionately represented. Some scholars use the plural form Candomblés to honour the many local variations. However, during the 1930s one version, the Bahian Candomblé with its emphasis on the Nagô nation, became hegemonic for the tradition.[19] However, this dominance of the Nagô branch has nothing to do, as early scholars declared, with the assumed superiority of the Yoruba (e.g. Nina Rodrigues) but rather with their overwhelming presence in the urban centres of Bahia (see Matory 1999).

Because of its hegemonic position, it became common to use the Yoruba name *orixás* (orishas) for African deities, though some traditions still call them other names in ritual contexts (e.g. *voduns* in the Jêje tradition or *nkisis* in the Congo tradition). Candomblé based on Jêje is regarded as being derived from the Ewe-Fon, while Candomblé Congo (also called Candomblé Angola) is connected to the so-called Bantu tradition. The division of Candomblé into specific *nações* (nations) represents the underlying structure of Candomblé, which Luis Nicolau Parés characterizes as 'meta-ethnic' with various 'subnations' (Parés 2006: 366). These nations are 'collectives that reflect the social reconstruction of identity from the epoch of slavery' (Johnson 2002: 190, n.7), and not essentialist categories, as some scholars argue. Johnson regards the nations as liturgical traditions but not African regions. He argues that the division reflects 'a reconstructed ethnicity and liturgical pattern, it is a social identity into which anyone may be initiated through the terreiros' (2002: 190, n.7). In some cases the proclaimed ethnic origin might even be completely fictive, for instance, the Xamba nation in Recife (Johnson 2002: 190, n.7, with reference to Motta 1998: 53.).

In addition to Candomblé, there are other African-derived traditions in Brazil that are recognized with other names despite sharing many similarities with Candomblé. These religions are often classified under the label *culto afro* or *matrix africana*. A crucial distinction is the location of their origin. The creation of Candomblé, for instance, is firmly connected to Bahia do Salvador. Xangô, named after the Yoruba deity with the same name, resembles Candomblé Nagô but was established in Recife. Tambor de Mina, which has a strong influence from Dahomey and consequently many similarities with the Haitian religion Vodou, was established in the state of Maranhão. Another Maranhão tradition is Terecô, which is quite similar to Tambor de Mina – it is sometimes even confused with it, even though it includes some elements that are missing in Tambor de Mina. Another group of Afro–Brazilian traditions that were established in the Rio Grande do Sul area and the Amazonia are summarized under the label Batuque. However, this list is not complete as there are some local names used only in specific areas and also originally pejorative labels (e.g. Macumba in Rio de Janeiro) later taken on by the adherents (see Harding 2005 for an overview).

Due to the strong link to a specific region in Brazil, Reginaldo Prandi categorizes the different forms of Candomblé and the other Afro–Brazilian religions as ethnic religions (2005: 13–14). It comes as no surprise that each developed in an area of Brazil with a strong historical link to slavery (e.g. slave markets or large sugar plantations). However, the label 'ethnic religion' does not imply that members of each variation are from one ethnic group. Prandi's category stresses the strong connection between one tradition and the locality (Bahia, Maranhão, Recife and so on), and hence regards people of one area as 'ethnic', disregarding their diverse ethnicity and even race. Nowadays, however, this categorization can no longer be applied due to the internal migration of all traditions throughout Brazil and beyond and the increasing diversification of the communities.

After the final abolition of slavery in 1888, the constitution of the new republic, in 1889, declared freedom of religion and abolished Roman Catholicism as the official religion of Brazil. However, Afro–Brazilian religions were still persecuted throughout the twentieth century, and Catholicism remained the 'almost official' religion (Mariano 2001: 145, quoted in Oro 2006a: 9), despite the constitutional separation of church and state. Only in 1965 did it become possible to legalize Afro–Brazilian places of worship by the civil registration of the *terreiro* (physical location of the community where ceremonies take place). This also enabled communities to apply for tax-exempt status as non-profit, charitable institutions (Brown 1986: 3). In particular animal sacrifice, which is an important obligation in all Afro–Brazilian religions and a crucial part of many rituals, was the target of legal persecution – and is still the target of campaigns against Afro–Brazilian religions (see Schmidt 2013b), despite all the efforts of some outstanding priests and priestesses of Afro–Brazilian religions to increase the visibility and acceptance of their religions. However, these are often only singular events that do not carry a nationwide impact. Prandi blames the lack of nationwide institutionalization for the negative growth of Afro–Brazilian religions in the twenty-first century (Prandi 2005: 223–32, quoted in Malandrino 2006: 40).

However, due to the growing internal migration within Brazil, the local religions have begun to migrate as well – a phenomenon which was further supported by the legalization of the Afro–Brazilian rituals throughout Brazil. Consequently, one can find different forms of Candomblé in every large city of Brazil, including São Paulo. This process increases competition for membership between different houses and for authority between different priests and priestesses. While earlier the degree of connection of one's *terreiro* and its priesthood to the oldest *terreiros* in Bahia was regarded as the most respected way of expressing seniority, today it is important to show that one's tradition is the most African one. Hence, Africanization became a means of demonstrating seniority – and authority (see also Matory 1999 on the link between Africa, in particular Yoruba, and Candomblé).

The process of re-Africanization was enforced in 1983 when *Mãe* (short for *mãe de santo*, mother of the saint, title of a priestess) Stella, head of the Candomblé house *Ilê Axé Opô Afonjá* in Salvador da Bahia, began a 'revolution in values' by prohibiting all syncretistic spirits and practices within her house (Sansi 2007: 20). Syncretism became defined by *Mãe* Stella and others as 'a disguise, a false construction, a façade under which real, authentic African cultural and religious traditions were preserved' (Sansi 2007: 20). This position is not uncontested, however, since it ignores the long history of Candomblé as a Brazilian tradition. Gonçalves da Silva even describes Candomblé as the 'reinvention of Africa in Brazil' (title of a book chapter,

1994: 43). Despite the open controversy about this process, which is elaborated below, the Candomblé version in Salvador da Bahia is still labelled the most African of all Afro–Brazilian religions. In a perhaps unexpected outcome, the Bahian *terreiros* have become the location of 'a tourist spectacle'. However, as van de Port writes (2005: 156), 'the gaze of tourists and other outsiders is not ... a threat to the authenticity of the spectacle, but a reinforcement of it' (van de Port 2005: 174). A relatively new development that might give a new turn to this process is the recent spread of the 'Yoruba tradition' in Brazil. Nigerian immigrants to Brazil aim to (re)introduce the 'correct' Yoruba tradition and in particular the cult of *ifá* in Brazil by establishing communities based on the 'original' West African Yoruba tradition. The impact of this addition into the religious repertoire is still undecided. We consider this at greater length below. However, what is already visible is a growing demarcation between *terreiros* and less willingness to cooperate among the leadership. Even when priests and priestesses attend ceremonies at other houses, they always insist, to members of their own community, that their own way of conducting rituals is the best, the only effective or the 'true' African way. However, the 'ordinary' adherents are 'shopping around' and are very open-minded towards new 'offers' on the market of religious traditions.

Nonetheless, Candomblé is still the best-known Afro–Brazilian religion and it occupies an important place in the public imagination of and about Brazil. The ritual music has inspired popular musicians; the mythology had – and still has – an impact on novelists, playwrights and filmmakers; and the rich symbolism of the material side of the religion is regarded as inspirational art (see van de Port 2005). Art galleries and museums are full of items whose symbolic meaning is connected to the Candomblé deities, the *orixás*.

The worship of the *orixás* is at the core of all traditions (though sometimes under other names). On one side, they are perceived as entities with elaborate personalities and even physical characteristics, while on the other side they are also described as forces of nature that go way beyond our simple human understanding. Oludumaré is regarded as the creator, the supreme deity whose breath gives life to the physical shape created by Oxalá. Without Oludumaré there would be no living beings, no *axé* (ashe, the spiritual force). Sometimes the *orixás* are even regarded as personifications of *axé*. Without *axé*, nothing exists. It is present in every living being, every plant, every animal and every human (see Schmidt 2012 for a discussion of ashe in the Afro–Cuban religion). If we live in an unbalanced way (e.g. by ignoring our ritual obligations to honour the *orixás*), *axé* in our bodies will decrease and our lives will become more and more problematic. However, we can renew *axé* through attending ceremonies and in particular by performing rituals such as initiation or sacrifice. Hence, devotees believe in a reciprocal relationship between human beings and *orixás* based on exchange of *axé*.

The initiation rituals and its periodic renewals (after one, three and seven years) reinforce the bond between the individual and the *orixás* as every person is believed to be connected to specific *orixás*. Every devotee commits to life-long obligations when going through the initiation. The highlight of the initiation is the moment when an orixá takes over the body of the new initiate in a new, more controlled form. While the first time when an orixá manifests in a human body is described as rough, uncontrolled and interpreted as the calling of the orixá, during the initiation process the adept learns the 'correct' style according to the house in which the adept is initiated, as I explain later below. The incorporation of an orixá into a human body is an integral part of the religious practice, crucial to most rituals. Equally important is the consultation of one's fate through oracle reading by the priest or priestess (*jogo de búzios*, set of cowrie shells) (see Figure 1.3). The *mãe* or *pai de santo* (mother or father of saint, titles of priestess and priest, also called with the Yoruba terms *yalorixa* and *babalorixa*) diagnoses the client's situation with the shells and prescribes a solution such as the performance of a ritual or the commitment to the *orixás* (from 'simple' initiation to full initiation to priesthood). Each community is structured around an extensive hierarchy of initiations with the priest or priestess as the undisputable leader. However, each *terreiro* (the physical location where the ceremonies are performed, used often as a synonym for the community) is independent despite a network of ritual connections between many communities. For instance, when someone establishes a *terreiro*, this person will still be connected to the *terreiro* where the initiation to priesthood took place. In addition to the priesthood, every community includes other ritual positions such as *iyakekere* or *mãe pequena* (small mother), whose role is to assist the priesthood. Another position is that of the *ogã* who, in distinction to all other *filhas* and *filhos de santo* (daughter and sons of the saint, the terms for initiated members), does not receive an

Figure 1.3 Candomblé priest with divination board, São Paulo

orixá but is nonetheless initiated and assists the priesthood. This role is often described as a public relations officer, and the person fulfils an important function in the fight for the public recognition of Candomblé.

Umbanda

Umbanda is the second group of traditions I want to introduce. As in the case of Candomblé, Umbanda is not a singular tradition but rather a huge field of different traditions with some common features. There are many different academic perspectives about Umbanda, from various explanations of the term 'Umbanda' and of the 'African origin' to the contested discussion of a Brazilian heritage. Nothing seems to be straightforward where Umbanda is concerned. While Roger Bastide, for instance, categorized Umbanda as an Afro–Brazilian religion in his book *The African Religions of Brazil* (1960), his student, Renato Ortiz, stated that Umbanda developed after Bastide's research from being an Afro–Brazilian religion in its infancy to a national religion later on.[20] The problem increases when we consider the many similarities

Umbanda shares with Candomblé and other traditions. It seems impossible to draw a line between Umbanda and Candomblé, in particular because many people practise both traditions – though often for different purposes. Malandrino states, for instance, that 42.1 per cent of the Umbanda priesthood with whom she worked had a Kardecist background (Malandrino 2006: 59). Most of the Umbandistas I interviewed, however, were also initiated into Candomblé, even among the priesthood. Hence, leaders of Umbanda have not only esoteric knowledge about Candomblé restricted to initiated devotees but also regularly practise two traditions. Sometimes an Umbanda priest or priestess is a 'normal' member of a Candomblé *terreiro*. I spoke to others who belonged to both priesthoods. Some of my interviewees claim that they prefer Umbanda because it is less esoteric; hence, access to knowledge is not restricted to initiated members only but is open for everyone who comes to a *terreiro*. Umbanda is also regarded as less hierarchical than Candomblé and without the many ritual obligations. Others have referred to animal sacrifice as their reason for avoiding Candomblé in spite of its better reputation (see also Hayes 2011: 19). These interconnections between Umbanda and Candomblé on the membership and priesthood level are possible because Umbanda is also centred on devotion to the *orixás*, though the interpretation of the entities differs slightly. Umbanda is also open towards new influences. The Umbanda cosmology represents indeed a paradigmatic *bricolage* of ideas and elements from various traditions. It offers something for everyone. However, the lack of conformity is also part of the problem and a reason why even some Umbanda leaders look for something else outside Umbanda.

Scholars (e.g. Brown 1986) usually date Umbanda's beginnings in the 1920s and 1930s, though elements existed before. Sometimes Zélio Fernandino de Moraes in Rio de Janeiro is identified as the founder (e.g. Jensen 1999: 280), though he was by no means the only one and the degree of his contribution to the establishment of Umbanda remains contested. Brown and others have located the origin of Umbanda among middle-class Brazilians in the cities, though in the general perception of Umbanda is often still connected to the lower classes. Nonetheless, one can state that from the beginning Umbanda has recruited followers from every sector of society (Brown and Bick 1987). Gonçalves da Silva states that Umbanda was dominated at the beginning by Kardecists in Rio de Janeiro, São Paulo and Rio Grande do

Sul who wanted to mix their practices with Afro–Brazilian elements in order to establish a new and officially accepted religion (Silva 1994: 106) but without the negative stigma of the Afro–Brazilian traditions.[21] While the Afro–Brazilian traditions were perceived as predominantly black and lower class at the beginning of the twentieth century, Umbanda aimed to offer an acceptable alternative that combined elements of these traditions with Spiritism and other traditions. Malandrino highlights in particular the ideas about karma and reincarnation as important Spiritist influences in Umbanda (Malandrino 2006: 59). However, despite these inclusions and the symbolic and ritual diversity of Umbanda, Malandrino categorizes Umbanda nonetheless as an Afro–Brazilian religion. She stresses in particular the influence from Bantu cults in the establishment of Umbanda (2006: 92). The Bantu belief system has offered Umbanda flexibility as well as consistency on a mythological level. Malandrino refers in particular to the ancestor cult, in which she sees the important connection between Umbanda (in Brazil) and Africa. One can, of course, argue that ancestor worship is also incorporated into Spiritism, which is based on communication with the spirits of the dead, that is, ancestors. It is also important to realize that Bantu is a relatively new label for a variation of mainly Central African traditions. Though the term 'Bantu' was already in use in the nineteenth century as a technical category for a group of languages of the Niger–Congo subdivision, it was regarded as too broad to be useful as an ethnic category. Its popularity arose, however, in the wake of the Negritude movement, and it is now used quite commonly as a reference to Central African culture, not only in the African Diaspora but increasingly also in Africa where the term 'Ubuntu' became a label for a general African philosophy.[22] In Brazil a similar tendency can be observed, in which Bantu increasingly carries the connotation of being 'pure' African, in contrast to the 'corrupted' Nagô traditions.

However, not everyone conforms to the interpretation of Umbanda as predominately Bantu, and Umbanda is still seen by many as the 'true' Brazilian religion because it brings together ideas as well as people from all sections of society. This interpretation was supported in the middle of the twentieth century with a growing impact on society. While Candomblé put people off with its extensive sacrificial rituals and obligations, Umbanda presented a less daunting way to worship the African deities on Brazilian soil. Though

Umbanda was also stigmatized as black magic and became the target of political oppression (Concone and Negrão 1985: 44), Umbandistas became increasingly institutionalized and politically influential (Concone and Negrão 1985: 78). In 1987, Brown and Bick estimated that 30 million Brazilians (in a population of 120 million) practise Umbanda (1987: 74). São Paulo alone counted at that time (1987) for 45,000 Umbanda *terreiros* in comparison to 'only' 3,000 Candomblé *terreiros* (Sjørslev 1999: 10). However, the time of growth seems to be over: the number of people openly confessing to practising Umbanda (and other Afro–Brazilian traditions) are declining, partly due to attacks by neo-Pentecostal churches (see Engler 2011). Though there are still important attempts to centralize and organize Umbanda *terreiros* (e.g. the attempt to establish an Umbanda study degree by the Faculdade de Teologia Umbandista in São Paulo), Umbanda is too diversified to be harmonized under one umbrella and one hierarchy.

Despite the wide range of variations, Umbanda cosmology is usually structured in similar ways. Above all is the belief in the creator God as well as the belief in the existence of pure angels. Usually (though not always) they are perceived as the Saints in Roman Catholicism and also, importantly as the *orixás* in Candomblé. Though they are not at the centre of ritual practice – which is occupied by the *guías* (spiritual guides) – they are nonetheless central in Umbanda as the main *orixás* present the source of specific *linhas* (lineages) which divide the spiritual worlds. The reason why the *orixás* carry less significance for the ritual practice than the (lower) spiritual entities is because the deities do not incorporate the mediums as they are regarded as too powerful: a medium would 'explode', as Pressel writes, if possessed by an *orixá* (1973: 285). Consequently *orixás* cannot be asked for advice during the possession rituals. However, according to Umbanda mythology, *orixás* have derived from living beings in Africa. Consequently, the cosmos included spirits of the deceased beings that became the deities – and these spirits can sometimes incorporate Umbanda mediums.

The ritual practice consists of the main function of Umbanda – consultation. The spiritual guides play the core roles here. In specific settings they incorporate the mediums through which they can be consulted by the clients. The range of entities with which a *terreiro* regularly works varies; however, each *terreiro* works usually with six or seven groups. *Caboclos* are the spirits

Figure 1.4 Umbanda altar, São Paulo

of Brazilian indigenous people from the Amazonian interior; *pretos velhos* are the spirits of old black slaves and runaways; *boiadeiros* are the spirits of cowboys from the *sertão*, the north-eastern hinterland of Brazil; *ciganos* are the spirits of gypsies; *marinheiros* are the spirits of sailors and fishermen; *baianos* honours the spirits of people from Bahia; *crianças* are spirits of deceased children; and last but not least, is the group of *exus* (male) and *pombagiras* (female) (see Figure 1.4). They are included in the cosmos of all Umbanda *terreiros*, while the presence of the other groups can vary. Though often portrayed as devils, *exus* are not perceived as evil but as a force to counterbalance the evil in the world. These are the most popular groups of *guias*; however, it is an open system and can incorporate other spiritual entities. In one *terreiro*, for instance, I also saw references to entities of other systems, for instance, to the goddess movement (from European Paganism), the extraterrestrial (New Age movement) and Native American (North American style). But they do not represent a common feature of Umbanda. Some categorize this type of Umbanda *terreiros* as esoteric Umbanda; however, I got the impression that the division of different types of Umbanda (e.g. Umbanda Pura, Umbanda

Branca and Umbanda Esotérico) is just an academic classification with little or no relevance for Umbandistas. As in the other Afro–Brazilian traditions, each Umbanda *terreiro* and each *mãe* or *pai de santo* is independent. Though there are some associations or federations as well as other attempts to create an all-embracing institution, their main function seems to be to organize meetings (e.g. congresses) to discuss joint strategies, for instance to fight back against the attacks of neo-Pentecostal churches or to increase the public recognition of the Afro–Brazilian traditions.

Spiritism

The third core element in this spectrum of different systems, Spiritism, is probably the most problematic to include here. It is not an Afro–Brazilian tradition, though it is sometimes listed under this label (e.g. Silva 1994; Jensen 1999; Wafer 1991), and quite a large number of practitioners would reject the notion that it could be labelled 'religious'. As mentioned above, the term *espiritismo* is sometimes even used as an umbrella for all Afro–Brazilian and Spiritist traditions. Wafer even states that religions may go by the name Spiritism (or Umbanda, as he clarifies), but that they are also accepted as Afro–Brazilian 'as long as they have a seated *exu* and members who receive the *orixás*' (Wafer 1991: 5). Spiritist elements are not only included in Umbanda as already explained but also Spiritism became the foundation of various other movements, some with religious connotations, though most with the aim of teaching people to develop their abilities in order to help others. Hence, the main aim of Spiritism is healing; therefore, it is therapeutic and not religious despite the fact that Spiritism is included on the national census as an option for religion. It is therefore possible for a Spiritist to self-identify as agnostic or even with a specific religion, though the majority of Brazilian Spiritists conform to Christian beliefs. In this way Brazilian Spiritists follow in the steps of the person who is regarded as the main source of inspiration, the French schoolteacher Hypolyte Léon Denizard Rivail (1804–69), whose publications codified Spiritist ideas and practices. He took on the alias Allan Kardec when he became involved in Spiritism in 1855, and consequently the main Brazilian Spiritists refer to Spiritism as Kardecism in order to honour his teachings.

However, there are also vast numbers of variations that have derived from Kardec's teachings by mixing his ideas with elements from other traditions. In order to distinguish these mixtures from Kardec's teaching, people refer in these cases to *espiritismo* (Spiritism), and sometimes scholars also distinguish between *baixo espiritismo* (lower Spiritism) and *alto espiritismo* (high Spiritism), with the former representing the mixtures with Afro–Brazilian elements and the latter the followers of Kardecism. When I studied Spiritism in Puerto Rico, I often used the term 'Spiritism' as an umbrella for Kardecism and its vernacular derivations, which I distinguished as 'popular Spiritism' or *espiritismo popular* (e.g. in Schmidt 1995). However, recently I have found it helpful to refer to Kardecism instead of Spiritism because the latter is increasingly confused with spiritualism, in particular by North American scholars, who overlook the different origins of the two systems. Though both originated in the nineteenth century and are based on the belief in the existence of spirits of the deceased and the possibility of communicating with them, the context is very different. Kardec firmly connected his ideas to the Christian faith. He regarded Spiritism as the only way out of the misery of the world that still suffered under the consequences of the Industrial Revolution. But in distinction to Karl Marx, who was also appalled by the misery in industrialized Europe, Kardec saw his ideas as connected to an early form of Christianity, before it became corrupted by institutions; he rejected Marxism vehemently (cf. Pérez García, 1988). He saw his teaching as an alternative to Marxism but also to the Christian churches, in particular Roman Catholicism. Not surprisingly, the Roman Catholic Church banned his books and even ordered that they be publicly burnt. In addition to Christianity, Kardec included elements from Hinduism, in particular the idea of karma and reincarnation. They mark the cornerstones of Spiritism in distinction to Spiritualism as they emphasize the central role of morality in the Spiritist worldview.

Kardec's main teaching is comprised of three aspects: the possibility of communicating with the spirits of the dead; spiritual evolution through reincarnation; and the need to do good and help others in order to achieve a higher position in one's next incarnation. The cornerstone of his system is therefore the spirits. They are perceived as non-material beings which can live for a limited time inside a human body. A human being is seen as consisting of three elements: the material element is the physical body; the spiritual element is the spirit that is reincarnated into the body during its existence; and the perispiritual element links the material body with the spirit. At the time of death, the spirit leaves the body, and after a while the spirit will choose another body in which to be reincarnated. The main goal of all spirits is to leave the physical world – and existence as human beings – behind, and hence to move on and leave all material aspects of existence behind. However, in order to achieve this goal, a spirit has to aim for perfection.

One way to achieve progress is during the incorporated period as a human being because this offers a spirit the chance to perfect its qualities. Another way of progression is offered to spirits by supporting troubled human beings. Based on the level of progression, spirits are categorized into different levels, from angels to good spirits to bad spirits. The latter are perceived as underdeveloped spirits, responsible for disturbances in the human world. Good spirits can be called upon for aid in these situations. Hence, helping others is at the core of Kardec's teachings, not only human beings but also spirits as well have to help in order to achieve perfection.

Kardec codified his teaching in various books and journal articles. His first book, for instance, *Le Livre des Esprits* (1857) contains 1,019 spirit responses to his questions about various aspects of human life. His second book (1861) focused on mediums, the individuals who enable communication between the human and spirit worlds. In order to work as mediums and help others, mediums have to live according to a rigid set of rules: they must behave in a morally upright and non-aggressive manner, and they must abstain from drugs that might affect their consciousness, including alcohol. Spiritists believe that everyone is born with the ability to receive messages from the spirit world, the afterlife. However, these abilities often remain undiscovered or underdeveloped. It is therefore important to train these mediumship abilities, as Kardec outlined in his book. Though he did not work as a medium personally, but always communicated with spirits via mediums, his teachings still present the crucial doctrine for all mediums (cf. Pérez García 1988).

Kardec's ideas reached Brazil around 1880 (Lewgoy 2006: 211), where they immediately won many followers, despite the fact that people had to be literate to follow them. Lewgoy states that at the beginning the anti-clerical attitude in particular – and its progressive, positivistic and free-thinking ideas – were attractive among the educated Brazilians (2006: 211). Unsurprisingly Kardecists were persecuted in Brazil during this early stage, until the separation of church and state in 1890 (Jensen 1999: 278). Spiritist ideas spread quickly, nonetheless, to wider sectors of society due to the central aim of Spiritists to do good deeds. Kardec's main teaching led to much charitable work in Brazil, such as the foundation of orphanages and hospitals (Brown and Bick 1987: 79) but also healing (Greenfield 2008: 39), though the latter resulted in severe persecution because it was regarded as illegal to offer medical treatment without a medical license (Jensen 1999: 278).

Nonetheless, the strong connection to charity brought Kardec's ideas into the wider society. As Lewgoy highlights, at a time when the state did not offer any official health support or other help, the charity aspect of Spiritism presented a huge attraction. The result was that Spiritist ideas appeared step by step, in little bags, as Lewgoy writes, in the cities. As in other parts of the Spanish and Portuguese colonial world,[23] Spiritism became seen in Brazil as an alternative to the Afro–Brazilian religions that were perceived negatively. While the practice of Afro–Brazilian religions was legally restricted until the 1970s, Kardecism met less opposition and was – legally at least – acceptable.[24] Hence, it carried a social prestige that outshone Afro–Brazilian practices, at least during the first stage of Spiritism in Brazil. Lewgoy regards the 1930s as the beginning of the second stage, which is connected in particular with the figure of Francisco Cândido (Chico) Xavier (1910–2002), probably the most famous medium in Brazil even today. During his lifetime he published over 400 books with messages from the spirits. However, his fame goes way beyond his books. He was a charismatic leader who became a national symbol in Brazil (Silva 2006; Stoll 2002). His supporters even started a national campaign for his nomination to the Nobel Peace Prize committee in 1981. Lewgoy mentions also that Chico Xavier is regularly compared with Saint Francis of Assisi (2006: 217). During my research time (in 2010), Brazil celebrated the one hundredth anniversary of his birth with various national events, including a movie that portrayed his struggle to become a medium and his path to fame; another movie about the afterlife, based on his teachings; and more recently, a third movie about the 'mothers of Chico Xavier', who re-encountered their dead children through Chico Xavier. On the whole one can say that Chico Xavier changed Spiritism in Brazil with his strong link to Roman Catholicism and his conservative attitude. As a result Spiritism became more structured with a set of ritualistic canon and doctrines (Lewgoy 2006: 219).

In the 1980s, however, Spiritism entered a third stage, which some perceived as the turning point. Spiritism became increasingly mixed with elements from other traditions, in particular New Age (Lewgoy 2006: 220), and to a certain degree even lost its Roman Catholic frame. Recent developments, in particular the move of some Spiritists towards selling advice on the Internet, have also shown a changed attitude towards the charity aspect that was central to Kardec's teaching. Brazilian Spiritism is, as Sandra Stoll writes, at a crossroads (Stoll 2006). Nowhere is this more visible than in the growing healing sector. From the beginning, healing was an important feature of Brazilian Spiritism and regarded as an important way of showing charity, to work (for free) for others. This link between Spiritists and healers is remarkably intense in Brazil and has created many variations, with various different treatments, from disobsession (persuading a spirit to let go and leave a person alone) over cleaning the aura of a client to surgery by a medium (often without medical training). One common feature among these treatments is the consultation of the spirits of deceased medical doctors, for instance Dr Fritz, who had become quite famous (Greenfield 2008). While usually these treatments are offered for free, Stoll notices the growing presence of a consumer-oriented attitude – Stoll uses the phrase 'ethic of prosperity' (2006: 271) – among Spiritist healers.

This development, however, should not obscure the fact that the central doctrine of Kardecism is still charity. Today one can still find copies of Kardec's books (in Portuguese) in every Spiritist centre, and sessions still start regularly with reading excerpts from one of his books. The main focus of each centre is teaching which aims to develop the mediumship ability. Developed mediums regularly offer consultations to clients. These are usually public events in which mediums sit around a table to communicate messages from spirits to the humans present in the audience. Some centres also offer private consultations. The most common mediumship abilities are feeling the presence of spirits, seeing them or hearing them. Some mediums have a premonition of something that will happen or has happened. The above-mentioned medium Chico Xavier received messages from the spirit world via automatic writing (called *psicografia* in Brazil). In other words, his arm and hand would move a pen across the paper, but he was unable to control it; he could not stop it nor influence the content of the message. And last but not least, another form of mediumship abil-ity is the temporal embodiment of a discarnate spirit in a human body, in order to enable this spirit to deliver a message to the world of the living by speaking (*psicofonia*). In Kardecist centres, in particular the ones belong-ing to the Federação Espírita Brasileira, this particular mediumship abil-ity is considered very rare, since it requires an extremely able and highly developed medium.

However, it is important to note that each of the abilities has to be used to help the living and the dead (the spirits), whether it is by delivering a mes-sage from the dead to the living or by healing, for instance via cleansing the aura of a person. Although the idea of reincarnation is less widespread among Brazilian Spiritists than in Kardec's teaching, doing good is regarded as the central aim of Brazilian Kardecism. Even centres that do not belong to the federation usually offer their consultations and treatments free of charge. However, Spiritism also shares a feature that represents, according to Kelly Hayes, the Afro–Brazilian religions: eclecticism. They all are 'religions that resist systematization, either by scholars or census takers' (2010: 102). They are organized in independent houses, either *terreiros* in case of the African matrix or centres in case of Spiritism. The leaders of each community do not bow to any non-spiritual authority and have the power to develop their own pantheon, rituals, doctrines and training programmes.

Other features of Brazilian religiosity: New Age and the charismatic turn of Brazil

I do not want to end my introduction with the impression that Candomblé, Umbanda and Spiritism are the only traditions (or even the only three vari-eties of vernacular tradition) in Brazil. There are many mixtures between these three cornerstones, for instance *umbandomblé* or *umbanda esotérica*. The way I have introduced the three traditions also does not indicate a hier-archical order. As one of my interviewees, a *mãe de santo* in Umbanda, firmly stated, it is not true that Umbanda is 'just' a low form of Spiritism or that Candomblé is stronger than Umbanda and Spiritism. All traditions as well as their various mixtures address people in different ways and have unique features. It is also common to move through various religious traditions during one's life. Sometimes they are even practised at the same time but for different purposes, though I have also encountered people criticizing these simultaneous practices as well as mixtures. Some Candomblé priests even reject all non-African elements in their cosmology, while some Kardecists discriminate against African deities.

However, apart from these debates at the border of the three ritual complexes, it is important to mention some of the other features of the Brazilian religious market. In addition to the religions which were carried to Brazil with various immigration streams (e.g. Lutheranism, Anglicanism, Baptism, Buddhism, Shinto, Islam and Judaism), there are also a growing number of New Age groups, in particular in urban centres such as São Paulo. Prokopy and Smith estimated in 1999 that there were already more than 1,000 New Age groups and establishments in both São Paulo and Rio de Janeiro (1999: 12). Today the number is much higher.

Some of the most vibrant developments are based on the intake of ayahuasca, a hallucinogenic drug that was traditionally used by indigenous shamans and healers based on indigenous traditions in the wider Amazonian area of Columbia, Bolivia, Peru, Venezuela, Ecuador and Brazil. In the 1920s and 1930s, however, ayahuasca inspired the establishment of various new religions that are still flourishing today among the urbanized population, even outside Brazil. The best known is Santo Daime, founded by Raimundo Irineu Serra, known as Mestre Irineu (1892–1971). Originally from Maranhão, he came to Acre to work in rubber production and then he encountered ayahuasca. In the 1930s he moved to Rio Branco where he established Santo Daime (Daime is the ritual name for ayahuasca). Shortly before his death he registered his community under the name Centro de Iluminação Cristã Luz Universal (in 1971). Capelinha de São Francisco, also called Barquinha, founded by Daniel Pereira de Mattos (Mestre Daniel) in 1945, is an early offspring of Santo Daime. In distinction to Santo Daime, Mestre Daniel incorporated several elements of Afro–Brazilian religions as well as the devotion of Saints. The third group in this sector is União do Vegetal (UDV), founded in 1961 by José Gabriel da Costa (Mestre Gabriel). Mestre Gabriel came from Bahia into the Amazon, also in search of work in the rubber production. Though he had no further connection to the other two groups when he founded UDV, there are similarities between UDV and those groups, in addition to the consumption of ayahuasca that marks the core of the ritual practice of each group. After the death of each founder, each group fragmented further and spread throughout Brazil and beyond (see Labate/MacRae 2010). One of the most successful groups is Culto Eclético da Fluente Luz Universal Raimundo Irineu Serra (Eclectic Centre of the Universal Flowing Light Raimundo Irineu Serra), CEFLURIS in short, founded by Sebastião Mota de Melo (1920–90) (Dawson 2010: 134–5). All of these groups – but CEFLURIS in particular – are very popular, especially among the more affluent middle and upper classes in Brazil and other countries. They support campaigns to save the environment and present themselves basically as green and environment friendly.

Though at first glance these groups seem to be relatively small and too insignificant to have an impact on Brazil, this superficial assessment fails to recognize the wider context, nationally and internationally. When Glauco Villas Boas, founder of the Céu de Maria Daime church in São Paulo, was killed outside his home in São Paulo in 2010, his murder made headlines and was reported nationally.[25] Even more impressive is the wide spread of Santo Daime groups outside Brazil. Due to the high degree of institutionalization, in particular of CEFLURIS, Santo Daime groups can be found in the United States, Canada, Japan, France, Italy, the Netherlands, Germany, the United Kingdom and many other countries. And here they demonstrate the possible impact these groups produce, for instance by changing constitutions: because it is usually illegal to consume ayahuasca due to its being classified as a drug, followers of Santo Daime are pursuing legal battles in each of these countries to get ayahuasca rituals accepted as religious (in Brazil it is legal to drink ayahuasca as part of a religious ritual). Hence, while the Afro–Brazilian traditions and Spiritism are ambivalent about being classified as religious, Santo Daime followers see this classification as their chance to become socially accepted, even to the degree of being allowed to consume ayahuasca openly. However, as previously mentioned, I decided against including this religious complex despite its connection to Afro–Brazilian traditions, Spiritism and Roman Catholicism, because its religious experiences are drug induced, which would have led the discussion in another direction. Nevertheless, it is important to be aware of this development because some Afro–Brazilian *terreiros* are popular in a similar sector of society as the Santo Daime groups.

The charismatic movements have a much stronger impact on the wider Brazilian population than the New Age groups, and I spend the remaining part of the introduction outlining their main features. David Lehman describes as charismatic a wide variety of churches and movements 'which have in common a belief in the gift of the spirit, which practice speaking in tongues, or glossolalia, and whose followers believe in the existence and prevalence of possession by devils' (2001: 46). He states that unlike other movements, the charismatic movements do not contextualize tradition but instead rework symbols and rituals to new purposes. We have to distinguish between two branches of the charismatic turn of Brazil: there is the increasingly important sector of evangelical and Pentecostal denominations and also the Charismatic Renewal of the Roman Catholic Church (Renovação Carismático Católico, abbreviated hereafter as RCC). The memberships of both are growing significantly. In just thirty years, the number of Protestants in Brazil rose from 6.6 per cent in 1980 to 22.2 per cent in 2010 – and the majority are Protestants who attend Pentecostal churches. As sociologists (e.g. Pierucci and Prandi 1996) have predicted for a while, the charismatic forms of Christianity will dominate Brazilian Christianity in the next decades. In particular, the Pentecostal movement shares some features with the Afro–Brazilian and Spiritist religions, not only in the type of religious experience but also sociologically, as Sidney Greenfield states: 'The African-derived, Spiritist and Evangelical Protestant religious groups in the urban centres likewise may be seen as systems of patronage and clientage in which a competition for followers is waged by offering access to different supernatural beings who in exchange for fealty provide resources – ranging from healing to employment to personal well being' (Greenfield and Calvacante 2006: 84).

RCC was introduced in Brazil in 1968. Coming from the United States,[26] RCC immediately spread through Brazil and confronted the other forms of Catholicism, in particular the base community movement, but also the Pentecostal movement that had gained dramatically in importance (Prandi 1998: 10). After centuries of being predominantly Roman Catholic, people started to look for other forms of belonging, and the Roman Catholic Church became increasingly divided by conflicts between radical liberation theologians, progressives and conservatives, all of them trying to strengthen the institutional church, though in different ways (Prokopy and Smith 1999: 1).

The Comunidades Eclesiais de Base (CEB; ecclesiastical grass-roots movement) drew attention in particular in the 1960s and 1970s and attracts now only 2 per cent of Catholics (Pierucci/Prandi 1998: 14). By shifting the focus to base communities the Church tried to address the needs of the wider population. However, though CEB still recruits more adherents from the lower social classes, it does not target the poorest members of society. Prokopy and Smith even argue that the emphasis on Bible interpretation enforced a new social barrier, this time between literate and illiterate members. The strong focus on sociopolitical and economic change also overlooks, as the authors point out, 'people's need for religious mystery' (1999: 13). As a consequence many people, illiterate and literate, left the base communities and converted to a Pentecostal church, where they received 'spiritual nourishment' instead of political and intellectual training.

Prokopy and Smith also point out that it became increasingly difficult for the relatively few pastoral workers in the base communities to compete with the much larger number of Protestant pastors (1999: 14). Here they refer to the growing number of evangelical and Pentecostal churches that dominate Protestantism today, against which the historical denominations (e.g. Lutherans, Anglicans and Baptists) are equally unable to compete. Alencar, who distinguishes between four stages of Protestantism in Brazil (Protestantism of immigrants, Protestantism of missionaries, Pentecostalism and contemporary Protestantism), explains how Protestantism developed from a foreign religion[27] into something 'made in Brazil' (2005: 37–51). Alencar points in particular to the bodily aspects of religious practice, the oral, festival, sensorial and experimental (2005: 149–50) when he outlines his concept of *Protestantismo Tupiniquim Mulato*. The charismatic revival of the Catholic Church mirrors the emotional worship style that emphasizes the physical dimension of religion – with the result that RCC attracts 4 per cent of Catholics, hence double the number of Catholics in support of the base community movement (Pierucci and Prandi 1998: 15). Pierucci and Prandi see significant similarities between RCC and the Pentecostal movement not only with regard to the charismatic form of religious practice but also on a sociological level. For instance, both attract predominately but not exclusively women – in distinction to traditional Catholicism, which has a slight majority of men. An important difference between RCC and the Pentecostal movement, however, is that devotion to the Virgin Mary takes a central place in RCC but is excluded from Pentecostal worship. Pierucci and Prandi explain the achievement of the RCC over CEB with the adaptation of techniques from the Pentecostal denominations, for instance, the reintroduction of miracles, the shift of emphasis to individuals and religious ecstasy, the 'trance of the Holy Spirit' as they write (1998: 23). While Liberation Theology as well as mainstream Catholicism and historical Protestantism tend to interpret the devil and demons as abstract beings or symbolic metaphors and push the belief in miracles and supernatural intervention away, the Pentecostal movement has these elements at the core of its belief and practice (Mariano 1995: 97). The charismatics in the Roman Catholic Church are following this turn and are also filling people's need for highly emotional religious experience. There are, of course, also sociological factors that supported the move from Roman Catholicism to Protestantism, for instance, the presence of local pastors instead of foreign clergy.

However, a main factor is the evangelization techniques that are, as Prokopy and Smith stress, highly experiential with a focus on healing and emotional prayer (1999: 10). By offering members a similar approach within Roman Catholicism, the Church accepts its need to change to a certain degree, despite internal attempts to reassert the authority of the hierarchical Church and to defend traditional Catholic morality and values in a changing world (1999: 14). Nonetheless, the reality is that it is possible in Brazil to be a member of a base community and also charismatic – even to attend an Afro–Brazilian *terreiro* at the same time. What Prokopy and Smith write about Latin America in general aptly describes the market in Brazil: 'it has simply become part of a religious and cultural process in which people see diverse faiths to meet a range of material, social, and spiritual needs that have been expanding rapidly as a result of urbanization and industrialization' (1999: 15). This pluralization seems even relatively unaffected by the struggle of the Pentecostal denominations against other forms of religious devotion, especially the worship of the saints in Roman Catholicism and the spirits and deities of the other Brazilian systems. Though the leaders of the Pentecostal denominations are even against any ecumenical relations with other churches (see overview table in Alcencar 2005: 151, appendix 1), people are still moving around as Greenfield points out (2008: 201–2). In a sense

Pentecostalism is just another player competing for followers in the diverse religious market – though a very important one. Corten, Dozer and Oro even compare the significance of Pentecostalism with the Protestant Reformation and state that Pentecostalism affects the history of the southern hemisphere as the Reformation did in the West (2003: 19). The increasing hostility of Pentecostal churches towards all vernacular forms of worship has started what some scholars call a 'war of possession' (e.g. Almeida 2003), which is examined in more detail below. At this point I introduce the main players on this field.

Pentecostalism was brought to Brazil from the United States in 1911 by two missionaries, Gunnar Vingren and Daniel Berg, who were originally Swedish. Though Vingren and Berg were not the first Pentecostals in Brazil (a year earlier the Italian Luis Francescon arrived in São Paulo, where he would later found the Congregaçã Christão), Vingren and Berg initiated what Chesnut describes as 'the birth of what was to become the Western Hemisphere's largest Pentecostal denomination, the Assembléia de Deus' (AD; the Assembly of God) (Chesnut 1997: 27). From the 1930s on, Brazilians began to take over the Pentecostal churches and to sever the ties of dependency with home organizations. In the 1950s, another wave of missionaries arrived in Brazil from the United States and founded more churches, which soon followed the 'classic patterns of Pentecostal schismatic growth' (Greenfield 2008: 140). The Igreja Pentecostal Deus É Amor (DEA; God is Love Pentecostal Church) was founded, for instance, in 1962 by David Miranda who was previously a member of the Brasil para Cristo (BPC; Brazil for Christ), founded by Manoel de Mello, a former AD member. In distinction to the more conservative Pentecostal denominations such as AD, Miranda incorporated aspects of popular Catholicism and Afro–Brazilian religions into DEA theology, and exorcism became (and still is, as I observed in São Paulo) the main activity of the DEA. In order to highlight the fundamental differences between 'traditional' Pentecostalism and the 'modern' forms, Ricardo Mariano successfully coined the term 'neo-Pentecostalism' for the latter (originally in his MPhil thesis in 1995, published in 1999), though Alencar prefers the more inclusive term contemporary or modern Protestantism (2005: 50). One of the main features is its Brazilian founder and leadership. The most successful Brazilian church is the Igreja Universal do Reino de Deus (IURD; Universal Church of the Kingdom of God), founded in 1977 by Edir Macedo Bezerra, a former lottery employee from Rio de Janeiro who is still at the head of the third-largest Pentecostal church in Brazil and 'one of Brazil's more unusual multinational corporations'(Greenfield 2008: 141). His former involvement in Umbanda might explain the significantly high number of former Umbandistas among IURD members: Chesnut reports that among IURD members there are three times more ex-Umbandistas than among members of the Assembly of God in Brazil (13% vs. 4.3%, Chesnut 1997: 69). The IURD owns numerous television and radio stations, a publishing company, daily newspapers and journals and a recording firm, as well as other important companies in Brazil alone. With its economic power comes political influence: IURD has managed to send several delegates to the Federal Congress, the Constituent National Assembly and other legislative assemblies on both the national and the local level (Oro 2003). And the IURD is not only vibrant in Brazil but it is also already present in more than thirty countries. Corten, Dozer and Oro regard the IURD as the largest and most important new church in the so-called developing world (2003: 13).

At the centre of IURD theology is the belief that Satan and demons are responsible for all the misery and evil in the world. They are classified as 'inferior spirits' (Oliva 1995: 99) who constantly disturb 'the mental, physical and spiritual order', which is the main problem, according to Macedo (Oliveira 1998: 112). It is the responsibility of everyone to intervene and to 'liberate' the world – and oneself – from demons. The liberation ceremony that is offered each Friday, during which demonic possession is initiated in order to exorcize the evil spirits, is therefore one of the core rituals. For the IURD, Satan and the demons exist as personified beings and not only in a symbolic manner. Demons were created by Satan, who is their leader, while Satan was created by God but was expelled from heaven. Demons can manifest themselves as spirits who bring evil into the world. Salvation can bring only God's word. Pimentel interprets the figure of Satan in the IURD as the result of syncretism between the perception of Satan in USP entecostalism and aspects of Afro–Brazilian traditions, in particular Umbanda in Rio de Janeiro (2005: 38), which Macedo practised before his conversion to Pentecostalism.

Another keystone of Macedo's ministry is the miraculous healing of the Holy Ghost, which can provide solutions to all kinds of problems – physical, psychological, social and even economic. Greenfield lists his 'theology of health and wealth' (2008: 142) as the third element which was critical to Macedo's success. Financial supporters are promised a life of abundance, and they do not have to wait for the next life because being blessed by God already carries fruits (e.g. material goods but also health) in this world. However, as Greenfield explains, health comes at a certain price. 'Should a prayer not be answered, Macedo tells the disappointed member of the congregation, he or she does not have sufficient faith and must petition God harder – which is to say, increase the value of his or her offering to the church' (Greenfield 2008: 142–3). The contribution comes first, therefore, and then in exchange for payment, God will provide whatever it is people are praying for. The doctrine of prosperity is not only a pillar of the IURD, but other churches have adopted it, too, as everyone can observe on the numerous religious television stations in Brazil. Healing has become big business and is firmly connected to conflicting local interpretations of the subjective experience of involuntary acts.

Gender, Race and Class: The Social Dimension of Religious Experience

Introduction

A most influential but also contested book about the social stratification of Candomblé *terreiros* is *City of Women*, by Ruth Landes (1947). Landes (1908–1991) was an American anthropologist in the tradition of Franz Boas and his student (and her PhD supervisor) Ruth Benedict. After completing her PhD (on Native American anthropology), she conducted a research project in Brazil. Between 1938 and 1939 she worked in collaboration with Brazilian scholars, especially with Edison Carneiro, in the areas of identity, race and gender in Bahian Candomblé. Her book *City of Women* presents Candomblé as a religion centred on women and homosexual men, who Landes considered to occupy a similar marginalized status in society. She argued that Candomblé gave both groups a position of power and enabled them to express and develop their creativity. Her findings, which became quite significant in studies of African American religions, confirmed a general impression that ascribed spirit possession, as Mary Keller writes, 'to women, the poor, and the religious other (the "primitive", the "tribal", the third-world woman, the black, the immigrant)' (Keller 2002: 4). However, as research in the last decades has shown, possession rituals are not always limited to the powerless, and even when the two coincide, they are not always causally linked (Cohen 2007: 93).[1]

When I started my PhD project in 1989, I had Landes's work in mind. My intention was to find out whether her findings could be applicable to Puerto

Rico; however, I soon learnt that it was not so easy. Nearly everyone with whom I spoke who was involved in either Puerto Rican Spiritism or the Afro–Cuban Orisha religion (called often Santería) denied any gender bias in favour of women. A quite common answer was that the spirits and deities do not make any difference between men and women, that only individual ability is important. I decided to adjust my research topic (see Schmidt 1995).[2] When my research took me to Brazil, however, I asked each interviewee what they thought about this gender preconception of the Afro–Brazilian traditions. As Landes's research is quite well known among the *terreiros*, it was even possible to enquire about reactions to her findings, sixty years later. This data provides the foundation of this chapter. I focus on the congregations and their social composition, though I did not conduct a survey on the social features of each *terreiro* I visited. Nonetheless, interview data and ritual observations enable me to discuss the common preconception in the academic literature, which still favours it as female practice, as well as in the public reception, which locates the practice among poor and socially marginalized Afro–Brazilians, in particular women and homosexual men. Unlike Landes's book, however, I do not focus only on Candomblé. My intention is to get a better understanding of the social stratification of people experiencing what we academics call spirit possession and trance. The comparison of Candomblé, Umbanda, Spiritism and charismatic-evangelical congregations provides a larger picture of the social diversity of people experiencing these involuntary acts of uncontrolled bodily movements, spontaneous vocalizations, unusual sensory experiences and alterations of consciousness and memory.

This decision is supported by Andrew Chesnut's comment that the ratio between women and men in Afro–Brazilian religions (2:1) is similar to that of Christian groups (2003: 108). Though members of the latter group disagree that their experiences can be likened to those of the others, I include them here, as have other scholars. Patricia Birman, for instance, combines Pentecostalism with possession cults and argues that possession is part of the exorcism performed by some neo-Pentecostal churches (1996: 99). I follow her lead in order to avoid unduly limiting my perspective. Each of the first three groups is usually described as 'deemed peripheral' vis-à-vis Christianity (Boddy 1994: 411–12). By including a Christian group, therefore, I avoid simplistic perceptions and misleading explanations, though my book overall focuses more on Afro–Brazilian and Spiritist practices than on Christianity. As outlined in the introduction, I respect the different local interpretations of the experience and will come back to their diversity later. However, in order to understand the impact of social setting on the practitioners and their experience I overlook the differences at this point.

The combination of the different forms of possession can be justified by referring to the diagnostic category 'dissociation', which combines a wide range of 'transcendent' phenomena, including spirit possession and so-called mystical experiences. With reference to analytical psychology, Lucy Huskinson regards dissociation as 'a healthy psychological disposition to life and to everyday experience generally' (2010: 72). It is 'a universal human capacity' which is, however, as Erika Bourguignon highlights, 'culturally modulated' (Bourguignon 2004: 558). I would like to extend Bourguignon's view by adding that we also need to consider the social setting. While Bourguignon sees the role of possession and trance as instruments of social change (1973: 338), I emphasize the opposite direction. My argument is that, when the structural factors of a society are changing, then the explanation of the experience has to adapt, too. Possession and trance are therefore not only instruments of social change but in their local explanations we also see a reflection of social change. Any change in socio-economic inequality, gender discrimination and political oppression carries a resonance in the interpretation of religious belonging and practice. I would therefore extend Keller's statement that 'representations of possession can give us information about marginalized persons and their struggle within and against the forces that have an impact upon their lives' (2002: 4). We receive not only information about marginalized people but also about the process of social stratification. It enables us to understand whether and how marginalized groups became elevated in society and why an experience that was formerly dominated by persons from the periphery became conquered by people from the centre of society. By including practices that are considered more 'mainstream', I want to stress the social recognition of the acts under consideration. In the background of this argument I look in this chapter at people experiencing spirit possession and trance under two angles, gender and social milieu. The latter is considered in relationship with race, since both characteristics are interwoven in Brazil.

Academic explanations and challenges
of the gender division

Erika Bourguignon, one of the first scholars to provide statistical data about
the presence of spirit possession and trance across the globe, argues that
'where individuals have little opportunity for achievement and little control
over their daily activities, possession trance is more likely to occur' (1976: 31).
This link between social marginalization and religious activities, in particular spirit possession, is often reported by scholars working in various areas of
the world and with different traditions, so it seems widely accepted as fact –
though with different explanations. However, it is important to avoid generalizations. It is seductive to apply general assumptions to a specific culture
without checking the data first, as a superficial glance at the gender division
of people experiencing spirit possession and trance shows. As Bourguignon,
Bellisari and McCabe also state, the simple equation women equals possession trance is not justified by the data we have at hand, despite impressionistic
accounts of a predominance of women in possession trance cults (1983: 414).
It seems to make sense to assume that spirit possession is a predominately
female occupation. It even confirms another preconception of religion being,
in general, predominately a female practice. Based on statistical data from
the World Value Survey, Rodney Stark, for instance, noted that throughout
history religious institutions and movements have generally recruited more
women than men (Stark 2002: 495), at least in cases where women were not cat-
egorically excluded from membership. Even when men dominate leadership
positions, there are usually more female members in congregations. Though
statistically this picture is correct, nonetheless it says little about specific cultures and traditions. And even when a scholar refers to a specific culture,
it is still alluring to apply one's own conception to the other culture, as did
Melville Herskovits (1948). He argued that the reason for the higher number
of priestesses in Afro–Brazilian religions was that women were less occupied
than men and had therefore more free time than men to spend in the *terreiros*. Not only did new studies show a missing correlation between occupation
and religious commitment (e.g. Miller and Hoffmann 1995) but Herskovits's
assumption about female occupation also betrays his ignorance of the harsh
social conditions under which these *mães de santo* lived in the 1940s. My

main argument, however, goes even further. People often overlook the significance of the social and political changes of a society when applying cross-cultural generalizations. Even if we assume that Landes's portrayal of the society was correct for the 1930s – and new research (e.g. Matory 2005) sheds much doubt on it as I elaborate later – Brazil has changed dramatically in the last eight decades. Brazil today and Brazil in the 1930s are two very different societies. And these changes have had an impact on the public recognition of spirit possession and trance. Consequently, they have also affected participation in ritual practice. When it is no longer regarded as inferior, the practice becomes more common, even among groups that traditionally shy away from it, such as, for instance, heterosexual men. To emphasize the significance of the social dimension, we need to go back to I. M. Lewis's study of shamanism and spirit possession (1971), which links the rituals with power asymmetries related to gender and class. Though I disagree with some of the generalizations about ecstatic religions made in the wake of this publication, Lewis's study still provides us, over forty years later, with a conceptual framework for new data (when applied with caution). Emma Cohen criticizes his lack of parameters and precise measurements, which makes his model widely applicable but superficial (2007: 93). I would rather interpret Lewis's intention with this study not as an ethnographic study but rather as a presentation of a framework of ideas open for discussion. As he pointed out some years after the first edition (1983), his study presents only prototypes and does not exclude variations or exceptions.

The core argument of his study is that there is sociological differentiation between central and peripheral possession cults. This differentiation is based on, as Lewis summarizes in the preface of the third edition of his book, 'whether they [the cults] are inspired by spirits which directly uphold public morality (central) or those "peripheral" agencies that threaten public order' (2003: xiv). The former constitute shamanistic trance and the latter subversive marginal cults. In a second step he then shows how gender influences the interpretation of spirit possession. He argues that '[w]here central and marginal possession religions exists side by side in the same society, the first is primarily reserved for men, while the second is restricted essentially to women, or men of lower status' (Lewis 1971: 135). For Lewis, the crucial feature that divides central and peripheral cults is morality and values, both concepts that are difficult to assess from the outside. Lewis argues that male-dominated cults sustain the prevailing moral values. Shamans and possession priests are leaders of the community and when they enter into trance, they represent authority and morality. Cults at the periphery of society, however, are dominated by marginalized social groups such as women, which use spirit possession as a strategy 'to achieve ends which they cannot readily obtain more directly' (Lewis 1971: 85). But, as Karen McCarthy Brown writes, Mama Lola, a Haitian Vodou priestess living in Brooklyn, can also be read as a case of moral leadership. On one side, Alourdes (Mama Lola is her alias given to her by Brown when she started her research) comes from a deprived social background and would qualify without any doubt as a socially marginalized person during her first years, or even decades, in New York (see Brown 2001). However, as Brown outlines in her article, within the Vodou communities in New York, Mama Lola is now a central figure, representing stability and leadership (Brown 1987; see also Schmidt 2008: 68). On the other side, Vodou still occupies a peripheral position in mainstream society, in the United States as well as Haiti, in particular vis-à-vis Christianity. To be accepted as a leader in Haitian Vodou does not make her a leader in the Haitian Diaspora, in spite of the fact that her voice is definitely heard not only by *vodouisants* but also by the wider Haitian Diaspora, the tenth Department (referring to the nine geographical departments that constitute Haiti), as I observed during my research in New York City. While Brown and others acknowledge her moral leadership, Lewis is more ambivalent towards Vodou. Referring to the rural version of Haitian Vodou, he writes that, while the rural population (the majority of Haitians) regards Vodou as a populist religion, the ruling elite (a small minority) rejects Vodou as 'insidious rural paganism' (Lewis 2003: 94, with reference to Métraux 1959). Though Lewis points to the changes in Vodou during the Duvalier regime, he locates it 'squarely within the periph-eral cult class' (2003: 115) before continuing to clarify that Vodou could also be seen as separatist ecstatic religion. As he acknowledges, Vodou and simi-lar traditions are difficult to classify appropriately, especially because of the attempts of the establishment to discredit them. While Brown works mainly in the urban Haitian diaspora – her main research field is Mama Lola's Vodou temple in Brooklyn – Lewis grounds his assessment on Métraux's monograph about Vodou in Haiti at the beginning of the Duvalier regime, which led to a dramatic increase in emigration. They refer therefore to different social and even cultural contexts in their assessment of Vodou. Nonetheless, even with information about the role of Vodou in Haiti today, it seems impossible to clarify whether Vodou has indeed moved from the periphery to the centre of society.[3] Consequently, it is also impossible to assess the impact of a priestess on public morality or the social order. However, the impact of the priesthood on the social order of society is, according to Lewis, the 'crucial bread-and-butter question' in studies about ecstatic religions. In Lewis's words, 'How does the incidence of ecstasy relate to the social order?, Why do people in certain social positions succumb to possession more readily than others? What does ecstasy offer them?' (Lewis 2003: 23). These questions make much sense; however, when one looks at specific cases such as Mama Lola and Vodou, the task becomes too ambiguous.

Lewis presents women's possession cults provocatively as 'thinly disguised protest movements directed against the dominant sex. They play a significant part in the sex-war in traditional societies and cultures where women lack more obvious and direct means for forwarding their aims. To a considerable extent they protect women from the exactions of men, and offer an effective vehicle for manipulating husbands and male relatives' (Lewis 2003: 26). However, Lewis vehemently disagrees with the assumption that he presents spirit possession in general as 'a product of the deprivation of women in male-dominated societies' (1967: 626). He even emphasizes that 'an initially negative possession indisposition is regularly transformed retrospectively into a beatific revelation' (2003: xiv). As an example he refers to St. Teresa of Avila (1515–1582), who – had she been less successful – could have been easily subjected to exorcism, because exorcism was employed to control, as Lewis confirms, 'unruly' and excessively enthusiastic ecstatics, especially women and men of a similar subordinate status (2003: xv, xvii). Despite the wealth of her family, she represents a typical marginalized figure in society due to her gender, marital status (single) and social status as member of a family of (forced) converts from Judaism to Christianity (Lewis 2003: xv, with reference to Evan Fales 1996). Her success is remarkable even after her death as her experiences could easily have been reclassified as demonic episodes by the ecclesiastical authorities; instead, they proceeded with her canonization. According to Lewis, therefore, the case of St. Teresa shows the impact of empowerment 'conferred by possession on those disadvantaged by gender and other social disabilities' (2003: xv).

Following Lewis and other scholars, a common feature of studies on ecstatic religious experience remains the association of possession rituals with women and other marginalized groups. An often-repeated explanation refers to deprivation, either social or psychological. In short, the deprivation theory assumes 'that people (and it seems, especially women) behave religiously because of social and psychological reasons rather than for religious reasons' (Sered 1994: 65). Consequently, possession is interpreted by scholars in this perspective, as Keller states, 'as a *symbol* of their deprivation', and women become perceived as 'needy bodies rather than firm minds' (2002: 58, 88). Challenging the deprivation theory, Sered stresses the voluntary character of possession rituals and argues that women have other choices for opposing the social situation. Sered especially criticizes the negative evaluation of women implied in deprivation theories and regards them as a misrepresentation of possession as a symptom of disempowerment (see also Keller 2002: 55).

Lewis's study is usually regarded as an example of the deprivation theory. However, one must recognize, as Lewis himself states, that he does not regard all cases of possession as derived from women's deprivation. He argues that only one type, the peripheral possession, is associated with it. He also insists that deprivation and peripherality are not themselves the cause of possession rituals and writes that his argument was only that 'in these circumstances such cults are likely to arise where other means of redress are excluded' (1967: 626, see also Lewis 1966). The crucial term in this sentence is 'likely'. Lewis regards spirit possession as an instrument of women in societies that provide women with no other means of assertiveness, but possession rituals are not the only strategy and are also not always linked to deprivation.

Lewis rejects Janice Boddy's feminist critique of his study and argues that she 'remains imprisoned by her own intellectual perceptions' (2003: xi). Boddy presents in her work about the *zar* [also written *saar*] cult a different reading as she sees it as counterhegemonic for the women, 'a feminine response to hegemonic praxis and the privileging of men that this ideologically entails' (Boddy 1989: 5). She elevates therefore the function of the *zar* cult for the women from a form of resistance to a sphere of dominance and creativity, of feminist consciousness. Men are mainly absent in her study as they worked as migrant workers outside the village during her research. The female practice is therefore not a peripheral cult but a central one, according to Boddy, as women have 'real' dominance over men (Boddy 1989: 136). Boddy even sees *zar* as 'an ambiguous metacommentary on local morality' (1994: 417). Though Lewis and Boddy both refer to the same tradition in their work, Bourguignon points out (2004: 561–2) that they worked in two different settings: Lewis worked in a Somali nomadic society where men had a major economic role, while Boddy worked in a Sudanese village where men were absent and women the majority. Also important are the two decades that passed between their respective fieldwork (Lewis carried out his research between 1955 and 1957, while Boddy was in Sudan in 1977 and in 1984), during which Africa became transformed.[4] But also the gender of the researchers, combined with a different historical time, played a role in the different approaches, in particular because Lewis's knowledge about *saar* derived largely from information given to him by men (Bourguignon 2004: 560). Both interpretations, however, refer to women's subordination, only with a different assessment of the influence (or dominance) of women over men.

In both studies Bourguignon criticizes the limited focus on conscious motives at the expense of unconscious processes. It is not enough, she argues, just to recognize the subordination of women. We need to understand women's role 'as a psychodynamic response to, and expression of, their powerlessness. It is not an attempt to gain power for its own sake but, rather, an attempt to gratify wishes whose satisfaction is ordinarily denied the women, wishes rooted in their situation' (Bourguignon 2004: 559). Bourguignon looks more at the symbolic dimension of the experience and sees the symbolic language used in the rituals as a vital clue. Her starting point is the comment that the language with which people speak about spirit possession is derived from women's experience. She refers here, for instance, to the custom of naming the human host as the 'wife' of the spirit (see also Schmidt 2010: 103–8) or to 'mounting' as a way to describe possession (in the sense that a spirit 'rides' a human host as a 'horse'). The sexual symbolism can even be found in cases without the horse and mount metaphor, as she argues, for instance, in Christianity, 'in which possession trancers may be referred to as "vessels", to be filled with the Holy Spirit' (Bourguignon 2004: 565). She regards the soul as female and the spirit as male and describes the relationship as libidinous.

A very different relationship is established, however, when the spirits are not invited but regarded as harmful. In these cases exorcism is initiated in order to expel the spirits instead of accommodating them. Though the cultural response is the opposite, Bourguignon puts it in the same category as other possession rituals, just with a different therapy (accommodation and initiation instead of exorcism). For Bourguignon, possession rituals offer women means to 'do unconsciously what they do not permit themselves to do consciously' (2004: 572). Hence, Bourguignon's underlying assumption is that women are indeed socialized to be subordinate and submissive. But, as Boddy asks quite correctly, '[b]y whose evaluation are women marginal? Does economic or political subordination fully determine women's positions in other spheres of life?' (1994: 415). Boddy's questions raise an important point: it is possible to be peripheral in the political arena but central in another sector of society. It is therefore crucial to understand the social variables that determine one's position and influence religious practice. However, this criticism does not affect Bourguignon's overall explanation of the gender stratification of people experiencing possession rituals, as she does not leave any doubt that she assumes women to be the primary target of these rituals. Like Lewis and other scholars, she states that 'for women, being receptive and passive to such entities is a situation that makes them powerful'; however, she then continues that the personalities of the spirits 'maintain the person's basic motivations, the motivations of the self, in spite of the temporary changes in identity' (2004: 571). Hence, according to Bourguignon, though the women are not regarded as responsible for anything that happens during these rituals, the possessing agencies nonetheless represent a continuity of motivation.

Another contribution in this debate about women's predominance in possession rituals comes from Sered, who criticizes a feature of many studies in this field (including those of Lewis and Boddy), namely, that they are based on the underlying hypothesis that possession is something abnormal. Sered insists that women's involvement in possession should be regarded as a normal human ability and not a reaction towards oppression because spirit possession itself is a normal human experience (Sered 1994: 190–1). Her own theory refers to the female body and its role in procreation. She argues that women's experiences during childbirth and heterosexual intercourse make them more receptive to others, including spiritual entities. Hence, she explains the predominance of women with receptivity to possession as a feminine-gendered ability, although Sered's theory does not explain why men can experience spirit possession, too (Lewis 2003: xx, see also Keller 2005: 8695). However, Sered clarifies in her work that 'a person's gender does not determine religiosity [though] it does influence the kinds of religions, rituals, communities and experiences that one is drawn to or which one finds meaningful'.[5]

Mary Keller goes in a different direction by criticizing Sered and others for ignoring the possessing agencies. She argues that the spirits are actively involved, as they will choose 'who will act as their instruments' (Keller 2002: 53). Keller states that scholars 'attribute it [the predominance of women in possession cults] to women's inferior gendered status in patriarchal culture. These analyses suggest that possessions are symptoms of the women's social and psychological deprivation that happen to find expression in culturally specific religious traditions' (Keller 2002: 2–3). But these scholars pay little or no attention to the possessing agency, the spirit, despite its importance. Though her critique of the way the West regards its own constructions as normative models is important, I have problems with her quite theological approach. The need to reorient possession studies is evident. However, to regard theology as the ground for comparative religious studies (2002: 227) goes too far for me, as I explain below. Keller is also aware of the problem, and she describes this step as 'the riskiest element of the blueprint' (2002: 227).

The debate about women's predominance in possession rituals in Brazil

Though experience with so-called abnormal phenomena is not gendered, as Machado's survey in São Paulo confirmed (Machado 2009: 234), in the literature about Brazilian religious practices many examples focus on women as mediums. The predominance of women in possession rituals in Brazil is documented in particular in traditions belonging to the so-called African matrix, while Spiritism seems to lack this feature and operates with male and female mediums equally. The explanations for the predominance of women in these traditions resemble the debate outlined above. Patricia Lerch (1982), for instance, explains the apparent predominance of women in Umbanda in Porto Alegre in terms of relative powerlessness, much like Lewis and other scholars. The role of a medium offers women, according to Lerch, 'access to "power" and thus offsets the relative powerlessness typical of comparable socio-economic roles available to them in the modern society' (Lerch 1982: 237–8). Though Donovan supports Lerch and others in their interpretation that people are drawn towards possession cults that are perceived as peripheral as a reaction to political powerlessness and socio-economic marginality, he challenges the generality: 'The question . . . is not whether the model is accurate, but whether it is complete' (2000: 361). Donovan points to his observation that many 'are attracted to these religious forms despite failing to be, by Lewis's standard, demographically predisposed' (2000: 363). Equally important is realizing that people fitting Lewis's (and Lerch's) pattern may have chosen the practice because of other reasons. He even argues that the female preponderance within possession cults can also be seen as epiphenomenal to some generic reasons as women outnumber men in almost every religious denomination. However, before I come to a general evaluation of women's predominance, I want to present some of the studies about it within the Brazilian context. But before I begin I will make one comment: Lewis's and other theories are based on traditions in which every participant is also a medium, and hence experiences spirit possession or another type of mediumship. The Brazilian religions I presented in the introduction, however, have different level of interaction and distinguish, for instance, between clients (who are searching for help from the spirits and deities) and mediums, the instrumental agencies who enable communication between humans and the spiritual world (see also Donovan 2000: 367). This diversity has some implications for the application of some of the theories discussed above on the Brazilian context.

I start with neo-Pentecostalism. Women are described as the main (sometimes even the exclusive) target for exorcism rituals in neo-Pentecostal churches. These possession rituals are often interpreted as 'symbolic rebellion on the part of socially disenfranchised Pentecostals. This rebellion functions as a catharsis, a safety-valve, accommodating them to their social condition' (Alexander 1989: 109). However, in his study about Pentecostal possession rituals in New York, Alexander questions 'the necessary relation of Pentecostal ritual to compensation and passivity as well as the conceptualisation of ritual that underlies this interpretation' and refers instead to Victor Turner's theory of 'ritual anti-structure' as 'a more illuminating interpretive frame of reference' (Alexander 1989: 109).

Fernanda da Silva Pimentel (2005), however, goes in a different direction in her study about women in the IURD and their role in the liberation rituals, the exorcism. In distinction to the African matrix in which the predominance of women seems to reflect the social value of the practice, Pimentel explains the neo-Pentecostal preference of women with a theological reason. As mentioned in the introduction, the IURD is the most prominent neo-Pentecostal church, with a global presence. The liberation ceremonies that are conducted each Friday are one of the core practices and regarded as one of the main functions of the IURD. Margarida Maria Cichelli Oliva describes their view in which Satan and the demons are regarded as inferior spirits (1995: 99) who are responsible for all misery and evil. They constantly disturb 'the mental, physical and spiritual order' which, according to the founder of the IURD, Edir Macedo, is the main problem of our existence (Oliveria 1998: 112). It is the responsibility of everyone, men and women, to intervene and to 'liberate' the world from demons. The IURD sends its members, for instance, to Afro–Brazilian *terreiros* with the instruction to prevent people from entering the *terreiro*.

However, the direct confrontation can contain a risk for the IURD members who believe that demons can infect everyone who approaches a *terreiro*. This disturbance can even affect the family members of someone who attends ceremonies. These disturbances are categorized as demonic possession, though generally the IURD rejects the terms 'possession' and 'incorporations' because body and soul are regarded as a unit that cannot be controlled by demons. Demonic possession is therefore carefully described as 'paralysing the will and distracting the conscience by a play of fantasy, or, in other words, by the demon' (Oliva 1995: 99–100). José Sorafim da Silva lists ten symptoms of demonic possession such as nervousness, headaches, insomnia, suicidal tendencies, depression, vision and hearing voices.[6] In these cases healing can only be achieved by reversing the affliction with a ceremony called 'depossession' (*despossessão* in Portuguese). While Lewis (referring to de Heusch) uses the term 'depossession of the self' in order to describe a state in which the soul is lost (Lewis 2003: 40), the IURD uses the term depossession to imply the loss of the demon, not the soul, which is regarded as inseparably connected to the body. The ritual can be seen as a cleansing of the body so that the Holy Ghost can enter, because the Holy Ghost will enter only if the individual is free of all demonic afflictions. It is initiated by shouting repeatedly, 'In the name of Jesus, in the name of Jesus, in the name of Jesus' (Sorafim da Silva 1998: 70) as it is believed that salvation lies in God's word alone. Everyone present in the congregation joins the pastor and his assistants in the constant shouting of 'Go away! Go away! Go away!' or 'In the name of Jesus!'– until someone collapses. I have also observed pastors enforcing the verbal attack by pressing their hands on or above the head of an individual in order to pass on positive energy. Members of the congregation are asked to support their effort by stretching their arms and hands towards the front of the church. While such an event embraces the whole congregation, the *sessão de descarrego* (literally the 'session of discharge') concentrates on certain individuals. The purpose is to initiate the manifestation of the demon that causes the affliction to the person or the family, in an individual, usually a woman, as Pimentel explains. Based on conservative gender stereotypes, the IURD preaches that women are seen predominately as housewives and mothers and should be quiet (Pimentel 2005: 116). Consequently, the main positions in the church hierarchy are occupied by men, though women constitute the majority of church members. However, in their roles as mothers and housewives it is their responsibility to keep evil away from the family. Thus, it is seen as the duty of women to fight demons that afflict members of their families. And exorcism is part of this battle against evil.

Pimentel outlines the exorcism in three steps: first, women have to be liberated (exorcized) from their own demonic affliction. In a second step they encourage the demons that affect their family to manifest in their bodies. And the third step is the exorcism of these demons out of the bodies of the women so that the Holy Spirit can fill their bodies and souls, and they and their families can be saved (Pimentel 2005: 121). Based on interviews with women in the IURD, Pimentel presents demonic possession as a crucial part of the female role as housewife and mother and even states that being the instrument for exorcism gives these women new significance: 'In other words, the demon takes from the devotees the blame for their actions, but not the responsibility of an individual to confront and liberate. The responsibility is placed on the shoulders of women' (Pimentel 2005: 123). Pimentel interprets exorcism not only as therapeutic for women but also as a means of empowerment, as their (only) opportunity to occupy a significant position in society. Her interpretation goes in a slightly different direction than the foregoing academic discourse about women's predominance. Instead of looking at the social deprivation of women in the IURD, Pimentel bases her argument on its members' conservative gender roles. Despite the fact that most (if not all) women in the IURD work outside the home and contribute to the family income, their role in society is limited to motherhood and to caring for the family. The liberation ritual is seen as an important healing ritual for the family as the basic social unit. The woman, whose body is used as an instrument for the liberation, becomes the scapegoat for the problems of her family. And as a result she receives a new, elevated social position. Though she is not the one who defeats the demon – the IURD believes that only God's word can defeat the demons; hence, the exorcism has to be conducted by a pastor who acts with the help of God – she is nonetheless a vital instrument for liberating the demons because only the manifestation of the demon in a body allows the pastor to identify the demon, which is the first step in an exorcism (Almeida 2003: 323). However, in comparison to other exorcism cases in which women gain a certain degree of social control and power (see e.g. Bourguignon 2004: 567–70), the women involved do not receive a permanent elevated status. It is regarded as their duty. It is therefore also not a possession illness which can be transformed into something positive (e.g. becoming a shaman), as described by Lewis (2003: 110–13). The case described here represents some intriguing contradictions. On the one side, the demon possession and the exorcism are conducted in a religious setting, the church building, and according to strict rules under the guidance of a senior pastor. On the other side, however, the pastors who initiate the manifestation of the demons will never experience them; instead, they are only experienced by women, who do not occupy any position of power in the IURD. Nonetheless, the ritual is one of the core events of the IURD's weekly calendars, and it is considered central to the preservation of morality and values. Though the role of women can be described purely as vehicles or instruments, they are essential for the performance of the rituals. I would therefore extend Pimentel's argumentation that the liberation rituals have a therapeutic function for the women (2005: 207) and the wider community, not only the family but also the congregation. To remain with Lewis's terminology, one can say that the ritual is central for the continuity of society, though performed by peripheral, socially marginalized individuals. The predominance of women can therefore be seen as the result of the conservative gender role division held by the IURD, according to which each gender has specific responsibilities. The outcome of the gender role classification within the IURD is, of course, the deprivation of women in peripheral positions of society. However, the IURD does not represent the majority religion in Brazil. Most members are still converts, and are not born into the IURD. Most female members have deliberately chosen to join the IURD, in spite or because of its conservative gender division. As the majority of members are female, one can only assume that they have no problem with the gender role associated with women in the IURD. It would be a mistake, therefore, to interpret the rituals as a strategy, as Lewis writes, 'to achieve ends which they cannot readily obtain more directly' (Lewis 1971: 85). It is also not a means of reversing the power structure or of celebrating femininity as Boddy suggests is the case with *saar*. The symbolic universe expressed in the role playing of the liberation rituals brings order into chaos, as Pimentel writes (2005: 209). It can even be seen, in light of Bourguignon's interpretation, as a psychodynamic response to, and expression of, powerlessness. The situation cannot be altered but at least expressed. Possession and exorcism become, in Bourguignon's words, 'an idiom of distress and of indirect self-assertion' (2004: 557).

However, the situation in the IURD (and a few other neo-Pentecostal churches that also focus on female members as instruments of liberation rituals) is quite unique and dissimilar to the gender stratification in the other traditions in which men are not excluded from the experience per se. As mentioned already, Spiritism does not have any restriction based on gender, and a medium can be male or female. More ambivalent is the gender division in the Afro–Brazilian religions that have been at the centre of the academic investigation of the predominance of women in possession rituals in Brazil. While the many mixtures and variations make it impossible to distinguish neatly between the traditions of the African matrix in Brazil, some features are different. For example, Birman (1995) describes the main difference between Umbanda and Candomblé as being their different positions with respect to homosexuality: while Candomblé *terreiros* welcome homosexual men, they are unwanted in most Umbanda *terreiros* (Birman 1995: 13). One interviewee who is *pai de santo* of an Umbanda *terreiro* but also *filho de santo* in Candomblé and even initiated into a Yoruba cult, attributed the different attitudes to homosexuality to Umbanda's Catholic influence. However, he stressed that this attitude is changing with the times. For *Pai* Ricardo, it is 'a reflection of society on religion and not religion on society'.[7] However, the less welcoming attitude towards homosexuality in Umbanda does not mean that men (homosexual and heterosexual) are excluded from the role of medium. Quite the opposite is documented by Pressel (1977), Brown (1986) and others who observed male mediums in Umbanda *terreiros*, though Pressel qualifies her observation in another article in which she states that 'men do not actively participate as mediums to the extent that women do' (Pressel 1982: 184). And even Birman refers to an Umbanda *pai de santo* whom she described as homosexual (1995: 6).

It is surprising, therefore, to see so many references to women dominating Umbanda, for instance in the work of Lerch (1982) quoted above. One possible explanation for this observation might be the gender distribution among active participants: female participants outnumbered males by a ratio of three to one.[8] It might be that some of the researchers took the sheer presence of a large female majority as a sign of women's predominance, but this presence does not suggest the non-existence of male participants in Umbanda. As Kelly Hayes comments, although women tend to outnumber men as mediums, Umbanda studies do not suggest that 'innate female traits predispose women to serve the spirits, as is sometimes asserted in Candomblé' (2010: 112). The common understanding is that both men and women have the ability to become mediums. The gender distribution depends, however, on the type of Umbanda under investigation. As Hayes highlights, women outnumber men at all levels (from clients to members and leaders) in most Umbanda *terreiros*. Only in the highly bureaucratic institutions do men predominate at the upper levels of the hierarchy (2010: 115). Though this kind of Umbanda does not represent the majority of Umbanda *terreiros* (where women outnumber men), it is nonetheless influential for the wider image of Umbanda. Most studies, for instance, refer to Zélio de Moraes as the founder of Umbanda, though his influence is debatable (e.g. by Brown 1986). Nonetheless, in most overviews of the history of Umbanda it seems that men dominate, 'at least as it has been preserved in the records of the religion's more institutionalized forms' (Hayes 2010: 114). This observation can also be applied to the Faculdade de Teologia Umbandista in São Paulo, though it also has women among its teachers and administrators. Even among its students men seem to dominate, though I do not have access to any official figures and can only reflect on my observations. Nonetheless, when we look at the ordinary Umbanda *terreiros*, female leadership is visible. During my research in São Paulo I only encountered one *terreiro* with exclusively female mediums (though men were present as drummers and among clients). When I asked the *mãe de santo* why, she said that her house is atypical and that the *terreiro* of the priest who initiated her also has *filhos de santo*. His *terreiro* is much larger than hers, and she likes it that her house is a house of women (referring here to Landes's book). She even said that she would refer a man to the *terreiro* of her *pai de santo* for initiation.[9] Despite this exception, the overall estimation is that two thirds of the *terreiros* are led by women. Negrão states, for instance, that 67 of the Umbanda *terreiros* she visited in São Paulo (i.e. 79.7%) have a female leader (1996: 175). This ratio is also mentioned by other scholars, though with different explanations: some account for the predominance with reference to motherhood and women's domestic duties, some focus on the healing aspect of Umbanda, and others spinpoint the centrality of spirit possession in Umbanda.

The first explanation is to a certain degree similar to Pimentel's explanation of women's role in the IURD, which stresses the conservative image of women in a patriarchal society: because women's traditional roles in society are to be housewives and mothers – and therefore to prepare and serve food, assist others in need, care for the house, organize parties and so on – they take over, almost as continuation of their 'normal' role, similar roles in the *terreiro*. This explanation is based on the family structure of Umbanda and other Afro–Brazilian religions, which 'provides a space in which women's experience and concerns are central' (Hayes 2010: 102). Activities that are traditionally associated with women (cooking, cleaning and caring) are elevated because they now have religious significance. Selka sees this focus on motherhood as related to Catholic notions of femininity and states that even in public politics women's roles are often understood in terms of motherhood and not citizenship (Selka 2009: 20). The ideal image is that of the Virgin Mary, and women are responsible for every task associated with biological and also social reproduction. Women gain access to power, therefore, grounded 'in the image of the mother who cares for others and protects her community' (Selka 2009: 20). While working as mothers and housewives is regarded as the ordinary duty of every woman, working in the *terreiro* is valued as sacred service and carries prestige. Behaviours that society, as Hayes summarizes, 'cultivates particularly in women, like obedience and submission, offer a route to increased authority' (Hayes 2010: 121). Ordinary women become powerful and sacred because the Afro–Brazilian religions 'provide a model of the world in which motherhood serves as an important route to and metaphor of religious leadership' (Hayes 2010: 102). This explanation, which confirms the stereotypical role models for women, overlooks societal changes as well as the availability of other opportunities for women. It also ignores the presence of male mediums in Umbanda. Hence, while it seems to be plausible at a first glance, it does not offer a thorough explanation of the gender stratification in Umbanda *terreiros*.

Andrew Chesnut explains the higher number of female participants in Umbanda based on the therapeutic function of the religion. Umbanda is widely accepted, as Diana Brown's research documents, as an alternative source of health. At the heart of all Afro–Brazilian religions, but particularly Umbanda, is a concern with easing suffering. Well-being is, as Hayes explains, 'the product of a dynamic state of equilibrium between these worlds [i.e. the human world and the supernatural world of spiritual beings] and results when ties of commitment and reciprocity are acknowledged through ritual means, facilitating the continuous flow of spiritual energy through the Universe' (Hayes 2010: 103). It is no wonder that the majority of people go to Umbanda *terreiros* and Spiritist centres in search of healing. The problem can be physiological, emotional, social or spiritual; hence, it can reach from headaches, stress or a problem with a partner or a child to an existential crisis. Healing can involve herbal remedies, prayers and offerings to pacify the spirits, and sometimes also the development of one's mediumship abilities. Hence, the patient has to learn how to serve the spiritual entity, even if this means that the patient has to become a medium. Chesnut argues now that, because women are perceived in Brazil as being 'responsible for the collective health of the family and the individual welfare of each member' (Chesnut 1997: 70), it would explain why more women than men go to Umbanda *terreiros*. Though Chesnut's figures were based on a survey among Pentecostal informants who admitted visiting an Umbanda *terreiro*, it is nonetheless interesting that his female interviewees explain their visits to Umbanda *terreiros* as a search for healing at a much greater rate than men (63% to 38.5%), while the latter explain their visits as motivated by looking for a cure but also searching for a job or earning a better wage. His observations, however, give no indication about the gender ratio among mediums. Though a client looking for help in an Umbanda *terreiro* can be advised to develop his or her mediumship abilities, there is still a significant gap between clients and mediums in a *terreiro*.

The third explanation focuses on the role of spirit possession as 'a means of direct contact with the sacred . . . [that] enables poor and working-class women greater access to status, power, autonomy, and authority than elsewhere in Brazil' (Hayes 2010: 121). An example of studies that take this direction is Lerch (1982), who applies Lewis's explanation to Umbanda. However, as Birman observes, 'To say that female mediums gain power through spirit possession is only half of the story. The other half, no less important to practitioners, concerns the limits [of this power]: they can't do everything because their control over these possessing entities is limited and follows a logic that goes beyond them' (quoted and translated by Hayes 2006: 157, from an unpublished paper of Birman 2005). Following Birman's approach, Hayes looks at the limits of spirit possession and argues – in line with Landes's observation – that being a bride of the spirits conflicts almost always with being a wife. Hayes sees the clash between the demands of the spiritual work (spirit possession) and the demands of their husbands (outside the religious sphere) as the most difficult challenge of female mediums. However, whether it is a reinterpretation of the traditional female role (Sered 1994) or an alternative to inadequate love relations (Brown 2001), Hayes argues that 'serving the spirits seems to be an attractive option for women struggling with normative conventions of gender and sexuality that prescribe for them a subordinate role in relationship to men, limit female power to the domestic sphere, and stigmatise female sexuality while permitting men a range of sexual outlets' (Hayes 2006: 159).

As an example, Hayes presents a detailed portrait of Maria Nazaré de Souza Oliveira (2011), a married, working-class, middle-aged medium of *pombagira* (also written *pomba gira*), the female counterpart of *exú* in the Umbanda pantheon. Hayes states that *pomba gira* spirit possession is most common among middle-aged housewives. The interesting aspect here is that the entity is commonly known as a prostitute. Or, in Hayes's words, 'Beholden to no man, she is often said to be the lover of seven, including Lucifer. Sexually independent and childless, she represents the antithesis of the docile, domestic, maternal female' (2006: 159). Someone incorporating *pombagira* expresses, according to Hayes, a particular kind of feminine power, in contrast to the normal role of faithful wife and mother. It enables her therefore to subvert the social norms that control her ordinary behaviour. However, Hayes highlights that this experience can have a negative outcome as *pombagira* can also introduce or exacerbate conflicts.

At this point Hayes differentiates herself from Stefania Capone (2010), who sees *pombagira* possession as an affiliation that enables a woman to act when confronted by violence or treachery of men (Capone 1999:182). Via the possession women therefore gain the authority to act even when the manner in which they respond contradicts their normal domestic, and hence subordinate, role. Hayes, however, emphasizes that it is not always the case 'that invoking the figure of Pomba Gira can successfully resolve gender conflicts, particularly when these involve entrenched social norms that encourage male violence and female quiescence' (Hayes 2006: 160). Hayes argues that Capone ignores the distinctions that mediums themselves make between their own wills as mediums and that of the possessing agency, the spirit. Referring to testimony of Nazaré, the spirit healer from Rio de Janeiro, and others, Hayes stresses that women can experience this conflict as 'different, if not actively antagonistic'.[10] Nazaré distinguishes carefully between her own desires and those of her spirits in her testimonies. In the end, the ménage-à-trois of male villain (husband), female victim (Nazaré) and spirit protector (*pombagira*), which is a common feature in the discourse about *pombagira* (Capone 2010), could not be resolved. As Hayes states, working with the spirit enabled Nazaré to cope with the infidelities of her husband. She became something else in addition to his wife and the mother of his children and gained autonomy, social recognition and prestige, even an independent income because

Umbanda provides social resources and access to a network of patron–client relationships that integrates healers such as Nazaré into an alternative economy (see Brown 1986; Greenfield and Prust 1990). However, it also increased the tensions at home and became counterproductive to some extent. Nazaré had to 'appease both sides' in order to keep her family; hence, she had to balance the demands of the spirit with the demands of her husband. But sometimes she found herself, as she said to Hayes, 'caught in the crossfire' (*fogo cruzado*) (2006: 169). In a way Hayes confirms the explanation of women's predominance in Umbanda as a means for socially marginalized people to gain prestige, a means of empowerment. Similar to Boddy's interpretation of the *saar* cult, Hayes interprets *pombagira* possession 'as a creative yet culturally sanctioned response to restrictive gender roles or inadequate love relationships, a way to express otherwise forbidden thoughts or feelings, and an economic strategy for women who have few options beyond the traditional wifely role' (2011: 9). But unlike other contributions to this approach, she highlights the tension that arises when women attempt to balance their ordinary roles with their spiritual roles.

Moving now to consider Candomblé, it is interesting to note that the majority of Candomblé studies still imply that 'Candomblé participants are primarily individuals with little access to power and resources' (Seligman 2005: 76). There is also a frequent appearance of homosexual mediums in studies about Candomblé. The general consensus seems to be that Candomblé mediums are overwhelmingly female because women represent, as Seligman and others emphasize, one of the social groups with the lowest social status in Brazilian society. Though men are also involved in the ritual practice of all Afro–Brazilian religions, including Candomblé – and some rituals are even performed exclusively by men – the common perception is that people who incorporate an *orixá* are women or homosexual men: that is to say, people from the periphery of society. When I discussed homosexuality with P., a practitioner of Tercerô (described sometimes as a subdivision of Tambor da Mina), he stressed the openness of religions in the African matrix towards all kinds of sexualities and gender. 'The issue is not that a religion makes people become gay, but because she is gay and feels more comfortable [in the *terreiros*] because of openness of the religion. For example: if the homosexual is in the *terreiro*, he can do whatever he wants, but not outside. In other religions it is not allowed.'[11] His observation reflects that at ceremonies today, one can observe women and men, both homosexual and heterosexual, embracing the possession experience without fear of public humiliation. In the same way as Umbanda changed its attitude towards homosexuality, Candomblé has also changed due to the shift in society. In some *terreiros* there are as many *filhas de santo* as *filhos de santo*, as well as an equal distribution of *iaôs* (male or female initiates who are trained in incarnating an *orixá*), without the strong emphasis on homosexuality.

In the literature about Candomblé it is generally acknowledged that women played an important role in the early transmission of African heritage to Brazil, though some of the explanations seem to neglect the historical evidence. Krippner, for instance, argues that the rites fell to women because male slaves in Brazil were preoccupied with manual labour (1989: 188), overlooking the fact that female slaves had to work as hard as male slaves on the plantations. Barbara Bush-Slimani (1993) even speaks of a 'dual burden' of hard physical work and child bearing that female slaves had to carry and that is often overlooked in studies about slavery.[12] Nonetheless, despite little historical evidence, it is commonly understood that in the *terreiros* founded by freed blacks and supported by a network of enslaved Africans in the late eighteenth and early nineteenth centuries, women were regarded as repositories of the heritage, embedded in myths, dances and songs as well as culinary and healing traditions. Through a complex system of symbols Candomblé practitioners honoured their links to Africa – and women played a central role in this process (Hayes 2010: 105). Rachel Harding acknowledges that the first *terreiros* were founded by Africans, but already in the middle of the nineteenth century a growing number of Brazilian-born descendants had become involved (2000). Several of the early and most prominent *terreiros*, according to Hayes, were founded by women in the late nineteenth and early twentieth centuries (2010: 107). However, that women excluded men intentionally, as Krippner states (1989: 188), is extremely unlikely (Matory 2005: 192). Nonetheless, the overwhelming presence of female leadership in Bahia led Landes to her description of Candomblé as a matriarchy (1947). She linked Candomblé in Bahia to female-centred households and portrayed the religion as not only statistically dominated by female practitioners but also led by women. Landes emphasized the significance of women in all hierarchical levels of Candomblé's structure, including as figures of authority. She even suggested that the presence of a heterosexual man in such a stage would be regarded as strange, even abnormal. Matory, however, questions her presentation of Jeje-Nagô Candomblé as matriarchal (2005: 189). He argues that male priests not only play a numerically equal and often politically dominant role in Candomblé's counterparts elsewhere in Brazil and around the Atlantic perimeter but also in Bahia at the time of Landes's research. He regards Landes's presentation of Candomblé as matriarchal as political motivated and misguided, but acknowledges the impact Landes's study had on Brazil, not only on academic studies but also on the religious practice: in the wake of her work the Black Mother become powerful icon of regionalist thought (2005: 200). However, he accuses Landes of falsifying her observations. Because she wanted to 'make real in Brazil her own subaltern North American vision of a primitive matriarchy' (Matory 2005: 190), she ignored, as Matory writes, the existence of male leaders in the Bahian Candomblé *terreiros*. Later, scholars in and outside Brazil followed her lead and overlooked the vibrant diversity among practitioners, including the mediums incorporating the *orixás*. Despite Matory's historical data about Candomblé in the 1930s I doubt, however, whether Landes would have indeed intentionally manufactured her research outcome to prove her argument. Her research was remarkable in her time, highlighting the dominant position of priestesses in Bahian Candomblé and their role in the codification of the version of Candomblé we know today.[13] *Mãe* Stella is just one of the more recent cases of a powerful priestess who dominates the tradition far beyond her own congregation Ilê Axé Opô Afonjá, even beyond Bahia (see Martins/Lody [eds.] 1999; Sansi 2007). Matory is certainly right that the presence of powerful priestesses is not enough to describe the whole tradition as matriarchal or to categorize even possession rituals as a female practice. It is also obvious that Landes focused on one form of Candomblé (Jeje-Nagô Candomblé) and ignored the others, which were – even in her time – much more diverse (e.g. Caboclo Candomblé). Unfortunately the outcome was that, as Matory and some of my interviewees in São Paulo remarked, one type of Candomblé practice became elevated to hegemonic status, while others became regarded as inferior. The *terreiros* described by Landes came to be seen as representing the correct way and other forms of Candomblé became ignored.[14] When I asked

Pai R., a *pai de santo* in Umbanda but also a practitioner of Candomblé and the Yoruba cult, about homosexuality, he agreed with Landes's portrayal of Candomblé as offering 'a place where homosexuality is accepted and allowed'. But he continued to say that 'there are other *terreiros* that do not accept them. For instance, Umbanda would not welcome homosexual [mediums] until not so long ago'.[15] Moreover, the situation has changed since the 1930s, as many anthropologists have confirmed (see Johnson 2002: 45), and the presence of men is now documented on all levels (e.g. Sjørslev 1999: 24), though women still outnumber men on all levels.

Similar to studies about Umbanda, quite a few scholars explain the even more visible predominance in Candomblé with reference to the 'natural mothering qualities' of women. Though my interviewees reject any perception of women being more religious than men (e.g. *Mãe I.* vehemently denied that men are less religious than women, despite the fact that women dominate in ceremonies), women are still sometimes portrayed in the literature as especially suited to care for the *orixás* as well as the congregation. The *mãe de santo* is compared to an idealized mother who is responsible to everyone under her care. Hayes quotes, for example, one devotee who said that the mother is 'the person who is most sought after . . . People are needy and women are more compassionate than men' (Hayes 2010: 107, referring to Maria Salete Joaquim 2001: 106). Sjørslev links the predominance of women to the socialization of girls through their mothers. While boys cut their connection to their mothers earlier in order to strengthen their identification with their fathers, girls develop their identity in relation to their mothers. However, as Sjørslev herself acknowledges, this Freudian explanation lacks empirical evidence and also ignores the wider network of adults among whom children are socialized (Sjørslev 1999: 108).

Other studies stress traditional gender roles and, like Lewis, explain the predominance of women in Candomblé as a female strategy to gain a degree of power that is normally beyond women's reach. Similar to the study about women in the IURD, serving the *orixás* is perceived as the duty of women because it involves so many domestic tasks such as cleaning, cooking and caring, all of which are traditionally performed by women. This explanation points therefore to the structure of Candomblé instead of to assumed female qualities. It is also reaffirmed in myths in which women are perceived as 'cool, reproductive, and contained – both in body and in the *terreiro* – while men carry the heat of bodies overindulgently open in the male domain of the street' (Johnson 2002: 44, alluding indirectly to Da Matta's idealized opposition of 'street' and 'house', see Da Matta 1991). In short, women are associated with reproduction and men with sex. However, as Johnson points out, the gendered structure of Candomblé transmitted in its mythology says little about the approach to 'engendering power' within Candomblé *terreiros*. Johnson explains that in one branch of Candomblé, what he labels the Ketu lineage nation (a sub-branch of Nagô Candomblé), the ideal leader of a *terreiro* is a postmenopausal woman who can devote most of her time to the *terreiro* and is regarded as 'doubly cool'. In other nations, however, the leadership ideal is less constrained, with the result that it has a higher number of *terreiros* with a male priest in charge (Johnson 2002: 44, 192, n.9). Nonetheless, regardless of the actual gender of the leader of the *terreiro*, according to Johnson the position is perceived as structurally female. The same is the case for the mediums who incorporate the *orixás*. During training they have to learn to submit to the authority of the *orixá*, who is perceived as *dono da cabeça* (master of the head). The trainees learn to endure and control the heat of the *orixá* during possession. This kind of behaviour, obedience and submission to authority is not only stereotypically associated with femininity (Hayes 2010: 107) but it is also described in gendered language. As mentioned above, possession is often symbolically referred to as a mounting of his wife, his *iaô*, even if the gender is the other way round – that is, even if the possessing agency is female and the possessed male. Johnson therefore states that 'being possessed by an orixá is symbolically a feminine, cool role' (2002: 44).

However, it is important to acknowledge that men and women are both involved in Candomblé. Ritual responsibilities are divided according to the grade of involvement (e.g. the stage of initiation) and the gender of the individual because all positions in a *terreiro* are gender specific, from preparing ceremonial food for the *orixás* (a female position) and the sacrifice of the animals (a male position) to drumming (usually a male role) and serving as ritual assistants (male and female). The latter are responsible for ensuring that the *fundamentos* (esoteric code of ritual practice) and *obrigações* (obligations) are followed by everyone present at the ceremonies (Hayes 2010: 109). Johnson also stresses that men as *ogã* are often the primary economic patrons of a *terreiro* and gain unprecedented access without the same obligations as other *filhos de santo* (2002: 48). Similar to Hayes's differentiated view on the Umbanda gendered structure, Johnson differentiates between the religious and the secular sphere. While women experience indeed power in the *terreiros*, he doubts whether this power can ever be transformed into the public sphere. He even comments that 'it may even reproduce and reinforce the gender stereotypes and gendered stratifications of Brazilian national culture'; however, he acknowledges that there is 'no source of prestige at the public, institutional level, at least for Afro–Brazilian women, that would compensate for the local forms of social capital offered within the religious hierarchies of the *terreiros*' (Johnson 2002: 48).

In order to come to a full understanding of the gender division of ritual practice in Candomblé and related traditions, some scholars look at the West African Yoruba tradition, though with different results. Mary Ann Clark, for instance, interprets possession in the so-called Orisha religions as a gendered female practice (2005). Clark uses the term 'Orisha religion' not only for the Cuban religion but also for other religions that have derived from the West African Yoruba tradition. Her label Orisha religions reaches from Nigeria and Niger to Cuba, Brazil and the United States, though most of her information seems to come from the Cuban Diaspora religion in the United States. Despite this generalization, Clark regards the Orisha religion as the only religion in which the female is normative because the religion valorizes feminine virtue and actions (2005: 143). Sex is no longer a limitation but the opposite: the gender role provides women 'the most important focal point of the entire ritual process' (2005: 120). And for Clark this is the reason why more women are drawn to the religion than men. As I have written elsewhere (Schmidt 2010: 100), Clark's assessment does not fit my own observation of the Cuban Diaspora religion. Though her critique of the misguided overemphasis on the significance of the *babalawos*[16] in the literature (e.g. Ortiz 1906, Cabrera 1954) is important,[17] Clark goes too far in her own interpretation of the role of the *diloggun* (a category of priesthood associated with cowry shell divination that is open to men and women). In her quest to present *diloggun* as more important than *ifá*, Clark imposes her ideas of the religion not only on other Cuban Diaspora houses in the United States but also on related religions of both past and present, ignoring the diversity of environments and historical developments. Even in Puerto Rico, which also belongs to the Cuban Diaspora, it is evident that the two branches of the religion, *regla de ifá* and *regla de ocha*, represent different gender structures but are equally important to the devotees (see Schmidt 2008). Clark's assessment of the significance of women in the Orisha religion also challenges Oyèrónké Oyêwùmí's presentation of the gender discourse among the West African Yoruba. Oyêwùmí argues that the Yoruba language is in principle genderfree (Oyêwùmí 1997: 29). By genderfree she does not mean that the language does not have any gender categories at all but rather that 'it is genderless because human attributes are not gender specific' (1997: 174). Because the language lacks many of the Western linguistic categories, they had to be introduced during the long process of colonization and missionary activities. Whether it was Islam, Christianity or British colonialism, all carried a different gendered perspective to Nigeria and influenced the Yoruba tradition. In particular, Christianity has changed the way the traditional religion is perceived, as Oyêwùmí argues. While originally the supernatural entities, deities and ancestor spirits were perceived without a fixed, static gender, Olodumare, the Creator God, came to be seen as male under the influence of Christian ideas of God (1997: 141). Though Oyêwùmí's analysis might have limited value when applied to specific cultural and historical contexts, it is important to keep in mind the fluid and complex gender construction in African indigenous religions such as the Yoruba (see also Olajuba 2005: 3402). Clark, however, challenges the idea of fluid gender constructions and writes that Oyêwùmí's descriptions 'seem to have ignored facts that suggest that among the Yoruba certain characteristics are attributed to women . . . and that these characteristics have an important place in their understanding of traditional religion in Africa and among Orisha worshippers in the Americas' (Clark 2005: 38). However, she does not present any evidence in support of her different reading of the past (see also the critique in Schmidt 2010).

Matory presents a more nuanced picture of women in Yoruba history by highlighting the changes that are due to the influences of Islam and Christianity as well as British colonialism. His argument is that we have to take into account the radical changes in women's position among the Yoruba that took place in the last centuries if we want to fully understand the gender division in ritual practice in Candomblé and other Yoruba-derived religions.

Instead of pointing towards the importance of women in traditional Yoruba religion, as, for instance, Clark does, we need to consider how the role of women was influenced by social and political changes. Matory argues that in the traditional Oyo-Yoruba religion, femininity has 'a privileged status', firmly connected to politico-religious authority, derived from the imperial past (Matory 1993: 58). Hence, women traditionally occupied positions of power. However, under the influence of Christian missionaries, women became systematically marginalized and later even excluded from some rituals, as Matory elaborates in detail (1993: 67). Women's role became restricted to fertility, without any political influence. But when the royal household in Oyo decreased in importance as a result of growing secularization, marginalized figures such as women and untitled rural men regained importance because the modern and secular king and his chiefs dissociated themselves from these rituals (1993: 70). Women's sexuality is used now as a metaphor; hence, women are seen as antithetical to the dominant forms of contemporary Nigeria. In particular, spirit possession rituals recall, as Matory writes, 'specific political orders of the past' (1993: 59), and by doing this they influence contemporary gender relations. 'These rites of spirit possession mobilize the norms of a defunct empire in the service of a rival modern order, which, unlike the modern hegemony, valorizes feminine authority' (Matory 1993: 64). Moving back to Candomblé, we see here the importance of avoiding an overly simplistic approach to gender relations. By stressing just one aspect, such as motherhood or women's association to fertility, one overlooks the political status they occupied and lost due to social and political changes. Stressing, for instance, the role of women in establishing the Candomblé *terreiros* and ritual in Salvador da Bahia in the late nineteenth and early twentieth centuries explains their influence in the past but does not provide an explanation about the predominance of women in possession rituals in the present. Recent decades have seen many changes in Brazilian society that have had an impact on women's position in society as well as in the *terreiros*, widening the opportunities open to them. Unfortunately, however, as Selka warns, these developments 'also contain the possibility of reproducing old inequalities when rural Afro–Brazilian women become the objects of a romanticizing gaze or commercializing projects that do not benefit them' (Selka 2009: 35). Selka's research in Cachoeira, Bahia, confirmed that women are in control within many *terreiros* in his research field and also in other organizations such as the Sisterhood of Boa Morte. Their influence can be seen not only within the narrow communities but also beyond. Referring to Rosalyn Terborg-Penn's research about African women who interpret similar groups as 'survival strategies', creating 'self-reliance through female networks' (1996: 25), Selka challenges the common perception of the ceremonial leadership in Candomblé and other religions as 'privilege without power' (e.g. Jules-Rosette 1996). He argues instead that Afro–Brazilian religions and public politics should not be seen as separate arenas. Candomblé is, as he writes, 'a potent source of power, even if this power is not specifically political in itself' (Selka 2009: 32). Though he later points to Candomblé in Cachoeira in particular, that is, in a rural town often portrayed as 'unaffected by modernization' (see also Sansi 2007), one can also apply his interpretation to other forms of Candomblé, including Candomblé paulista. Access to power is provided by the quite common Brazilian practice of patronage (see da Matta 1991) that structures the work of each *terreiro*. However, this practice is not associated to the possession rituals but relies more on the other divination techniques, especially *jogo de búzios*. Oracle reading can establish an extensive network of clients surrounding the leader of the *terreiro*. Clients provide income but also political influence and therefore power, in particular if regular clients can be transformed into official patrons of the *terreiro*. Through *jogo de búzios* and other practices that are mainly religious, priests and priestesses therefore gain some influence in the political realm (Selka 2009: 32, see also Brown 1986 about patronage in Umbanda). Clientelism becomes the crucial link between power on a religious level (as leader of a *terreiro*) and power in the public arena that can extend, as one can observe in the case of *Mãe* Stella, even to a national level. With an overwhelming presence of female leaders of Candomblé *terreiros*, women therefore have access to power via a religious practice. However, going back now to Lewis's explanation of women's predominance, access to power is not associated primarily with possession rituals but with divination, which Lewis takes to be a central, not peripheral, practice.

On the whole, studies confirm that there are no 'theological' explanations for the predominance of women in the African matrix. It can only be explained by a withdrawal of men from these rituals due to social pressure. Hence, the predominance of women in Candomblé rituals during the first half of the twentieth century follows a similar path to the process in Nigeria in which men were given a secular role model, leading to power positions, while women became marginalized. It only changed when Candomblé and the other traditions in the African matrix lost their strong 'ethnic' association with Afro–Brazilians and became globalized religions, or, as Gonçalves da Silva writes (1995: 290), universal traditions (*religião universal*). The performance of possession rituals lost – to a certain degree – its gender-biased connotation. Though still regarded as a feminine activity, the experience of possession rituals is less associated with social inferiority and instead with prestige. As Michael Lambek states, power and hierarchy are socially constructed categories, 'generated in the rituals and system of communication through which possession is constituted' (Lambek 1989: 50–1). Women and other marginalized groups learned to access power via Candomblé rituals. They were not helpless victims but empowered by their role in the *terreiros*. Nowadays other groups compete for the same power as the marginalized groups and again change the dynamic in the African matrix. These changes make it impossible to apply any of the dominant discourses on gender stratification to the Brazilian situation, as Brown and Bick commented with regard to Umbanda:

> Our examination of Umbanda, in relation to other Afro–Brazilian religions and to the Catholic Church, points to the fallacy of arguments that see the encounter between the religions of dominant and dominated groups as simply unidirectional. As Umbanda's early leaders sought to whiten the Afro–Brazilian tradition, like some practitioners of Candomblé, elements in Umbanda today seek to re-Africanize it. In no simple sense has any religion established hegemony in Brazil. Instead, Brazilians move freely among religions, seeing themselves as adherents of more than one religion at the same time. To whatever degree models of unidirectional change in the realm of religion apply elsewhere, such models clearly do not apply to Brazil. (1987: 88)

At this point I return to Donovan and his assessment of the validity of Lewis's theory in Brazil. Donovan criticizes Lewis in particular because of his lack of definitions, which makes it impossible to fully characterize the individuals drawn towards possession cults. In a sense, everyone seems impotent and inferior in comparison to someone else, even the upper classes. Even the social deprivation highlighted by Lewis is handled by everyone in a different way, in particular in Brazil, as Donovan points out with reference to Daniel Halperin's comment about Brazilians: 'despite "overwhelming political-economic exigencies", many still appear to enjoy a high quality of life' (Donovan 2000: 364 with reference to Halperin 1996: 4). Donovan argues therefore that not the objective deprivation (economic or social) is relevant but the perceived one; hence, the *reaction* to difficulty distinguishes between a new medium and non-mediums (Donovan referring here to Zinnbauer and Pargament 1998, among others). Consequently Lewis's model has to be altered as it is not the low socio-economic status that correlates with participation in possession cuts but how it is perceived by individuals. Connected to it is another of Donovan's points: that the valuation of a socio-economic status depends on the standard of comparison (Donovan 2000: 365). This point is quite a common remark for anthropologists, though Donovan does not refer only to different societies but also to the impact of rising expectations. A status can be perceived therefore by an individual as stress-relieving as well as stress-inducing depending on the moment in his or her life. Consequently, it can draw individuals who are objectively in the same position to different religions. Mariz's comments in relation to Spiritism can be applied to other traditions, too: 'No specific element or situation helps characterize Afro–Brazilian Spiritists as distinct from Brazilians belonging to other religions. What distinguishes the Afro–Spiritists are their subjective experiences' (Mariz 1994: 53, quoted in Donovan 2000: 365).

Donovan also points to the presence of alternatives in Brazilian society, for instance carnival organizations but also football clubs (referring here to Da Matta 1991). Donovan therefore argues that 'the availability of alternatives blunts the inevitability which Lewis tried to build into his model' (2000: 366). However, while his critical comments resonate with some of my concerns, his test cases do not convince. This is mainly due to the lack of data, in particular when looking at the national statistical data but also when looking at a small sample of questionnaires. It even seems sometimes that he is unaware of the reluctance of Brazilians to openly confess that they belong to an Afro-Brazilian religion or Spiritism, which has an impact on the data. Nonetheless, his comments on the applicability of Lewis's theory to Brazil highlight the complex relationship between religious affiliation and social variables and the need to supplement the current model (Donavan 2002: 373–4). The socio-economic variables are important but 'only to the extent to which they generate not merely stress, but "identity-threatening" stress' (Donovan 2000: 374). As Lewis also pointed out, 'the common factor linked with possession seems to be the experience of identity-threatening stress, exacerbated by conditions of confinement and exclusion' (Lewis 1991: 10, see also the preface in Lewis 2003). In a sense Donovan confirms Lewis's revised position of mediumship 'as a reaction to a personal interpretation of the individual's social situation' (Donovan 2000: 375).

The social stratification of people experiencing ecstatic religions in Brazil

Shortly after I arrived in Brazil for my research, a colleague from the University of São Paulo invited me to accompany him and some friends to a ceremony in a Candomblé *terreiro* at the edge of São Paulo (see Figure 2.1). Still struggling with jetlag, I was delighted, of course, and looked forward to my first ever Candomblé ceremony. The occasion was the seven-year anniversary, which is an important occasion in the life of an individual and also of the *terreiro*. This ceremony was even more special as the *filho de santo* was an *ogã* who occupies an important role in the *terreiro*. Though the person does not experience the merger with his *orixás*, and hence does not become possessed, he has elevated social prestige in the congregation. His *orixás* were nonetheless present at the ceremony but in different human bodies. Looking at the photos I took at the ceremony, I am once again enchanted by the colours and decorations. From the first step I took into the *terreiro* it was evident that this was a rich congregation, not only because of the size of the *terreiro* and its many buildings (including a museum) but also the cars in which the participants arrived. More striking than the presence of so many *filhos* and *filhas de santo* was to observe how many of them experienced their *orixás* during the evening. In some cases the merger between human and supernatural being did not come to a full conclusion but ended after a few moments of initial contact. In some other cases, however, the

Figure 2.1 Candomblé ceremony, São Paulo

orixás successfully incorporated into the bodies of the *filhos* and *filhas de santo* and took control over them. As it was the first time I had attended a ceremony in Brazil, I noticed first and foremost the differences and similarities to ceremonies of Caribbean religions. One striking factor that hit me from the beginning was that I saw men and women incorporating the *orixás*. And as I had noticed some of the participants arriving with partners and children, I could guess that some of the men, at least, lived in heterosexual relationships (it was, however, not possible to enquire any further in this direction). As I observed at other ceremonies, and later confirmed in the literature (e.g. Gonçalves da Silva 1995) and in my interviews, Candomblé in São Paulo can be characterized by an extreme openness and adaptability to the urban environment. Candomblé is, of course, firmly located in an urban setting, whether it is Salvador da Bahia, Rio de Janeiro or Recife. But, as Gonçalves da Silva writes, Candomblé is not always the same (1995: 288). When Candomblé expanded into São Paulo during the 1960s, it adapted to the metropolitan surroundings. During this time São Paulo embraced immigrants from various parts of Brazil who arrived in the city mainly in search of work and better living conditions. The industrial development of São Paulo together with a rising mobility of people made São Paulo a culturally exuberant centre that became a perfect setting for Candomblé and other traditions to prosper and flourish. However, one should not forget the social mobility that changed Brazilian society in the second part of the twentieth century.

The vast majority of Brazilians (over 80%) live now in urban cities such as São Paulo. The massive influx of rural migrants met the cities unprepared, which led to the growth of favelas at the margins of each city, including São Paulo. Though the situation has improved a little, Brazil is still, as Greenfield states, one of the most unjust nations in the world with regard to economic stratification. Unemployment is officially around 10 per cent, though probably much higher. And even if someone has a job, it does not mean that their income can sustain proper living conditions: 32 per cent earn just the minimum wage (in 2007). The result is that 44.8 million Brazilians live below the misery line (in 2004), with 41.8 million living without access to water, sewers or trash collection (Greenfield 2008: 147–9). President Lula has used the natural wealth of Brazil (in particular gas and petrol) to fund some relatively successful governmental programmes to help the poor. Nonetheless, Brazil still faces incredible social problems, as the religious leaders and their congregations experience on a daily basis.

This is the background of religious mobility in Brazil: 'Each encounter with a new religion and its supernatural(s) presents an opportunity for the resolution of a specific problem by someone in need. . . . The result is that Brazilians trek from one religious group to the next until they obtain what they request, but once they convert, there is no guarantee they will remain loyal' (Greenfield 2008: 151). It is consequently impossible to draw firm lines between the communities. Members change their affiliation constantly but also attend more than one *terreiro* or church at the same time. It is also quite common that members of the same household go to different, even hostile religious communities. The religious marketplace is wide open, not only in São Paulo. As a result, the religions have adapted, too.

One of the outcomes of the arrival of Candomblé, a traditionally ethnic religion, in São Paulo, a multi-ethnic and pluricultural setting, is the outreach of Candomblé beyond the Afro–Brazilian population (Gonçalves da Silva 1995: 290). The documentary *Somos Filhos de Orixás*, made by Andreas

Hofbauer in 1989, confirmed how quickly its ethnic and social composition has changed. Hofbauer portrayed Candomblé *terreiros* in São Paulo first and foremost as a black domain, as a space for Afro–Brazilians to express their creativity and to develop a sense of self-awareness: Candomblé is seen as instrument for empowerment for the marginalized poor Afro–Brazilians who have arrived in the city with little access to any resources. Twenty years later, this is no longer the case, at least not in São Paulo. Though a *mãe de santo* I met in Londrina vehemently stressed the function of her religion as an expression of the Afro–Brazilian identity and sees her work in and outside the *terreiro* as a struggle for equal rights for Afro–Brazilians, race no longer seems to be as important as the freedom of religious expression in *candomblé paulista*. In particular the struggle with some neo-Pentecostal churches enrages the *filhos* and *filhas de santo* and the priesthood, but less the fight for political rights and equality for Afro–Brazilians. This does not mean that Brazil has overcome its struggle with racism; rather, quite the opposite. Nor is it the case that the devotees have stepped out of all anti-racist campaigns. Race is still an important issue in Brazil on a daily basis because its social stratification is largely racially constructed. In a sense the ongoing fights for religious freedom have strengthened people's awareness of social injustice and their willingness to work together. The growing willingness to cooperate has a positive and negative impact. On one side the lack of institutionalization of the African matrix is always seen as weakness in the fight for equal rights. Prandi, for instance, complains that the lack of a nationwide institutionalization affects the growth of Afro–Brazilian religions (Prandi 2005: 223–32, quoted in Malandrino 2006: 40), though he also acknowledges elsewhere the rich creativity that is associated with the individual character of Candomblé. Roger Bastide goes even further in seeing the individualization as a result of the proletarianization of the Afro–Brazilian population in the cities. He describes the possession (or, 'ecstatic trance' in his words) in Afro–Brazilian religions as a sociological creation through which the individual becomes controlled by the group (Bastide 1978: 191). However, as a consequence of the urbanization and industrialization of society, he notices a shift towards individual interest which threatened such control. However, the degree of control is 'inversely correlated with the degree of "hysterical violence" in the trance' (Cohen 2007: 91 summarizing Bastide 1978). In

Bastide's words, 'The susceptibility of this trance to infiltration by personal drives seems to me to be associated with the individualization of the black in the industrialized big cities as he has been proletarianized through contact with whites' (1978: 381). Recent developments, however, indicate that more and more *terreiros* begin cooperating, though usually for wider social and not religious goals. For instance, the *Marcha do Axé*, which attracted around 2,000 people to the Parque Ibirapuera in São Paulo on 28 April 2012, was organized by devotees of Candomblé and Umbanda to demonstrate against intolerance and religious prejudice. However, in addition to devotees of the Afro–Brazilian religions, secular groups such as GLBTT (a group in support of the rights of gay, lesbian, bisexual and transgender people) and other non-governmental organizations against racism supported the event. This shows that Candomblé has become, at least in São Paulo, a truly universal religion, as Gonçalves da Silva explains (1995: 290), and is no longer ethnically con-strued as a religion for Afro–Brazilians. However, there is a vast difference between *terreiros*. As mentioned previously, Landes's research had an impact on Candomblé because it led to the representation of one type of Candomblé practice as hegemonic. This created an imbalance between the different branches, as other types came to be seen as inferior. As a kind of counter-strategy, however, I noticed that some *terreiros* highlight the uniqueness of their practice in order to distance themselves from the former orthodox style, which is losing gradually its hegemonic status. Image, in either way, can increase status, which then increases the income of a *terreiro*: more prestige means more clients and more spectators at the public parts of the ceremonies, which then will lead to more important patrons and growing public attention and so on. It is therefore understandable that some *terreiros* (members of all levels) refer to *City of Women* either to confirm their orthodoxy or to high-light their uniqueness.

To a certain degree present-day Candomblé resembles Umbanda in the early twentieth century, in that it appeals to all major ethnic and racial groups while remaining popular among Afro–Brazilians. Brown and Bick describe Umbanda as a prime example of the dramatic changes that 'Afro–Brazilian religions have undergone over the past century in their identification with the African heritage, the class locus, size, and composition of their mem-berships, and in their acceptance into the mainstream of Brazilian culture'

(1987: 74). This process can be observed now in Candomblé *terreiros* in São Paulo. While still identified as a part of Afro–Brazilian heritage, today *terreiros* attract a wide range of members, from various ethnic and social backgrounds. Africa remains, of course, the main point of reference, as I have outlined elsewhere (see Schmidt 2014b). However, the link to Africa can be established today with visits to the continent which convey similar prestige, even more sometimes, than African ancestry. Even the Oduduwa Templo dos Orixá, founded and led by the Nigerian *babalorixá* Sikiru King Salami (see Iyakemi Ribeiro [draft]), now seems to be dominated by Brazilians of all colours, in spite of being associated firmly with the traditional West African Yoruba religion. Ronilda Iyakemi Ribeiro states that more than 500 *ifá* initiations were performed by the Nigerian *babalawo* Fabunmi Sowinmi in the temple. According to Iyakemi Ribeiro, both Brazilians and Europeans were initiated, as *babalorixá* Sikiru King Salami has extended his work to Europe and regularly invites his European followers to Brazil, in particular when *babalawo* Fabunmi or his successor, *babalawo* Awodiran Sowunmi, visit Brazil.[18] According to my information, *babalorixá* King travels regularly to Spain and Slovenia and nowadays spends much of the year either in Europe or in Nigeria. Nonetheless, his Odudawa temple is very successful and has now a large site in Monaguá, on the coast of São Paulo state. The rituals I observed were very different from any Candomblé ceremony I attended despite the fact that *orixás* are the central entities in both traditions (from the music and songs to the clothing and decoration). While Candomblé and other traditions of the African matrix have been derived from the Yoruba tradition, and most members of the Odudawa temple are also members of a *terreiro* in the African matrix (mainly but not exclusively Umbanda), the (Brazilian) Yoruba tradition is nonetheless different from the (Brazilian) African matrix. *Babalorixá* King attempts to highlight the hegemonic character of his Odudawa temple as the traditional Yoruba form. Even before he founded the Odudawa temple, he established the Centro Cultural Odudawa (CCO) in São Paulo in 1988. Today the centre still offers several classes, not only in the Yoruba language[19] but also in Yoruba theology and other topics. Iyakemi Ribeiro describes as the goal of CCO to spread knowledge about the oral culture of the Yoruba, to promote the language as one of the most important and widespread African languages, to offer educational courses, to develop research projects, to stimulate dialogue not only on a local base but also with larger organizations in order to develop a network, and, last but not least, to participate in the Africanization of the religious traditions associated with the *orixás* cult (Ribeiro [draft]). However, in addition to these more secular objectives, CCO also has several religious offers such as classes in the songs that are necessary for the communication between humans and deities as well as oracle readings that have to be regularly conducted for every devotee (see Figure 2.2). *Babalorixá* King uses both the cultural centre and the temple as the main instruments to transmit his authority, which is derived from his national background, his ability to speak and write in Yoruba (which is regarded as the language of the deities), and his support by Nigerian *babalawos*, who are associated with the *ifá*-ritual. Nonetheless, despite his strong focus on Nigeria, his congregation is not restricted to Afro–Brazilians but includes a high number of white Brazilians, to certain degree quite similar to *Candomblé paulista*. It seems that with his many educational offers at the CCO, King attracts slightly more educated, middle-class individuals to his temple than other *terreiros* in the African matrix, though only time will tell whether he will be able to maintain his position.[20] The wider

Figure 2.2 Templo de Orixás, São Paulo

priesthood in Candomblé and also in some other Afro–Brazilian traditions usually keep their distance from him and reject any claims to submit to his authority. As already mentioned, several Umbanda priests and priestesses are also members of the temple and undergo initiations offered by *babalorixá* King. These initiations are, however, not their main point of reference within Umbanda and are seen only as additional 'qualifications'.

What is interesting to note is the widening of the ethnic stratification of the temple and its similarity to Candomblé *terreiros*. To a certain degree, the process is similar to the assimilation of ethnic minorities into the wider Brazilian population. Evandro Camara explains that Brazil has a tendency to amalgamate and assimilate ethnic minorities. He argues that no differentiation is visible between people from the dominant and minority ethnic communities as the basic patterns of language, aesthetics, morality and social ethics are common, though distinctions are maintained on the basis of class (1997: 55). Camara sees race and ethnicity consequently transcended by culture, or, in his words, culture 'triumphed over race and ethnicity' (1997: 221). However, despite a greater conceptual fluidity than in the United States, where ethnic difference is equated with racial difference, according to Camara, Brazil is by no means a heaven of racial equality, as was claimed in the 1930s by Freyre and others (e.g. Freyre 1956), only a more complex one (see Hofbauer 2006). Though most Brazilians consider themselves, as Selka writes, 'neither black nor white, but brown (Moreno or pardo) or mixed (mulato or mestiço)' (Selka 2009: 19), race plays a role in the class stratification of Brazil: the so-called non-white population is generally more disadvantaged than the so-called white population. Nonetheless, the conceptual fluidity between race, ethnicity, class and culture has enabled the widening of the Afro–Brazilian religions towards people of non-Afro–Brazilian ethnicity. Even the Candomblé priesthood is no longer a group of exclusively Afro–Brazilians. I actually noticed a few Brazilians of Asian descent among the elders in some *terreiros*, but especially remarkable was the high number of white Brazilians among the leaders in the *terreiros* I visited. While even early descriptions of Candomblé rituals noted the presence of white Brazilians among participants, the leadership remained predominately black for a long time. The changes are even more visible among the other ranks. Although I did not conduct a survey about the racial self-identification among the *filhos* and *filhas de santo*, the demographic change in *candomblé paulista* is clearly visible. Asian Brazilians are still exceptions, but the majority of the *filhos* and *filhas de santo* are mixed race or white Brazilians with an equally number of Afro–Brazilians and mulattos. This 'whiting' of the membership points to the loss of the ethnic base of the Afro–Brazilian religions but not to a significant widening of the class catchment. Despite the presence of intellectuals and university students, most members still come from the lower social classes, though with a grow-ing number of middle-class Brazilians. However, Candomblé has gained the image of being expensive due to the colourful costumes and decorations needed for the ceremonies. Though I have seen members creating the decora-tions and the costumes in order to lower cost, this image might push some away – or attract others. Nonetheless, my impression is slightly different from that of other scholars, who still stress the association of Afro–Brazilian reli-gions to socially marginalized sectors of society. Chesnut, for instance, states that religions of the African Diaspora attract a larger portion of devotees who are subaltern, for example a significant presence of male homosexuals. The religions also appeal, as he continues, to people whose illicit economic activities are condemned as sinful by Christian denominations (e.g. pros-titutes, smugglers, drug traffickers) because Candomblé, Umbanda and so on offer spiritual protection for these activities (Chesnut 2003: 1008–109). Nonetheless, he also confirms the changes from essentially ethnic religions until the 1960s to a wider recruitment field with a growing number of white and mixed-race believers (2003: 110).

These changes also affect gender stratification. Despite an ongoing influence of the early studies about Candomblé that established one type of Candomblé as superior to others, São Paulo Candomblé differs from these early descrip-tions, as some of my interviewees point out. *Mãe* I., for instance, disagrees strongly with the general perception of a female dominance in Candomblé, which she traced back to the early studies about Afro–Brazilian religions by Nina Rodrigues in the nineteenth century. She argues that Rodrigues was wrong but that because no one challenged his view, it is still accepted. 'Now there is the idea that Candomblé has more women than men. Women are more visible in Candomblé of Bahia because most men do not dance. They may even represent an orixá [i.e. getting possessed] but when it comes ... they do not dance in the circle. Only women are dancing there.' However, as she clarifies, while men do not dance in the circle in the Casa Branca [seen as the most hegemonic *terreiro* in Bahia], they dance in São Paulo. For her the social division of labour is important. *Mãe* I. argues that 'there is a social division of labour in which there are certain things that men do and certain things that women do'. Consequently, Candomblé also has a social division, and 'men must have and need women'. However, women sometimes appear to be more visible, while men are more in the background. She refers, for instance, to drummers who are usually male[21] and *ogãs*, a position that does not rely on possession experience.[22]

The Umbanda *terreiros* are even more diverse. Though their members also represent all main ethnic and racial groups, the composition of the religious pantheon worshipped in the Umbanda *terreiro* seems to have an impact on the demographic structure. For instance, a more esoteric Umbanda mixture attracts mainly (but not exclusively) white Brazilians, while a *terreiro* representing the more common diversity of spiritual guides with a focus on healing draws its members from all ethnic groups, especially (but not exclusively) Afro–Brazilians. Brown and Bick highlight that 'Umbanda represents a reinterpretation of Afro–Brazilian religions by the white middle sectors' (1987: 81). This is visible in particular in the more institutionalized form of Umbanda, for instance, in the Faculdade Teologia Umbandista in São Paulo (see Figure 2.3). However, the majority of Umbanda *terreiros* still attract the majority of its clients from the lower social classes. As Engler confirms, Umbandists are 'more likely to be *pardo* or black, poor, and poorly educated', though at the 'white' end of the spectrum of Umbanda one can see higher middle-class and white participation (Engler 2009a: 486). However, on the whole, the link to the African heritage remains intact as far as I could observe, even in *terreiros* with predominately white membership.

Spiritism, however, has little connection to Africa, as already mentioned. Originally it was always described as predominately white. However, the offers of healing made by some centres also attract a relatively high number of Brazilians of other ethnic groups, including Afro–Brazilians. It depends here on the general orientation of the centre. Some centres that focus on spiritual education are nearly exclusively white and middle class. Other centres with a focus on healing include some African entities in their spiritual pantheon and allow a bridge to Umbanda and the other Afro–Brazilian traditions.

Figure 2.3 Faculdade de Teologia Umbandista, São Paulo

Here one can find a slightly higher number of Afro–Brazilians, though still a minority. The clients seem to represent the ethnically diverse subgroups of the wider society, though mainly from the middle to lower classes of society. Though Carmargo states that membership in Spiritist cults is restricted to lower classes (Carmargo 1973: 18, quoted in Donovan 2000: 370), my observations do not confirm this perception, in particular because the majority of members remain white. Engler also describes Kardecists as being 'more likely white, middle-class, and well educated', hence on average Kardecists have 'significantly more social and economic capital within Brazilian society' (2009: 486).[23]

The charismatic churches overlap Spiritism and Umbanda to a certain degree because they work in a similar sector of society. Chesnut, for instance, states that Umbanda and the charismatic and Pentecostal churches recruit in the same socioeconomic sectors (2003: 108). Hence, the congregations contain predominately Brazilians from the lower and aspiring middle classes, most of them mixed race. As reported above, many practised Umbanda before converting to one of the Charismatic Christian churches. Among the leaders, however, one still finds more white Brazilians than Afro–Brazilians. Alencar even points to an underlying racism in many Protestant churches and asks, for instance, why German, English or indigenous dances appear to the Protestant leaders less 'demonic' than African? (2005: 144–5). A similar bias can be seen with regard to gender stratification as most (if not all) higher positions in the hierarchy of Pentecostal churches are occupied by men, though theoretically women can also become pastors, at least in more liberal Protestant denominations. In the public reception, however, the Roman Catholic Church is usually portrayed as being gender biased towards men as well as representing a socially unjust picture of society. *Pai R.*, for instance, blamed the impact of Roman Catholicism on Umbanda for its (former) rejection of homosexual men. He argues that the conservative gender bias of the Church discriminates against women and female religious experience. He explains the changed tendency in Umbanda towards a more open attitude towards sexuality as being due to a decreasing influence of Roman Catholicism in Brazil (interview with *Pai* R. in São Paulo on 14 April 2010). Though he overlooks the increase in evangelical and in particular Pentecostal churches, which are at least as conservative as the Roman Catholic Church, he makes a valid point in highlighting changing attitudes in Brazil that have an impact on the society.

These comments lead me to my final point. Socially marginalized groups may use religions to increase their social position and even political power; however, it would be too superficial to categorize the Afro–Brazilian and Spiritist traditions, as well as the Charismatic forms of Christianity, purely as peripheral. Though it is impossible to provide statistical data or objective evidence because mediumship and possession practice is still handicapped by its negative perception in wider society – and therefore people shy away from openly admitting to their practice – it is widely accepted that Brazilians move around various communities in search of help and support. Consequently, there is a constant flux in clients and members who have an impact on the prestige of the leadership but also contribute to the wider status of the traditions. Yes, the dominant religion in Brazil is still Roman Catholicism. But people rely on different systems of belief and practices in most questions concerning life and death, from personal life decisions to psychological, social and even physical problems. All the traditions that include mediumship practice in a wider sense, including possession and depossession, provide people with a sense of morality and values, that is to say, with characteristics of central cults in Lewis's model. However, as previously mentioned, an important difference between Lewis's (and others') ecstatic religions and the Brazilian case is that in all traditions presented here only some individuals will experience the involuntary acts with uncontrolled bodily movements, spontaneous vocalizations, unusual sensory experiences and alterations of consciousness and memory. And these mediums are not always the leaders of the communities. Nonetheless, it is still crucial to notice that the traditions are not restricted at all to socially marginalized groups but have spread to the middle classes and beyond. This observation does not contradict the earlier comment about the traditions as providers of a unique access to social prestige and power. In line with Donovan's critique, I argue for a wider perspective that is not restricted to one explanation. McCutcheon asserts that our task is not simply concerned with 'interpreting a mysterious phenomenon rather than explaining one aspect of human culture in relation to other aspects' (McCutcheon 1997: 11). His claim can be also applied to the interpretation of possession rituals. In the same way that we cannot look at religions as autonomous entities because it would limit our understanding of the meaning of religion for people practising religions, we also cannot look at possession rituals only as an arena for socially marginalized people. The key to understanding the social importance of possession traditions lies in understanding the agencies involved. Following Engler, I regard the possession rituals I observed in Brazil as 'a social space, like and unlike that of non-ritual action, in which distinct forms of agency, characterized by the displacement of agency, play themselves out' (2009: 469). This space is available for everyone, marginalized or non-marginalized. The decision to engage in this ritual activity depends on various variables such as political pressure, religious tension and personal strain but also individual creativity.

Experiencing and Explaining Ecstatic Religions: Religious Experience Revisited

Introduction

I do not remember anything about the first time except that the sensation was a strong heat, the sensation of heat and sleep at the same time. I felt a huge weight in my back and neck, and I began to feel my heart. The heart accelerated! And it was the sensation of two hearts beating inside me. There was a kind of force in my throat, a very strong energy in the throat, and I felt like it was about to speak. But in that moment, at the first time, I was very afraid, because when it began to happen, I had doubts about whether it would be good or bad. I tried to stop it and I was left with the sensation that I would begin the communication in a trance.

(Interview on 21 May 2010 in São Paulo)

I feel differences between the deities in Umbanda. When I incorporate some deities, I do not feel anything. And I have other deities that make me feel ecstatic, even though I did not enter them. The feeling is different from my normal waking state. But when I incorporate an orixá, I usually I have no control of my movements. In most deities, in the Yoruba tradition, I have no control of my movements. Often when I am conscious, I want to stop, but I cannot.

(Interview on 14 April 2010, in São Paulo)

These two excerpts from interviews I took with people experiencing spirit possession or other forms of communication with supernatural entities illustrate two poles of the range of variations between individual recollections. They highlight lack of control, loss of memory and an awareness of an extraordinary presence in their body. The outcome is described like an increased creativity, a new sense of achievement and even self-empowerment but also a feeling of loss shortly afterwards. While some experiencers point towards the contribution of the possessing agency and describe how the *orixás* influence what they feel and experience in this moment, others struggle against the dominant presence of another entity in their bodies until they surrender and learn to control the extraordinary form of communication. And while one side emphasizes a divine or spiritual feature, others stress the technical aspect of communication. The commonality is the reference to something extraordinary, outside oneself and often outside the human body. From an academic point of view, the problem is now how to deal with this 'extraordinary' element. As I outlined in the introduction, Ann Taves describes the experience quite passively as uncontrolled bodily movements and alterations of consciousness, lack of memory, unusual sensory experiences and so on. But what about the 'agency of supernatural agents' (Engler)? How do we academics charged with the task of explaining the experience, deal with the 'possession agency' (Keller)? As an anthropologist I am used to referring to subjective narratives I collected in the field; however, often scholars from social scientific disciplines regard ethnographic monographs as just another 'story' firmly embedded in a cultural context but without much wider significance. We are sometimes even accused of 'going native' when arguing from the perspective of our interviewees. A similar discussion goes on among religious studies scholars who want to distance themselves from theology. It is no wonder therefore that the possessing agency is often overlooked in studies about ecstatic religions. But in order to understand what is going on, we also should take into account the point of view of those involved. And our respect for other religions should prevent us from dismissing their feelings as wrong (as little as we may be able to participate in them), but on the contrary lead us to ask, at least, what is their system? Keller, who challenges studies about ecstatic religions for ignoring the importance of the possessing agencies, argues that the spirits choose 'who will act as their instruments'

(Keller 2002: 53). She regards the possessing agency as a crucial element of the triangle that constitutes possession rituals (the mediums, the possessing agencies and the observers). Keller argues that, when asked about their experience, people usually begin by explaining the possessing agency and its role, whether it is regarded as mediumship, trance or possession. However, this approach contains a problem, as Keller acknowledges: 'On the one hand, the possession is described as a *real belief*, but on the other hand it is *not* the belief of the scholar, who then presents an alternative interpretation of the *real* processes at hand. . . . [Consequently,] agency is a central dilemma for these scholars' (2002: 29, italics in the original).

Keller seems to me to give disproportional emphasis to one aspect of the triangle, which should be, as I argue, considered together. Hence, we need a way to balance the attitudes towards agencies. Nonetheless, an important point of Keller's argument is her critique of the common scholarly practice of transferring possession to a matter of belief: 'As long as the power of the possession is located in the bubble of other people's beliefs, the scholar constructs him or her as safely neutral and objective, reasonable and unaffected' (2002: 7). Hence, Keller forces us to come out of the safe haven of academic distance and confront the normative model of subjectivity underlying the analysis of possession rituals. In her work she suggests a new way of looking at possessed bodies without disregarding them as figments of belief (see for instance Lambek 1996: 238–9). Keller draws on Charles Long's concept of signifying, which he describes as 'a complex relationship between the meaning and nature of religion as a subject of academic study of religion and the reality of the peoples and cultures who were conquered and colonized during the same period' (Long 1986: 4). Based on Long, Keller argues that translated representations of possession always carry a devaluation of the rituals. A study of possession rituals is therefore, according to Keller, a study of the representations of possession (Keller 2002: 13). Without promoting a naive understanding of possession rituals, Keller interprets possessed bodies as instrumental agencies, firmly connected in postcolonial discourses of power relationship, autonomy and identity. Her work is, nonetheless, quite 'theological' as she also states in her conclusion, and in danger of opening up the well-known pitfall of a non-critical, biased 'religious by sympathy' approach of Otto and others. Keller opposes the common trend of promoting a study of religion 'free of hidden theological agendas' (Strenski 1993: 3). Though she writes that she would not insist on the term 'theology', she is 'committed to the argument that a discursive space is needed in order to discuss the unique power struggles engaged in by religious bodies' (Keller 2002: 227).

Keller's critique of the academic approaches to spirit possession and the representation of possessed bodies in the literature echoes Taves's critique of the studies of religious experience. As mentioned in the introduction, Taves's approach combines the two (usually opposing) branches of people experiencing religion and people explaining experience. Scholars used to offer explanations that disregarded the explanations of the people having experiences, but overlook the fact that people experiencing acts such as possession trance do not live in isolation from the surrounding discourses. The boundary between scholars explaining experiences and people living them is increasingly blurred, in particular in Brazil, where several of my interviewees are pursuing an academic degree in order to learn how scholars analyse their experience. However, it is extremely difficult to find the right balance between explaining and experiencing religion, as Taves explains in her study of Anglo–American Protestants and ex-Protestants (Taves 1999). She criticizes the dualistic view that divides experiencing religion and explaining experiences as being 'antithetical' (Taves 1999: 6) and promotes a threefold typology. Instead of developing theories based on the dichotomy between natural and supernatural or between secular and religious, Taves includes a third position, which she calls 'the mediating tradition' (1999: 348). Referring to William James as the 'quintessential theorist of the mediating tradition', Taves notes that 'the mediators believed that the way in which they accessed religion was scientific rather than simply a matter of faith and that the character of their methods legitimated the religious reality of that which they discovered as a result of their method' (1999: 349). As a result of the threefold typology, Taves defines the experiences she investigates as 'abilities or capacities that can be discouraged or cultivated'. She further argues that in the West the controlling aspect of this ability has been stressed, while in other cultures the ability 'has been cultivated in service of complex group interactions' (1999: 357, pointing to African cultures). She insists therefore that seemingly involuntary acts that include uncontrolled bodily movements, spontaneous vocalizations, unusual sensory experiences and alterations of consciousness and/or memory should not be regarded as symptoms of mental weakness or an expression of false religion, but should be understood in terms of skill development. Taves urges us here to follow James's interest in the interplay between theories of religion and living religion. Even though theories are 'the farthest removed and the most fragmented', they inform the 'making and unmaking of experience at the level of narrative in varied and complicated ways' (1999: 361), since people experiencing these involuntary acts do not live in isolation from the surrounding discourses. In this chapter I follow her path and present the various ideas about experiencing and explaining possession and mediumship.

After an overview of the academic discourse, I present the ideas about divine transformation that dominate the discourse among Afro–Brazilian practitioners and then the debate about mediumship as form of communication. I end this chapter with an observation of a case of opposite readings of the spiritual entities, in which they are viewed as demons instead of deities and require exorcizing rather than celebration.

Academic debate about the experience of ecstatic (and other) religions

A key text in the study of religious experience is still William James's *Varieties of Religious Experience*, published more than one hundred years ago and based on his Gifford Lectures in Edinburgh in 1901/1902. In a letter to Fanny Morse, written on 12 April 1900, he outlined his plan for the lecture series:

> *First* to defend (against all the prejudices of my 'class') experience against philosophy as being the real backbone of the world's religious life – I mean prayer, guidance and all that sort of thing immediately and privately felt, as against high and noble general views of our destiny and the world's meaning; and *second*, to make the reader or hearer believe, what I myself invincibly do believe, that, although all the special manifestations of religion have been absurd (I mean its creeds and theories) yet the life of it as a whole is mankind's most important function. (James and James 2008: 127, italics in the original)

His primary intention was to highlight the importance of personal experiences, even over any theological dimension such as doctrinal and institutional aspects of religions. This approach already indicated that James saw religion per se as a collective entity and why he challenged any effort of his contemporaries to find the essence of religion. As a psychologist his focus was on emotion, and he even argued that the type of person someone is determines the form of religious experience this person will undergo. His work had and still has a vast impact on the study of religious experience, not the least due to his interdisciplinary approach to the field: he frequently referred to anthropology, philosophy, biology and other disciplines in addition to his own field, psychology.

In his various publications, in particular in *The Varieties of Religious Experience*, he illustrates his points with personal accounts of people's experiences, usually drawn from their life stories. However, he also insists that religious experience is ineffable, which he later confirmed when trying to describe his own experience in the Adirondack Mountains:

> The streaming moonlight lit up things in a magical checkered play, and it seemed as if the God of all the nature mythologies were holding an indescribable meeting in my breast with the moral Gods of the inner life . . . the intense significance of some sort, of the whole scene, if one could only *tell* the significance; the intense inhuman remoteness of its inner life, and yet the intense *appeal* of it; . . . In point of fact, I can't find a single word for all that significance, and don't know what it was significant of, so there it remains, and mere boulder of *impression*. (James and James 2008: 76–7, italics in the original)

Though he was unable to describe his experience, it illustrates that James's interest was mainly in personal experiences.

Most important, however, is that James saw religious experience not as something different from ordinary experiences or as contradicting the laws of nature. Hence, he tried to clear religious experience from any reference to the supernatural, though he often cited the personal experiences of key religious figures such as the Buddha, Jesus and Muhammad. James argued that founders of religions 'owed their power originally to the fact of their direct personal communion with the divine' (James 2008: 31). However, in addition to experiences of founders of religions, he also included experiences of ordinary members because he argued that the maintenance of religious traditions relies on a constant process of revalidation that happens when other members have further personal experiences, similar to the founder of the tradition. He argued that someone's beliefs and knowledge, or, in other words, cultural and personal context, influences the experience and also the way someone relates to it. For instance, whether someone interprets the experience as demonic or divine depends on the context in which someone lives. But James went further. He also wrote that it depends on pre-existing belief systems, for instance whether specific elements (e.g. seeing a light in a near-death experience) are regarded as important and will be narrated, or will be regarded as unimportant and soon forgotten. Hence, James argued that aspects that do not conform to the pre-existing belief system of the person experiencing it will be neglected in narratives about it. He highlights here an important point which affects the interpretation of any narrative: every narrative is influenced by the subjective perspective of the narrator. Though the person describing the experience might regard the description as accurate, the narrative reflects the subjectivity of this person, including pre-existing ideas and information. We therefore have to contextualize and assess the narratives with care.

However, James's approach to what constitutes a 'religious' experience was vague and influenced by his Western background. He defined religion as 'the feelings, acts and experiences of individual men in their solitude, so far as they apprehend themselves to stand in relation to whatever they may consider the divine' (James 2008: 31). Consequently, James regarded religious experience predominantly as a mystical element, linked to internal and private feelings, quite similar to his contemporary, the theologian Rudolf Otto (1859–1937), who also emphasizes the internal attributes of religion. However, while both argued that religion arises out of an experience that is potentially in each of us, James promoted the idea of a variety of experiences. Otto, in contrast, supported the idea of a pure religious experience that he described as *mysterium tremendum et fascinans*. Otto acknowledged this feeling himself as he wrote in a letter: 'In whatever language they resound, these most exalted words that have ever come from human lips always grip one in the depths of the soul, with a mighty shudder exciting and calling into play the mystery of the other world latent therein' (in Turner and Mackenzie n.d.: 4). While he referred mainly to Jewish and Christian rituals that inspired the feeling, during his various journeys he attended rituals of different religious traditions that also inspired in him feelings of awe and fascination. For Otto, religious rituals such as the Sufi Mevlevi (whirling dervishes), the observation of silence in Quaker meetings and the cantillation in a synagogue were the core of religious experience.

Otto was inspired by the theologian Friedrich Schleiermacher's (1768–1834) *Speeches on Religion to its Cultured Despisers* (1799), in which he outlined that religion is about feeling and relationship and not morality or metaphysics. In the heart of all living religion is the feeling of *Frömmigkeit* (piety). Schleiermacher even argued that theology itself centred on religious experience. 'It is not . . . a description of God as he is in himself, for God is not an Object to be differentiated from other objects, but an articulation of the feeling men and women have of their relationship with the divine apprehended as the ground of both their own being and that of the world' (Thrower 1999: 53). Otto developed these ideas further and argued that the primal form of the encounter between divine and human beings is neither rational nor moral. Otto insisted that religious experience is unique from other forms of experiences and feelings and that we need specific tools for its understanding. In order to stress its importance, Otto created the phrase *mysterium tremendum et fascinans* as a descriptor of religious experience as a feeling of awe and fear in the presence of God, seen by Otto as the wholly Other. Otto's position is at odds with the academic need to explain and analyse all aspects of human experience and actions in an objective, scientific way. Consequently, he is widely disregarded as biased and judgemental. Unfortunately, his critics often overlook that Otto can provide access to an understanding of the perspective of people experiencing these involuntary acts.

Scholars in the culturalist perspective, who look at religion as a human construct, disregard any notion of a sacred ontological entity, from which the practitioners' understanding of possession experience derives. For the Jungian psychotherapist José Jorge de Morais Zacharias, whom I interviewed about his involvement in Afro–Brazilian religions, it is crucial to explain every experience within its cultural framework if it is to become meaningful and structured:

> Suppose a teenager begins to see figures and people sometimes talk to her. If she is in a very Catholic or Protestant church, she's crazy, she's in trouble, because you cannot see such things. The idea that you are seeing

something is regarded as a hallucination; it's crazy and will pose a threat to your identity. As a result her identity is threatened, she feels like she's going crazy. This threat of disintegration of identity generates anxiety. This anxiety accentuates the feeling of disorder and brings fear, and can even cause panic. The person can develop a disorder and will be sent to hospital where he or she will be given a psychiatric drug. You can create a disruption in the brain chemistry that actually disrupts the ego.

On the other hand, and I've seen this happen a lot, a relative or a neighbour of the individual says, 'We take her to the centre, she must be seeing spirits'. When this information is passed to the person who is living with it, she thinks, 'I see spirits'. Who are these spirits? Oh, and there are spirits in the spiritual plane, and appear to some people who have a gift. 'Ah, but I'm seeing it, I'm not going crazy, even though others do not see them'. The new identity is reinforced. 'I am not going crazy, I see spirits'. . . . After some training in the spiritual centre the individual begins to learn the meaning of the phenomenon and becomes an active member of the group because it becomes a means of communication. Then a process of indoctrination begins, where she or he will see the spirits during the sessions, and beyond. The experience becomes structured. There is no pathology, but a set of ideas. You think in a set of beliefs and values that make sense of human experience. When we do not have that, the experience is meaningless. If it does not make sense, then something is threatening. If I see a fireball in the sky, I might say 'oh, it's an angel, God, and Yahweh', or nowadays, "'t's a flying saucer, or an extraterrestrial'. Now, if I do not have those references, I may collapse with fear.[1]

We need to understand the set of beliefs and values which provide the cultural framework in which the experience is embedded. For Otto, being a Lutheran theologian, Christianity provided his set of beliefs and values, in particular Protestant Christianity. For Brazilian practitioners, the answer to this question is much more complex – as indicated in the introduction – because it is impossible to construe a single belief set despite all efforts. André Droogers (1987) promotes, for instance, the idea of *religiosidade minimal brasileira* (minimal Brazilian religiosity). Among the core features of the minimal Brazilian religiosity (MBR) he lists God and God's counterpart, the devil, Jesus, the power of prayer and others (Droogers 1987: 77–8). Droogers argues that through the common idea of God and the other features, Brazilians are able to recognize each other and accept the manifestations of the other despite all differences. Following Carlos Brandão's proposal of 'a grand symbolic matrix of common usage' (1978: 77, quoted by Droogers 1987: 64), Droogers describes MBR as the natural order of the universe for Brazilians; it manifests itself publicly in secular contexts and constitutes the Brazilian culture. MBR is product as well as producer; it establishes unity and construes cultural identity (Droogers 1987: 82). And it enables people to freely express their ideas about the experiences that refer to spiritual entities, though not everyone will experience the same type of religious experiences or even any type at all. Hence, despite fundamental differences between the religions, the concept of MBR points towards a sense of continuity. Nonetheless, despite being quite persuasive, Drooger's essentialist approach to religion (and culture in general) has become less convincing over time (see, e.g. Dickie 2007), and Dickie insists that 'having religiosity as a constituent of culture does not produce an equal concept of religious experience' (2007: 9). She points not only to the difference between each tradition but also to the internal differences of each group.

> So, it is possible to say that there is a Catholic deep culture in Brazil – which underlies and informs different religious practices – but as we address the different denominations or designations, their ostensive differences become very clear. These differences also manifest as relevant in the unveiling of the fundamental meanings of the religious concepts and feelings associated with them, thus having an effect on how the expression 'religious experience' might be understood. The cases studied show the complexity of the religious field in Brazil and the problems in assuming that experience is an idea as clearly present as that of religion. (Dickie 2007: 9)

Dickie's critique of the MBR concept of Droogers – or, more precisely, of the essentialist grounding of the terms 'religion' and 'culture' – highlights not only the diversity within the communities as well as traditions but also the problem around any interpretation of experiences that are highly subjective.

Dickie therefore locates the study of experiences firmly inside a social scientific framework, contrary to Otto, who grounded his concept of the Holy 'on the necessary existence of an unobservable transcendental other. [However,] while such a transcendental other may or may not exist, it cannot serve as an explanatory basis because it is unobservable and therefore not amenable to social scientific analysis' (Kunin 2003: 66). But instead of abandoning the study of experience, scholars such as Taves argue that 'we should disaggregate the concept of "religious experience" and study the wide range of experiences to which religious significance has been attributed' (2009: 8). And this is the direction Dickie takes in her research project about religious experience in Brazil. She decided to start the research with a test of the applicability of the term 'religious experience' due to the multilayered Brazilian society as she was concerned with 'producing material to subsidize the formulation of a questionnaire about religious experience' (2007: 7, n.4). Echoing Taves by referring the concept of religious experience back to the reformist movements of European modernity (Taves 1999: 271), Dickie challenges the term itself due to its European connotation and states that it cannot be used without a risk of 'cultural dyslexia' (Pálsson 1993):

> From a strict Social Anthropology methodological and theoretical perspective, culture not only creates names but conditions their understanding. From this we assume that the meaning conveyed by the expression 'religious experience' will vary according to the culture in which the person addressed is immersed. We could suppose that within the range of the educated Western world a reference to Schleiermacher's definition would be recurrent. However, when the research aims to investigate religious experience in a country as culturally diverse and religiously multi-faceted like Brazil we have to depart from a test of the applicability of the expression as one of our research instruments. . . . there is a literal translation of the expression in Portuguese. However, it does not guarantee an adequate translation of its meaning. (Dickie 2007: 6)

Lack of funding made it impossible for Dickie and her colleagues to continue with the research on a large scale. Nonetheless, based on her pilot study she argues that we need to explore 'the range of possibilities suggested by the word experience to guarantee a parameter for the investigation' (2007: 15). At this point she turns to Victor Turner and his description of the concept 'experience': 'An experience stands out from the evenness of passing hours and years . . . and forms a structure of experience. In other words, it does not have an arbitrary beginning and ending, cut out of the stream of chronological temporality, but has what Dewey called "an initiation and a consummation"' '

(Turner 1986: 35). Following his lead, Dickie proposes that 'an experience would also be formative and transformative – with isolatable sequences of external events and internal responses to them – like an initiation into a new life' (2007: 16). A common aspect of my interviews was also to speak with the interviewees about their initial experience with the extraordinary phenomena and how it affected their lives. However, I decided to include subsequent events; hence, I did not restrict 'experience' to the initial incident that was truly transformative and formative but also included the following events, when the transformative experience became familiar to the individual and further integrated into the local conceptual context.

The term 'experience' has a wider pitfall, as Robert Sharf points out. Sharf states that 'the term is often used rhetorically to thwart the authority of the "objective" or the "empirical", and to valorize instead the subjective, the personal, the private' (1998: 94). The aim of these scholars is to counter a materialist approach to religion which is dismissed by many as reductionist. As an alternative to an empirical approach which argues that truth claims must be subject to empirical or scientific verification, some scholars claim that we can overcome cultural bias by turning our attention towards the collective or 'lived' experience of a religious community. Hence, phenomenologists argue that by bracketing our presuppositions and 'ingrained sense of cultural superiority' over foreign traditions, we can find that 'their *experience* of the world possesses its own rationality, its own coherence, its own truth' (Sharf 1998: 95, italics in original). But is there a limit and how far can we go? Sharf effectively illustrates the problem by looking at reports of alien abduction. The consensus among scholars in the case of alien abduction is that the abductions did not take place, that the memory is faulty as there is 'no originary event behind the memories' (1998: 109). But if we read these reports as religious narratives, as some do, 'there is no reason to assume that the reports of experiences by mystics, shamans, or meditation masters are any more credible as "phenomenological descriptions" than those of the abductees' (Sharf 1998: 110). This case highlights a wider problem with the concept of 'experience'. James, Otto and others use the term experience as if we can distinguish between a core experience and 'the divergent culturally conditioned expressions of that core' (1998: 97). James, for instance, isolates in his lectures on the varieties of religious experience four universal features of mystical experience (noetic quality, ineffability, transiency and passivity). However, as for instance Proudfoot (1985) shows, we do not have access to such a core mystical experience, only to texts that describe the experience, whether it is the experience of an abductee, a shaman or a mystic. Challenging the notion of a perennial core of the concept 'experience', Sharf writes that there is little evidence to indicate 'that these very disparate accounts are actually referring to one and the same experience'. And, as he continues, it is therefore impossible to separate 'experience' from 'a culturally determined description of that experience'. We need to take the environment of the person having the experience into consideration, hence the cultural context, 'personal history, doctrinal commitments, religious training, expectations, aspirations, and so on' (1998: 97–8).

I agree with Sharf's critique as my notion of spirit possession as a deictic term shows. I argue that the meaning of 'spirit possession', which I see as a specific type of religious experience, depends on the given context. Instead of extracting universal features, we need to provincialize the experience and acknowledge its many local features. Religious experience as well as its subcategory spirit possession are context-dependent concepts. Or, in Sharf's words, the terms such as mystical or religious experience function only referentially, 'that is, their signification lies in the signifieds to which they allegedly refer' (1998: 103).

Other scholars approach the topic of religious experience in a more descriptive way and often without the rigorous challenge of defining the terms religious or experience. Caroline Franks Davis (1989), for instance, is one of the many scholars who categorizes various types of experiences under the label religious. These experiences have in common that the experiencer describes it in – as she writes – religious terms or – and here it gets even more vague – in terms that are intrinsically religious. Her six types are called Interpretive; Quasi-Sensory, Revelatory; Regenerative; Numinous; and Mystical. 'Interpretive' means that the experiencer interprets events within the framework of the belief system. 'Quasi-Sensory' refers to specific physical sensations such as hearing voices, seeing visions, feelings of being touched, feelings of motion or levitation. 'Revelatory' indicates sudden inspiration, enlightenment, insight or revelation. 'Regenerative' means experiences which will renew the individual spiritually. 'Numinous' refers, in line with Otto, to feelings of awe and insignificance at the power and majesty of the divine or some other sort of transpersonal ultimate reality. And 'Mystical' embraces four characteristics of apprehending an ultimate reality, freedom from limitations of space and time, a sense of oneness and feelings of bliss or serenity (Franks Davis 1989: 33–65). These types are quite similar to other categorizations done by Hardy (1979), Hay (1982) or others. They have in common a descriptive nature that is helpful in categorizing individual narratives, such as those collected in the Alister Hardy archive of the Religious Experience Research Centre, but are less effective within the wider academic debate, as Sharf shows.

There is another important point that we need to consider – the inclusion of experiences that might not be categorized as religious. As Ann Taves writes, we own the description of the specific experience to followers of the person or observers but usually not to the person who had the experience, the ostensible subject. These reports often do not use the terms religion or religious but rather describe the experience in culturally specific terms. We should therefore, as Taves warns, not become too protective of the term religious but use it in an inclusive manner. By including experiences such as the mediumship communications practised by Brazilian Spiritists that are not necessarily labelled as religious, it is possible to compare various types of experiences 'deemed religious and non-religious by practitioners and/or observers and to recognize and examine boundary issues (e.g. between experiences deemed psychical, psychopathological, religious, mystical and so on) typically suppressed by scholarly definitions of religion' (Taves 2005: 45). In her monograph *Religious Experience Reconsidered* (2009), she consequently suggests describing the experiences labelled under 'religious experience' as 'experiences people consider special' within a broader field (2009: 12). However, this does not mean that she expands her comparison to all kinds of experiences. Her examples remain, as a critic of her book, Timothy Fitzgerald, states, 'within the already conventionally-established contours of religious studies' (2010: 297). Fitzgerald would like Taves to expand her work outside the realm of religious studies. He argues that '[t]o successfully deconstruct practices normally "deemed to be religious" (including "experiences deemed to be religious") might in this kind of way lead to the interrogation of practices and experiences usually deemed to be secular as well' (2010: 297). He suggests, for instance, the inclusion of the justice system or even the way scientists work. Fitzgerald argues that the experiences that scientists such as Sir Isaac Newton and Charles Darwin have in the course of their work can also be seen as 'deemed special'. He questions therefore why their experiences are seen as different from so-called religious experiences. While no one would look into Newton's insight into gravity, scholars are investigating, as Fitzgerald highlights, Gotama Shakyamuni's insight about the emptiness of dhammas. 'Why has this insight, and the consequent theorization of a path of carefully monitored empirical observation, been classified differently from the insights of Newton et al., that is as "religious" rather than "scientific"?' (Fitzgerald 2010: 299).

But this is not Taves's pathway. Though Taves argues for a broader approach and challenges the sui generis approach to religion and religious experience, she nonetheless focuses in her work on 'experiences deemed religious' (2009: 15). The aim is to identify 'marks of specialness', hence what sets things apart, in a quite Durkheimian way. In relation to the Brazilian varieties of ecstatic experiences, one can therefore argue that mediumship, though not classified as religious by observers or followers, can still be regarded as 'special' or, in Taves's terminology, 'deemed religious'. When we then look at the descriptions of experiences I collected in my interviews, I can easily compare the subjective narratives according to types or levels of consciousness, or according to the embodiment of the experience. As Taves argues, 'viewing experience in this way allows us to consider how we gain access to experience (our own and that of others) and how it acquires meaning as it arises in the body and through interaction with others' (2009: 12). Instead of pushing religious experience to the outset of society, I argue with Taves against the division of social and sacred, of religious experience and other, non-religious experiences. This way I can take into account all kinds of categories of ecstatic experiences, including the quite technical approach to mediumship as communication. To a certain degree Taves follows here Csordas in his challenge of Émile Durkheim's definition of the sacred as a social construct. Though Csordas agrees with Durkheim's definition of the sacred as 'something radically other', he rejects Durkheim's limitation of human experience of otherness to the category of the social (1990: 33, referring to Durkheim 1915).

> The *sui generis* nature of the sacred is defined not by the capacity to have such experiences, but by the human propensity to thematize them as radically other.

> With this conception, the question of what is religious about religious heal-
> ing can be posed, since the sacred is operationalized by the criterion of the
> 'other'. However, since otherness is a characteristic of human conscious-
> ness rather than of an objective reality, anything can be perceived as 'other'
> depending on the conditions and configuration of circumstances, so that
> defining the sacred becomes an ethnographic problem. (Csordas 1990: 34)

The experience of ecstatic religions is the ultimate Other. It is also to a high
degree ineffable. Though sometimes my interviewees were willing to describe
their feelings going in or coming out of the state of altered consciousness,
often they could not remember or would not reveal their memories about
the incident itself. Nonetheless, despite being ineffable, the 'radically other'
defines not only the experience but also the tradition as it is at the core of its
practice despite its different function and ontology.

The divine transformation and the role of the possessing agency in Candomblé

The experience of the divine is a central aspect of Candomblé rituals and
also very important for the devotees. By incorporating the *orixás*, ordinary
members of the Candomblé *terreiros* are transformed into new beings who
embrace the divine. In order to explain the Candomblé concept, I outline,
first, Candomblé ideas about divine transformation, which refer to the body
concept in Candomblé. Afterwards I use the differences between *orixás*
and *caboclos* to explain the role of the possessing agencies in Candomblé.
However, it is important to remember what I highlighted in the introduction: the diversity of Candomblé. It is impossible to present the topic in a
way that it does justice to all internal controversies and debates. I ground my
reflection on my interviews, which give me only a selection of the numerous perspectives within the wide range of Candomblé varieties. It is not my
intention to present an ultimate definition of the ecstatic experience within
Candomblé but to further the understanding of it.

Candomblé devotees discuss the purpose of the ecstatic experience in
Candomblé quite controversially. Members of the priesthood usually argue
that the *orixás* convey their messages to human beings via oracle readings

(*buzios* or *ifa*). Hence, the incorporation of the *orixás* is not described as the main means of communication. However, it is nonetheless a core practice and highly significant for devotees.

Priests and priestesses usually disregard the idea of possession as communication because the majority of mediums do not speak during the incorporation. While I was told that it is possible, it is regarded as very difficult for the human medium to cope with and therefore highly unusual. Another problem is the language: *Pai F.*, a Candomblé priest from Salvador de Bahia but who was living and working in São Paulo, told me that the *orixás* are African. They do not speak Portuguese but may convey their message with other means. Hand gestures, for instance, can be very elaborate and convey meaning to the initiated followers. Body language is, in the whole, crucial in the interpretation of the message from the *orixás* because an *orixá* expresses emotions and wishes through bodily movement, whether dancing, walking or standing.[2]

The interview with *Pai Z.*, another Candomblé priest and leader of a Candomblé Fon community that is usually quite reclusive, offers an explanation for why mediums cannot transmit messages from the *orixás* during the incorporation. The key is that the *orixás* are regarded as too powerful for human beings to incorporate. They are like forces of nature. Since it is impossible for a human being to become a thunderstorm or a flash of lightning, it is also impossible to become possessed by one. *Pai Z.* therefore strongly rejects the term 'possession' and even incorporation as a limited explanation for what is going on during the event. As I had the opportunity to stay several days in his *terreiro* during the initiation of a new member, I was able to observe how difficult it is to teach someone undergoing initiation the correct body movements. Though I was not allowed in the sacred chamber of the *terreiro* where the novice stayed most of the time, I was able to observe the various presentations of the new initiate to the other members of the *terreiro* during which *Pai Z.* showed her and simultaneously her *orixás* the correct movements in his *terreiro*. He walked slowly in front of her and carefully corrected the way she walked, bowed, turned, danced, prostrated and so on. Every step was carefully monitored and, if necessary, corrected by showing her the correct way and indicating the mistake. She seemed unconscious the whole time. She did not acknowledge anyone else in the ceremonial hall and seemed unaware of everything around her, apart from *Pai Z.* and his assistants in this ritual. Sometimes she even seemed to stumble.

When I asked *Pai Z.* about this, he said that when the *orixás* make their first contact, everything is new to the person. 'The body is not accustomed to that energy, [but] the energy is also not accustomed to the body. At these times the person exists in a state of shock and can fall or have very strong spasms.'[3] He continued that when a first contact with the *orixás* happens prior to the initiation, the person will fall to the ground and have a kind of seizure. He said that this would be extremely hard for the person because the *orixá* is not yet inside; hence, is not yet linked to the human body, which does not yet have the knowledge. Before an initiation a person would be in a state of tremor. The person 'loses the notion of the body, the notion of everything, trembles and falls. This is symbolical for the *orixá* who knocks down the person to the ground in order to show that it [the *orixá*] has to be initiated in that person.'[4] This involuntary contact can happen anywhere – at work, when talking to friends or even in the movie theatre – whenever an *orixá* is next to the person and wants to initiate initiation and when the *ori* of the person needs this to take place. *Pai Z.* insists that only a *babalorixá* or someone familiar with the initiation process can then bring a person back to consciousness.

During the initiation process a person is regarded as innocent and ignorant like a child. The initiate I accompanied for a short while was already very familiar with the religion prior to the time of the initiation – she had attended several ceremonies, knew a lot about the religion, had already fulfilled the first obligations and had passed through the first rituals. Nonetheless, during the initiation she behaved and was treated like a child who has to learn everything. During the nights, when I heard her talking in the other room, sometimes her voice even seemed like that of a child, singing cheerfully, talking or even joking to the other person in the room. She stayed in this chamber day and night during her initiation, apart from the daily presentations to the members of the *terreiro* and when attending certain ceremonies outside the room. *Pai Z.* explained that, while at the beginning the movements of every novice were always rough and unfinished, with time the new devotee will learn how to behave and how to move. The style of movement depends on the *terreiro*'s lineage but also on the priest or priestess since every *terreiro* develops in time its own style. It is therefore important to teach the new initiate during the initiation process the style of the *terreiro*. Interestingly, *Pai Z.* insists that 'as much as the person learns, the *orixá* as well will learn.

They will learn how to move, the dances and the rituals. They are taught to make everything according to the tradition of the house because each nation, each house, each place tends to keep to a specific form. Each house has its tradition, each house has its way to deal with the *orixás,* and the *orixá* needs to learn how to carry them out.'[5] I was surprised by this explanation because it seems to contradict the powerful position of the *orixás.* However, *Pai Z.'s* description of the possession itself points to the reason for this alleged contradiction. According to his explanation, the *orixá* is firmly placed in the body of the new initiate during the initiation. Hence, after the initial encounter, something will remain in the body of the devotee, who has only now become complete; the missing item has been included into the human body. From now on, whenever the *orixá* takes control of the body, the *orixá* raises from within the human body to the head. Hence, the *orixá* does not overtake the head of the human medium from outside as it is in Umbanda, but from within the human body because it has become part of it. Though this link was firmly established during the initial initiation, the links between a person and the *orixás* are already prepared beforehand and then discovered by the *babalorixá* during oracle reading prior to the initiation. The initial initiation prepares the seat for the main *orixá,* but there is also a 'nest' for a second and even third *orixá.* During the next seven years after the initial initiation, the newly initiated will learn how to handle these *orixás.* Only after seven years will the devotee be considered as fully initiated and then elevated to the position of an elder of the *terreiro* or even a priest or priestess with his or her own *terreiro.* During these seven years, the person learns and extends his or her abilities. *Pai Z.* said that 'at time the person can be in a semi-conscious state, however, after many times, and after the person is initiated, the *orixá* takes the consciousness of the person . . . sometimes completely, depending on the sensitivity of the person'.[6] Consequently, seven years after the original initiation the experience is much stronger and is regarded then as complete.

Pai Z.'s view that the event should not be classified as possession or incorporation from an outside spirit but as the transformation of a human body from within is supported by some explanations in the literature. The *orixás* are perceived as surpassing individuality. After the initial initiation, when the merger has been completed, the divine never totally leaves the human body, according to the Candomblé notion of the body. The human being

is transformed by the initial merger with the divine. During the following encounters, the human part of the consciousness is taken over by the
divine part. Hence, the Candomblé medium does not handle two or more
consciousnesses, but allows a section of it to outshine the other. Followers of
Carl Gustav Jung would perhaps like to argue that the *orixá* constitutes part
of the consciousness of the medium (see Zacharias 1998 and his interpretation of the *orixás*), which justifies resisting the labelling of this experience as
possession. Candomblé devotees therefore clearly distinguish between their
experience and the experience of Umbanda and Spiritist mediums due to
Candomblé's conceptualization of the body. Barros and Teixeira even argue
that Candomblé ideas go beyond the division of body and mind. According
to their argumentation, the soul is not only spiritual but also has a material aspect, and the body is not only material but also has a spiritual aspect
(2004: 110), since it serves as a connection to the divine. They describe the
human body therefore as a vehicle for communication with the deities. The
body can receive the *orixás*, but it is also a means of personal individuality.
Consequently, it is impossible, according to the two authors, to distinguish
clearly between body and mind: the deities are not (only) phenomena of the
mind, and the body is not (only) a material unit.

Their explanation is consistent with Berkenbrock's statement that
in Candomblé thought a human being consists of different elements.
Berkenbrock explains that the body, which becomes earth again after death,
consists of *emi* (breath), which provides the body with life, *ori* (intelligence
or consciousness), and something from *Orum* (explained by Berkenbrock as
the divine creator, though other terms are more common for the creator god),
which means that every person has some elements of his or her *orixás* inside
the human body (1998: 285–6). The trance provides human beings with a
moment of harmony because all fragments are temporarily unified.

Marcio Goldman also presents an elaborate explanation for what happens
during the encounter and differentiates the transformation hypothesis more
emphatically. He argues that the world of the gods and the humans converse
during a possession. Human and *orixá* almost overlap and create two new
agencies together, a person and an individual *orixá*. Goldman insists that
possession involves more than the enactment of a rite, 'it amounts to a lived-
experience ritual' (Goldman 2007: 112). Being possessed means, according to

Goldman, that a person has become an 'almost' divine entity, the possessed person is not transformed into an *orixá* but becomes one (2007:114). While *Pai Z.*'s description of the transformation process echoes Eduardo Viveiros de Castro's explanation that transformation is 'not a process but a relation. Nothing "happened", but everything has changed' (2004: 473, 470), Goldman states that 'becoming' is not identical with transformation, the latter term includes the view at an active and creative process that will not (necessarily) result in a transformed entity. He highlights that a person is not born ready-made but constructed during the long process of initiation. Hence, the initial possession creates the person and also the *orixá* (2007: 111–12). Goldman argues that the generic *orixá* has no individuality but is a generic and gender-free entity that becomes an individual (and often but not always gendered) being during the initial possession of a human being. The outcome of an initiation is that 'a more or less undifferentiated individual . . . becomes a structured person and a generic *orixá* . . . is actualized as an individual *orixá*' (Goldman 2007: 112). Goldman here offers a different interpretation of the mental processes during possession that explains why the *orixás* are regarded as forces of nature on one side and individual spiritual entities on the other. He therefore makes a distinction between the *orixás* whose stories are told in myths, and the *orixás* who can possess a human body. He categorizes the first one as 'generic' and declares that initiation never involves the consecration of the initiate to one of these generic Orishas. Initiation means 'the ritual production of two individualizes entities out of two generic substrates' (Goldman 2007: 112). The initial possession ritual is, according to Goldman, the crucial moment in which the individuality of a person and of the *orixás* is construed. Goldman bases his interpretation on the perception that a person 'is presumed to be multiple and layered, composed of agencies of natural and immaterial elements', including a main *orixá* and a number of secondary *orixás*, ancestral spirits and a soul (2007: 111). An uninitiated human being is regarded 'close to Non-Being', and only the initiation finishes the creation process; hence, a person is 'made' during the initiation. Similar to the human being, the *orixá*, too, has no individuality prior to the initiation; therefore, the initial possession transforms a generic *orixá* into an individual entity and an unfinished, undifferentiated human being into a structured person (Goldman 2007: 112). This is why each incorporation is different: because the human element also plays a role in the transformation process. Each initiation ritual creates one specific being within the human; possessed agency and possessing agency become inseparably merged and create a unique entity. To a certain degree his argumentation echoes Klass's distinction between biological organism and personhood, but with a fundamental difference. While Klass regards personhood as a characteristic of every human being (2003, with reference to Radcliffe-Brown 1940), Goldman argues that a human being is imperfect until initiation. At birth a human being is not yet finished because an important piece is missing. Hence, Goldman argues that a person is not born readymade but constructed during the long process of initiation (Goldman 2007: 111–12). A human being is unstructured, while a person after the initiation is structured. While in the vast literature about spirit possession the possessed is often described as lacking a sense of self or losing the individual personality, the Candomblé ontology argues differently, that the self is only fully construed by the initial possession. Hence, in the Candomblé concept the aspect of the *orixás* that remains after the initiation is part of the self and constitutes a vital aspect of the individuality of the person (see the

Figure 3.1 The goddess Oxum in a transformed human body

goddess Oxum in a transformed human body during a Candomblé ceremony, Figure 3.1).

With this explanation I turn now to the possessing agencies and to the distinction between *orixás* and *caboclos* as it will shed a light on the differences between the possessing agency in Candomblé and Umbanda. As mentioned above, the *orixás* are seen in Candomblé as divine entities, forces of nature, too powerful for the human being to incorporate. *Caboclos*, in contrast, as well as other spirits such as the *egums* (spirits of ancestors) are regarded as limited entities. Though these entities are also perceived as more powerful than human beings, the devotees regard them as distinct from the *orixás* due to their former physical life on earth. Some Candomblé priests and priestesses use the ontology of *caboclos* in distinction to the *orixás* to differentiate between Candomblé and Umbanda. Perhaps not surprisingly, there has been a tendency in some Candomblé *terreiros* in the last years to disregard *caboclos* from the Candomblé pantheon, despite the fact that *caboclos* have been a constant presence in Candomblé for decades (for a longer discussion, see Schmidt 2013a). Nonetheless, many Candomblé devotees still acknowledge the presence of *caboclos* in the Candomblé pantheon as an important element of Afro–Brazilian religions because *caboclos* represent their Brazilian roots. *Pai* F., for instance, explained his attitude towards the *caboclo* Pena Branca (White Feather) in these words:

> As I am Brazilian, although I have been initiated in an African cult, I also have a Brazilian entity that it is the Pena Branca. . . . He is an Indian born in the interior of Goiás, inside of the bushes, according to his own information. It says that it belonged to another *pai de santo* who did not take care of him correctly, this is why it ended the connection to this *pai de santo* and caught me, still a novice. Really, before I made Oxum, the caboclo revealed him to me.

When I asked him why some Candomblé priests and priestesses are against the *caboclos*, he referred to local differences and insisted that in the Northeast where he came from, many houses have *caboclos*.

> Because before being initiated, they pass already *caboclos* [=are possessed by *caboclos*] and these *caboclos* are there to express the local (indigenous) identity. They say that an *orixá* is not an *egum*, a spirit of the deceased similar to a father, a mother, a person who lived here and died. But it is not correct because *Oxum* also lived, in Africa but it lived. *Iansã* also could be

an *egum*, it also lived, *Ogum* the same. *Xangô* was also a human until he got killed and died.[7]

I asked him whether he feels any differences between the incorporation of White Feather or Oxum, his major *orixá*. But he insisted that the difference was only between people and that the sensation of the approach was quite similar. He described it as a sensation of 'having lost the contact with the world'. It is, as he explained, 'as if I had to lean over in a building of more than 20 floors, and look down. There is the moment as if somebody arrives and pushes me down. Then there is panic. It always was as if I am in a high place, very high, looking down, then I turn round and somebody is there and he pushes me.'[8] This sensation is there when Oxum or the *caboclo* arrives. However, he cannot tell me what happens during the incorporation. From the moment of the approach he does not see or feel nothing. The people around him recognize the entity and they say that he danced White Feather or that Oxum is very pretty today. But he does not have any memory.

Pai Z., however, insists that the feeling between the encounter with a *caboclo* or an *orixá* is totally different. When I asked him what would happen if a *caboclo* approaches someone during a Candomblé ceremony, he replied that this would be very difficult as all of the ceremonies that he conducts in his community house consist of several rituals that call the *orixás*. 'And if someone is touched by an *orixá* it would be very difficult, almost impossible, to incorporate a *caboclo*.'[9] Pai Z. connects *caboclos* with a different version of Candomblé but in particular with Umbanda. For him, *caboclos* are derived from Angola Candomblé, but they have no place in Fon Candomblé, to which lineage his *terreiro* belongs. He said that 'in Fon there is no place for the *caboclos*. The *caboclo* rituals are part of the Angolan rituals. In order to perform a ritual for *caboclos*, it would be necessary to perform a rituals from Angola Candomblé. We [i.e. in the Fon ritual tradition] do not have proper rituals for the *caboclos*. To perform an Angolan ritual would be a mixture – and I do not encourage mixtures.' Pai Z., who has described the divine transformation in case of the *orixás* so eloquently, explains,

> Spirits have had a human body and can speak. A spirit can come and take control over the head of a person as a caboclo. Umbanda *caboclos* exists as an old black person, an ox-driver, for instance. [But] I do not perform

caboclo rituals because it would encourage in the head of a person the vision that the *orixá* is also there, in the head, and not here, inside the body. [At this moment he put his hand on his heart.] This would support the understanding that the *orixás* come from the outside and take control of the head of a person. However, they are inside.[10]

Pai Z. describes this as the most crucial distinction between Umbanda and Candomblé: while in the first case the spirit takes complete control of the human body and leaves the mediums after the possession, the Candomblé *orixás* arise from inside the body. 'The sensation is another one, the weight is another one, it [the experience] is a completely different thing.' It is, of course, understandable that every tradition has its own essentialist definition of the spiritual entities since the ontology of the supernatural beings is at the core of each tradition. The remarkable aspect in Brazil, however, is that many devotees practise, as has already been mentioned, more than one tradition. Many of my interviewees were even initiated members of more than one *terreiro*. Even priests and priestesses, in particular in Umbanda, also practised Candomblé and regularly attended rituals in a Candomblé *terreiro* to which they belonged. This flexibility is less evident among the Candomblé priesthood, as the account of *Pai Z.* indicates. Though some Candomblé priests and priestesses include spirits in the pantheon of spiritual beings of their *terreiro* and perform rituals not only for the *orixás* but also for other entities such as *caboclos* (e.g. *Pai F.*), they nonetheless highlight the unique relationship between humans and *orixás* and regard the other entities as secondary. In Umbanda, *orixás* are also considered as special entities, above all others; however, in the rituals the focus is on other groups of spiritual entities. These entities are approachable by the Umbanda mediums who will work with them during the weekly sessions. These weekly (or fortnightly) rituals, during which the mediums incorporate the Umbanda entities, provide the crucial means of communication between humans and spiritual beings, the core feature of Umbanda. Even the only priestess among my interviewees, who is a priestess in Umbanda and Candomblé, performs rituals in both traditions in her *terreiro*, but they are strictly divided (in different weeks and some parts even in a different space inside her *terreiro*). In her attempt to explain the difference between Candomblé and Umbanda, *Mãe I.* described the Candomblé *orixás* as energy, as a living energy that is in nature. It is awake and manifests in various ways. 'When one embraces this energy and captures it from the nature, it will form a new being which has quite a bit of you [i.e. a human person] and the energy of nature.' The Umbanda spirits, however, are removed because, as she explains, 'the energy of the dead does not live well with the energy of the living'.[11] Each entity has a specific 'vibration', and its meaning and interpretation are regarded as very different. Nonetheless, the fact that in one weekend someone can experience Umbanda entities taking control of her body and the next month experience an encounter with Candomblé *orixás* highlights the significance of understanding the different ontologies.

Mediumship as means of communication: A secular approach to trance?

In Candomblé, the *orixás* communicate their messages mainly via the oracle and not via possession rituals. The priesthood is the main interface between the *orixás* and human beings because they interpret the oracle for clients and therefore transmit the messages from the *orixás*. The personal encounter with the *orixás* during the so-called possession experience, however, also fulfils important functions for the devotees, enriching them by enabling them to experience the divine in a unique way. As Bateson suggests, dance – and the encounter with the *orixás* manifests itself often in dancing – can serve as an 'interface between conscious and unconscious' (Bateson 2000 [1972]: 138), or, from the perspective of the devotees, between divine and human. Bateson also regards this experience as a means of understanding messages, but highlights that the dancer is consciously unaware of these messages. In Candomblé, however, the movement of the mediums is highly influenced by the tradition of the house to which the practitioner belongs. During the long initiation process, the new initiate as well as the *orixá* inside the body have to learn how to move, how to prostrate, how to dance, as *Pai* Z. explained (see above). This experience is regarded as a fulfilment of a religious obligation but not as a means of communication. Nonetheless, I was told that a highly experienced priest, several years after the original initiation, can develop the ability to speak during trance. Though the main way to convey a message is via hand gestures and bodily movements, an experienced devotee is sometimes able to

speak a few words during the possession ritual. Whether anyone can understand the message is a different question, since the *orixás* speak usually in
Yoruba, not Portuguese.

Language, however, is not generally a problem in Umbanda as most of the
spiritual guides are regarded as Brazilian. The message by the spiritual guides
is considered more powerful than any advice given by members of the priesthood, as *Mãe* M. explains:

> People like to work with the guides in order to help someone. It is very
> popular for these guides to be incorporated in Umbanda, everybody likes
> it because it allows people to talk directly with the spirit. It is very dif-
> ferent from talking directly with a medium. You can say the same thing
> that the spiritual guide says but it has a different weight (when the guide
> is talking). . . . Five minutes of conversation with a spiritual guide about
> something personal is like directing a person for an hour and a half about
> an individual query. It does not have the same weight as spending five min-
> utes with a spiritual entity. It is therefore absolutely clear that the spiritual
> vibration of a spiritual entity is different from ours, and this sums it up.[12]

In Umbanda as well as in Spiritism, the focus is on helping clients by giving them advice in moments of crisis, whether it affects the health or general well-being of the client or their social environment. However, while
Umbanda embraces rituals of personal devotion to the spiritual entities in
addition to the public consultation session, Spiritism focuses on the communication between the human and the spiritual world, and the communication is perceived as secular. This strong emphasis is one of the reasons
why Spiritists often reject categorizing Spiritism as a religious tradition. For
them it is a technique, a means of communication, and therefore regarded
as secular. Though there are also Spiritist churches in Brazil, the majority of Spiritists follow the secular approach. They are text oriented and
study, for instance, the writings of Allan Kardec but also other Spiritists
in weekly classes and at home. Unlike Umbanda, Spiritists usually receive
'evolved' spirits that are considered 'good', full of positive energy, though
Spiritist centres also offer to 'disobsess' clients, that is, to cleanse them from
negative influences caused, for instance, by some of the spiritual entities of
Umbanda.

Spiritist mediums usually remain fully conscious of what is going on, though some have described their situation to me as semi-conscious in order to stress that they do not have control over their body during the trance. But mediums are considered to be at least partly responsible for what happens. Only one Spiritist (C.) told me that she does not remember anything.

> In my first contact with Dr. Marsec I was 18 years old. My mother had a seizure and she was bedridden. I woke up very early to go to work and when I said goodbye to her at five in the morning she could not move in her bed; she only moaned in pain. I told her 'Mom, I'll say a prayer because I need to go to work. I'll say a prayer for you to calm down, and I'm going to work.' When I started praying, I lost awareness of what was going on, and the Doctor came for the first time. When I came to, my mother was sitting up in bed and had nothing, no pain. She told me what happened and I was very scared because someone had entered my body, took over and did this to me. I was angry, happy to see her well, but very upset because this was not right.
>
> Then with time, I understand that it was not someone coming into my body, but it is a psychic power that is now almost instinct. . . . I gradually understood that my psychic power was not the same as with most other mediums, who are conscious or semi-conscious. In the beginning everything was very difficult, because sometimes when I returned I was off balance. Sometimes I had the impression that I was missing my legs and I would fall. Not today, today I think that training and extensive work with these brothers has given me a physical strength and knowledge . . . But I always need someone to hold me.[13]

Even in her Spiritist centre, medium C. is seen as an exception, and when I asked other Spiritists I was usually told that mediums are conscious or semi-conscious of themselves during the trance. A common characteristic between C. and other Spiritists is the tendency in Spiritism to receive so-called evolved spirits, in particular medical doctors but also other intellectuals (e.g. Greek philosophers). The preference is logical as the main goals of the communication are healing and education. Hence, it is not as common to communicate with the spirits of dead family members as it was in spiritualism in the nineteenth century in Europe and North America, though messages of the deceased are also transmitted via the guides of mediums. Chico Xavier, for instance, became famous for delivering messages of deceased children to their parents. These messages, however, are usually transmitted via spirit writing, also called automatic writing or *psicografia* (psychography). Though these sessions play a central role in most Spiritist centres and take on a ritualized form, the feeling they convey to participants is more like an evening class than a ceremony. The format emphasizes the secular character of Spiritism from the perspective of its participants (e.g. the sessions usually start with a reading from one of Kardec's books and often includes a Q&A session to discuss its meaning). But it would be wrong to describe mediumship as a purely technical process. I heard it, for instance, once described as 'an immense metaphysical telephone' (Rodrígues Vázquez 1994). This nickname gives the wrong impression, since mediumship involves a relatively long training period of the medium's special abilities, or, in Madeleine Michtom's words, the 'mystical powers which require training, practice and time' (1980: 168). Spiritists believe that everyone has certain powers but needs to develop and train them before one can use them for a good cause. Hence, the powers are given to human beings in order to help others. Spiritists therefore reject any notion of economic profit, as this excerpt from my interview with medium C. demonstrates:

> We believe that those who are making an income are still very attached to earthly matters. As incarnated spirits, we eat, drink, and have physiological needs, but the disembodied do not. So what's the point of communities saying, as they often do, that a spirit is going to benefit from the energies of those foods? A spirit would need to consume them. But a spirit that is disconnected from the world is in a different spiritual condition (and) will have no needs. So to say that this is for the spirit is rubbish. What is good for us when we are embodied does not justify the use of any of this (in the Afterlife). [. . .] God does not charge, God has left us with our consciences which is the judge of everything. You may fool another person, even in a court, but not your conscience. This is impossible . . . God has made this mechanism perfectly, however much you want to hide – you cannot hide your mistakes or your failures from yourself.[14]

This excerpt again points to the medium's responsibility for what happens during the trance. Even when a medium becomes unconscious of herself, as does medium C., she does not cease to be liable for her actions, even under the influence of a spirit guide.

In the majority of cases, however, Spiritists step away from incorporating a spirit. One Spiritist (J.) even describes it as a waste of time which would only prevent a medium's intellectual development:

> Nobody came to this world to receive the spirit of the third. We came here for our spirit, and what is our spirit, is our truth, our obligations, the ethics that we must learn to live together. Usually people do not want to know more, they want to come here to receive a spirit. . . . They are talking about a future life, or they are talking about a past life. But no one can really say anything about it because nobody knows. . . . We will just lose time. . . . We do not believe in a spirit that speaks. . . . Working with spirits [i.e. mediumship] is very difficult. So we have a separate group dedicated to developing guidelines for work with spirits, but not for one person. The spirits do not reveal anything about a person. They have no such right to do so because there is free will. They cannot say 'do this or do that.' The most they can do is enlighten the doctor for a proper diagnosis and to give us a good lecture, so that the patient feels compelled to take the medication, modify the diet, modify their habits, improve and be happy. None of this comes via incorporation. The merger is a primary process in psychic development. Let's say we have a range of therapeutic possibilities to help someone. The merger is the last, the very last chances we launched there.[15]

Though he acknowledges that it is possible to incorporate a spirit, it is not the right way. He receives his instructions via spirit writing though he had experienced incorporation by a spirit in the early days of his involvement with Spiritism. He argues that a constant incorporation of a spirit into a human body would create a 'supercreature', but this is not the intention of the spirits. He refers here also to highly evolved spirits, the spirits of light, whose instruction the mediums are receiving. Instead of the individual consultation of a spirit, as in the case in Umbanda, with their instructions spirits guide the mediums to apply their abilities for the good of the patient. He insists that the spirits work by guiding the system but not by incorporating a person. In other centres, he said,

> people are too involved. Sometimes the spirits require more attention than the patient. We do not have this kind of work, it does not work. The mediums here are trained to develop themselves intellectually. We develop spiritually through intellectual education, and that is not done by receiving

spirits. This is not allowed because much of the practice of receiving spirits is mechanical; it is more mental, pathological than strictly religious.[16]

With their insistence that Spiritism is a technique, without a religious connotation, Spiritism stands out among the numerous Brazilian traditions. However, one has to differentiate here between Kardecism and Spiritism. Though so far I have used the terms interchangeably, as most Brazilians do, there is a slight distinction. Kardecism refers more strictly to the ideas of Allan Kardec, and hence is descended from the nineteenth-century French movement. While Kardec saw his ideas in line with early Christianity – though not in line with the Church – he promoted a scientific approach to the world of spirits. He rejected any suggestion that his teaching might found a religious movement and described Spiritism as a philosophy or a science but never as a religion. In Latin America, however, his ideas merged with those of popular Catholicism as well as elements of other traditions, which led to the establishment of popular religious systems such as Puerto Rican *espiritismo popular*. Spiritism became seen as an alternative spirituality that lacked the negative image of African-derived belief systems. Though under the colonial rule Kardec's books were prohibited because he opposed the Roman Catholic Church, in the twentieth century Spiritism met less political opposition and became – legally at least – acceptable. In Brazil, the term Spiritism was gradually used to describe Kardec's ideas as well as a range of beliefs under the umbrella *espírita*. The latter then even made an entry into the national census – under the heading religious beliefs. The result is that 3.8 million Brazilians ticked the box *espírita* in the national census in 2010 – but it is not clear whether all the self-identified Spiritists actually followed Kardec's teaching or just tried to avoid the negative connotation of Umbanda or other Afro–Brazilian religions by identifying with Spiritism, as some scholars indicate (e.g. Malandrino 2006). Nonetheless, the fact is that Chico Xavier's many publications have sold over 25 million copies (Stoll 2006: 265) and are still bestsellers in Brazil. Lewgoy (2006) argues that Spiritism has to be understood before the background of the all-embracing Catholic culture of Brazil. While at the beginning Spiritism struggled with the Roman Catholic Church, it succeeded in converting eminent members of the elite, in particular republicans and abolitionists but also Catholics (Lewgoy 2006: 211).

With its anti-clerical tendency and its strong promotion of progressive think-ing, Spiritism became widespread, especially in Brazil's cities. However, two strands of Spiritism quickly emerged – one pushed the scientific angle, while the other promoted a more mystical approach. Nonetheless, Lewgoy char-acterizes Spiritism in the beginning of the twentieth century as 'an invis-ible Catholic influence', which he attributes to the fact that Catholicism was naturalized as the national ethos of Brazil. Spiritism became seen as secu-lar religion (*religião laica da ordem*) that promoted evolution by individual merit (2006: 213). While Spiritism originated among Brazilian intellectuals, under the influence of Chico Xavier, Spiritism expanded to a wider, popular movement that embraced, as Lewgoy states, a different form of Catholicism, derived from Xavier's life. As Stoll (2002) highlights, Chico Xavier played a crucial role in 'designing the Catholic ethos that is shaped Spiritismin Brazil' (Stoll 2002: 363). He consolidated Spiritism with Catholicism, as Stoll states, by introducing both Catholic practical and doctrinal elements into Spiritism. The clues to this development lie, according to Stoll, in Xavier's biography. She refers especially to his narratives of his experience with the spirits which featured elements of popular Catholicism and, second, to his public image, which represented an ideal of holiness inspired by the life of Catholic monas-tic principles (2002: 370). The outcome was a syncretic mosaic that included, for instance, the figure of Jesus as a 'superior spirit' as well as the introduc-tion of images of Catholic saints and candles in Spiritist centres and even pilgrimages to Uberaba in order to pray to Chico Xavier (Stoll 2006: 215–16). Lewgoy interprets the syncretism within Chico Xavier's form of Spiritism as a sign of an approach between Catholicism and Spiritism that led to the spread of Spiritism in wider sectors of society. Hence, despite the strong ther-apeutic frame of Spiritism today, which has led to the emphasis on medi-umship as technique, Lewgoy sees a strong connection between Spiritism and Catholicism, based on Brazilian culture but also on the impact of Chico Xavier's life and teachings. While most Spiritists reject the notion of Spiritism as a religion, it has incorporated some religious aspects, though the level of significance the participants assign these elements varies from one centre to another. Nonetheless, can mediumship just be reduced to a technique, with-out any religious connotation? And why do Spiritists oppose any connection to 'possession' or 'incorporation'? The answer to these questions lies in the notion of personhood within Spiritism, which supports (as mentioned above) a different attitude towards agency.

MariaLaura Viveiros de Castro Cavalcanti explains that 'the whole spiritist religious realm is based on the relationship between the two Worlds' (2006: 4), hence the world of the living and the world of the spirits. However, this relationship coexists, as she outlines, with the individual factors that point in the other direction, towards responsibility for one's own actions. These two poles coexist under constant tension, as Sandra Stoll (2009) explains. Referring to Cavalcanti (1983), Stoll defines personhood in Spiritism as captured between two opposite images: on the one side we have the notion of autonomous beings, producers of one's own history and subjects with free will, and on the other side we see the laws of evolution, karma and reincarnation, which characterize submission of the living to the spirits.

Cavalcanti explains that the relationship between the two worlds is connected along two logical-temporal axes, one diachronic and one synchronous. The first one describes the 'great cosmic path where everything unfolds under the eye of God' (2006: 4). Hence, connected to this axis are the concepts of reincarnation, karma and evolution. The second axis concerns the relation between the two worlds based 'on the perspective of the incarnate spirit, whose unity between body and soul is contingent on a unique incarnation' (2006: 4). On this axis mediumship is the key concept, hence the communication between the living and spirits, or, in Spiritist terms, between incarnate and disincarnate. Cavalcanti states that 'mediumship and reincarnation determine each other where the significance of human acts is necessarily dense' – though according to Spiritism nothing happens randomly, 'a true drama unfolds, necessarily experienced by each incarnate spirit: the confrontation between what we could call the incarnate spirit's own free will and the will of others (the free will of disincarnate spirits)' (Cavalcanti 2006: 5). While Stoll (2009) argues that the happiness and well-being of a person depend largely on free will and being responsible for one's own destiny and that ideas of karma and the universal law are less significant to Spiritists, Cavalcanti focuses on the tension between reincarnation and mediumship in her explanation of personhood in Spiritism. Cavalcanti states that

> reincarnation and mediumship shatter any idea of an eventual unity of the 'self', however, there is an immediate proposal to complete such a unit.

> Reincarnation implies the idea of inherent incompleteness regarding any
> spiritual entity (by definition: in progress, on a long cosmic journey of suc-
> cessive incarnations). In addition, mediumship implies the intrinsically
> *fragmentary* nature of the incarnate spiritual entity (the human being here
> and now), who is in search of meaning. . . . Therefore . . . reincarnation
> in diachrony and mediumship in synchrony, both configure the complex
> spiritist concept of the person, i.e. that which a spiritist beliefs he/she is, i.e.,
> him/herself. (2006: 5, italics in the original)

Because of this complex notion of self, mediumship is very different from
spirit possession. Though Stoll acknowledges some similarities between the
Candomblé experience in Goldman's interpretation (outlined above) and
Spiritism, since both involve mediums as well as their spirit guides, the perception of the entities in Spiritism is unlike that of Candomblé. As Stoll
points out, Spiritism is based on the individuality of all entities involved,
mediums as well as spirits, which includes their differences and affinities
as well as life histories (Stoll 2009: 15). Consequently the possession experience does not produce new, synthetic identities as in Goldman's interpretation of the Candomblé merger, but confirms the individuality of the entities.
Stoll describes mediumship as a vertical shaft, a meeting of beings of the
same kind but who are unequal due to the different degree of their spiritual
development. It can be seen, as Stoll outlines, as a virtual field of coexistent
relations between living beings and spirits, complementing each other and
building links in support of a moral order (Stoll 2009: 16). Through training, a medium will gain control of the ecstatic experience whenever mediumship is voluntarily initiated. Stoll insists that a medium 'is not someone
who is simply a subject to the will of the "spirits". A medium is described
as someone who "gives way", "enters in harmony", "opens your field of
vibration" for the manifestation of Others' (Stoll 2009: 16). Stoll therefore
points to the free will of mediums and the preservation of the individuality of medium and spirit in order to distinguish between mediumship and
possession and adds that Spiritists use 'possession' only in the context of
'obsession', hence as a negative experience that involves an experience of
annihilation of individuality and which needs treatment (desobsession).
Stoll argues that possession is regarded in this way as negative because it

dissolves the boundaries between the two worlds, something no good spirit would do.

Hence, to answer the questions raised above, mediumship, one of the two main characteristics of Spiritism, is interpreted by its practitioners as a (secular) communication technique, though in order to understand it one has to consider the cosmology of the two realms of existence in Spiritism (the living and the spirits), which is, essentially, a religious worldview. However, its strong emphasis on free will, hence a predominately reactive attitude to the agency of the mediums, explains the rejection of spirit possession since the latter is seen as undermining free will. To summarize, I cite from Cavalcanti's article:

> Dramatizing the tension between free will and determinism to the extreme, Spiritism features a unique profile within the Brazilian religious realm. It simultaneously constructs fabulous, imaginary, active worlds where the living and the dead constantly communicate, and counterbalances this fabled vision, which feeds in the Beyond, with a variation of the ethics of intra-world action, by placing incarnate life in the unique privileged place of **probation**, of gradual construction of **free will**, of the sense of responsibility for every action and behaviour, of **merit** and **blame**. Thus, an individual will have to evoke the whole universe inhabited by spirits in order to live his own life, as Chico Xavier exemplarily did. (2006: 11–12, bold used in the original)

Exorcism and the interpretation of the *Orixás* and spirits as demons

My last section in this chapter looks at the possession experience from the opposite angle. I focus on the interpretation of spiritual entities as demons from which one needs to be liberated, hence exorcized. As Kramer writes, the battle 'against the demons and forces of darkness that possess individuals, cities, and even regions, is not unique to the Universal Church . . . [but] has become something of a Universal Church trademark' (Kramer 2005: 108–9). When I observed an exorcism for the first time at a branch of the Universal Church of the Kingdom of God (IURD) in São Paulo, I was surprised to see how familiar the body language of the possessed women looked. I was reminded instantaneously of Umbanda mediums as well as mediums in a Xangô *terreiro* in Recife. I was surprised because several years earlier I had attended a series of IURD services, including exorcism, in New York City (Schmidt 2008), but the body language of the possessed in New York was very different from that in Brazil. IURD in New York provided for the large and ethnically diverse Hispanic/Latino community. The pastors preached in Spanish, and the whole setting addressed a largely Puerto Rican/Dominican audience as well as Spanish-speaking South American immigrants. There was no reference to any spirits or African deities; instead, the devil or Satan was the main focus of the exorcism, or liberation. Though the elements of the exorcism were translated into the Latino context, the spiritual entities that had to be exorcized were different. Even when I asked the main pastor, who was Brazilian, about the *orixás*, he did not acknowledge them at all. This shift is understandable because of the different composition of the congregation. While evil remains the target of the liberation, it shows itself, according to the IURD worldview, in different shapes, depending on the cultural environment.

Because I have already discussed exorcism in Chapter 3 (in the context of the role of women in the IURD), I focus here on the ontology of the spiritual entities and the possession experience itself. This is considered particularly in light of religious experiences in Pentecostal churches, connected to the Holy Ghost. Though in Pentecostal terms these are not described as possessions, the religious experience of divine revelation shows some similarities to those of Candomblé and other Afro–Brazilian religions. I largely refer to the IURD, but I also attended – and interviewed members of – other neo-Pentecostal churches such as the Igreja Pentecostal Deus é Amor (Pentecostal Church God and Love), one of the oldest Brazilian neo-Pentecostal churches in São Paulo (founded in 1962), though nationwide it is second in size after the IURD and the Igreja Assembléia de Deus (Assembly of God Church), the largest Pentecostal church in Brazil.

Pentecostal theology distinguishes between different origins of religious experience, with some attributed to the Holy Ghost, Christ and the Father. William Kay states that according to the Trinitarian orthodoxy of most Pentecostals, 'it becomes much more important to work from a biblical basis to define what it is the Holy Spirit does and how the Holy Spirit relates both to the Christ and the Father' (Kay 2005: 6). Referring to passages in John 14–16 and Acts 2:33, which show a differentiated notion of the persons of the Trinity, Kay argues that it is possible in Pentecostal churches to attribute religious phenomena to one of the three figures of the Trinity with great precision. 'It is not just a case of saying that an experience or event is attributable to God. Rather, there is the potential for specification about whether an event took place through the Holy Spirit or as a result of the power of Christ, or the Father, or all Persons of the Trinity working jointly' (Kay 2005: 6). Pentecostal theology puts a strong emphasis on religious experience but also relies on a correlation between religious experience and doctrine. While the baptism of the Holy Ghost – and subsequent conversion – has the most prominent role among the range of religious experiences, Pentecostals expect that the Holy Ghost will continue to work through the manifestation of *charismata*, as Kay explains. One core element is the charisma of divine healing. However, while Kay stresses 'an automatic feedback loop' that points towards the charisma (when the person remains ill, the charisma has not done its work), in Brazil, especially in neo-Pentecostal churches, I observed a stronger emphasis on the person's responsibility (when the person remains ill, the faith of the person is not strong enough). Though the Assembly of God follows a more moderate practice in line with Kay's explanation, other churches such as the Igreja Pentecostal Deus é Amor, which advertises its successes in divine healing, put the patients under such enormous pressure to demonstrate even a little success that some of them collapse under the stress.

Kay describes demonology as one of the challenges of traditional Pentecostalism. He traces the influence back to Derek Prince (1915–2003), whose radio programmes were broadcast worldwide. He distinguished, as Kay summarizes, between angels and demons, with both groups subdivided in different ranks. Angels 'never sought embodiment within the material world since they had spiritual bodies of their own', while demons, 'as bodiless spirits, [would] constantly [seek] to live within the material world and to utilise animate beings to express themselves' (Kay 2005: 9–10). The only solution would be to expel the demons by exorcism 'through the authority of Christ'. But, as Kay acknowledges, demonology is difficult to prove. Though an improvement in the exorcized person would indicate a successful exorcism and a failed improvement a continued presence of the demons, it is not possible, as Kay states, to verify the initial diagnosis, the possession itself. 'In other words, once the presumption is made that exorcism is necessary, attempts to carry this out cannot be tested against the condition of the exorcisee unless he or she dramatically and permanently improves' (Kay 2005: 6).

Prince described demons as spirits of pre-Adamic races who 'lust for embodiment', while evil angels 'were those who were hurled out of heaven during the Satanic revolt against God described in the apocalypse' (Kay 2005: 10). The IURD characterizes all deities in any religion as demons, from the Greek Antic to the *orixás* of the Afro–Brazilian traditions, and describes them as descendants of Satan and the cause of all evil in the world. The targets are nowadays often described as evil spirits under the general, unspecific name *encostos*, which can also include the spirit of a deceased relative that interferes with someone's life (Kramer 2005: 111). Kramer interprets the growing usage of *encostos* instead of *orixás* as a result of the 1989 law that prohibited religious discrimination, since the use of *encostos* 'blurs the legal definition of what could be construed as acts of religious discrimination' (Kramer 2005: 117, n.6). Nonetheless, IURD theology seems not to differentiate between demons according to their geographical locations or origin, as Prince suggested, but rather modifies the features of the entities according to the other religious discourses. However, 'in this new voicing, the sense of encosto changes as its field of reference is extended to include all manner of spirits from Afro–Brazilian religions' (Kramer 2005: 111). This re-interpretation of indigenous spirits as demons is widespread among Pentecostal churches worldwide, as Robbins (2004) shows. In her case study among the Ewe in Ghana, Birgit Meyer traces this diabolization of indigenous entities back to the missionaries who 'based the claim that the gods and ghosts served by the Ewe were real agents of the Devil on their interpretation of the New Testament' (Meyer 1999: 83). The Ewe religion became represented as satanic, and the missionaries were called to destroy Satan and his creatures. Meyer describes the Devil as the link between missionaries and the Ewes' worldview: 'to state that Ewe religion was a work of Satan made it meaningful in the light of Christianity, and subordinate to it' (Meyer 1999: 84). As a result, the image of the Devil also mediated between old and new ways of life, hence became a sign of the dispute with modernity. While

Christianity signified modernity and offered people a path towards 'civilization', the relationship of the Ewe to the elements of the modern society remained ambivalent. And the image of the Devil helped people, as Meyer points out, deal with modernity but also the traditions they wanted to break with, but 'from which they could not fully dissociate themselves' (Meyer 1999: 111). Baptism signifies the crucial rupture with the past, but equally important are the other 'rituals of rupture' (Robbins 2004) that are aimed at deepening the break with the past. Probably the most important one in the IURD and other neo-Pentecostal churches in Brazil is the *libertação* (deliverance) ritual, hence the exorcism. Kramer writes that deliverance is different from the initial conversion, the act of accepting Jesus. He describes deliverance 'as a liminal stage in the process of freeing oneself from the lingering influence of demons' (Kramer 2005: 102). The aim is to distance oneself from the past (e.g. to give up vices) and to fully embrace the faith.

According to Robbins, we need to understand these rituals of rupture in the context of the dualistic scheme that shapes the Pentecostal worldview. He states that 'dualism divides the world into those whose lives are directed by God and those who follow the devil' (Robbins 2004: 128, with reference to Droogers 2001). Both realms operate as symbols, as Robbins writes, 'with an open-ended range of referents': it can signify the opposition between the past and the present, as in Meyer's case study, or the differences between the Church and the world, between the public and the private. Since the dualism refers to strict moral codes which prohibit alcohol and drugs, extramarital sex and much more, it therefore has an impact on private conduct. This is also the case in Brazil, where the dualism between God and evil, the Holy Ghost and Satan, addresses the individual behaviour of the devotees. Exorcism rituals allow the participants to confront and problematize their own traditions, their own past and also their own life. Hence, while Meyer interprets the diabolization of the Ewe religion as an expression of ambivalence towards modernity, the Brazilian context localizes the 'spiritual warfare' (Robbins) within the private realm. By preserving the Afro–Brazilian ontologies and by continuously engaging with them on a ritual level, the IURD and other churches offer 'meaningful idioms for talking about the past and about current social problems – for spirits always are a language for talking about broader concerns' (Robbins 2004: 129). Satan and the demons are not only addressed in the exorcism rituals but are also part of most other services in the IURD as spiritual warfare is the most prominent topic of sermons and also the ritual practice. Nonetheless, exorcism is the most spectacular event. Kramer even writes that in these rituals the IURD 'dramatizes the realization of faith *itself* as a ramifying spectacle of empowerment' (2005: 103, italics in the original). It functions 'as a ritual process for producing truth and affirming the power of a superior being' (2005: 110). Kramer sees the exorcism rituals therefore as rhetorically constructing 'forms of authority and concepts of power that depend on spectacular manifestation. The unfolding drama, then, is not simply an exorcism but a broader demonstration of value that points to church authority and concepts such as fidelity, which in turn reflect back on participation' (2005: 110).

As an example, I cite a short excerpt from a much longer sermon given by Bishop Romualdo in July 2002 in Rio de Janeiro, quoted by Kramer (2005: 113–14), since I did not record the rituals I attended in São Paulo:

> You can come out, encosto
> You can come out
> The encosto who's in that man
> Who's in the marriage of that woman
> The encosto who doesn't let that man be happy
> You can come out.
> Gradually, he began to name the encostos, identifying each with the specific affliction it caused and its social origin:

> That's right, come out . . .
> The spirit of darkness
> Whose name is Pombagira
> With the name of Maria Padilha
> And who is in the marriage of that woman
>
> . . .

The spell (*trabalho*) that was done to separate the couple:

> A lover performed sorcery with a piece of that man's underwear
> The lover put his name in the cemetery
> . . .
> You can come out, Pombagira.

And, after an interval of prayers the bishop addresses the spirits individually:

Exu Farrapo
Exu da Lama
I want to hear your scream
Pombagira Maria Mulambo
Pombagira Maria Farrapo
The encosto who was gifted at the trash dump
Down at the dump in Caxias
They performed sorcery so she would be reduced to trash
So her life would become dust.

The climax comes with collective cries of 'in the name of Jesus' and loud shouts of *sai!* (out). What Kramer here describes is the quite typical collective part of a *sessão de descarrego* (discharge or unloading session) in which the whole audience is included. The exorcism afterwards addresses usually only a handful of people, generally women, as I explained previously. In these cases the exorcist addresses the spirit directly, asks for its name and 'exposes' the spirit to the audience. I again cite Kramer (2005: 115, insertion by Kramer):

The bishop now turned to interrogate the encosto. When asked its name, the rebellious spirit replied, Lucifer'. Bishop Romualdo began ordering the encosto to stand up, kneel, and throw back its head. Grabbing hold of the possessed woman's hair, he forced the spirit to turn around to show the congregation its 'claws', the visible sign of an incorporation. (The names, the posture, and the claw like hands of the possessing spirits clearly identify them with Afro–Brazilian religions, Umbanda in particular.) He then demanded to know what the spirit was doing to her. The encosto replied and said she had cancer. As yet another proof of his power over the spirit, the bishop now told us that, on his command, the woman would return to her normal state. A few more questions to the encosto revealed that the spirit had put a cancer in her uterus and that it was preventing her from having a relationship with a divorced man. The bishop ordered the spirit to return to its original state. The woman came out of the trance with no memory of her possession. Romualdo noted her physical transformation and asked her a series of questions to check her knowledge against what the encosto had said. Her testimony confirmed tangentially the things that the spirit had confessed under interrogation: that she had lower abdominal pain and that the ex-wife of her boyfriend was causing problems. Upon this, the bishop looked up and rhetorically addressed the congregation: 'Pretty clear, isn't it?' He then told the woman what the encosto had said and counseled her to see a doctor, to follow the medical recommendations and do all the tests, but also to put her faith in God.

Next, he forced the spirit to return and again asked its name and what it was doing. Having finally identified the spirit as Exú Caveira, he then invited us to assist him in the final push to exorcise the exú. After a lengthy struggle, repeatedly ordering the spirit to expel the illness, the pastor called on us to extend our hands. Once more the auditorium filled with the sound of hundreds of people shouting, 'Burn!''Burn!''Burn!' and then 'Out!' On that triumph, we applauded and thanked Jesus.

While all other traditions I presented above focus on living with the spirits and deities, this case illustrates an opposite pattern – the rejection of the experience, while maintaining it in its repertoire of weekly practices. Exorcists acknowledge the presence of the supernatural entities but interpret them as evil. Firmly embedded in a Christian worldview of good and evil, exorcists present a different approach to the experience and its meaning for society and the individual.

***

To conclude this chapter, I want to address once again the relevance of subjective narratives to academic debate. Pyysiäinen argues that 'whether a given explanation is valid should be judged on the basis of evidence and logical coherence of the argument, not on the basis of a religious [or anti-religious] agenda' (2008: 3). He rejects the perspective of the practitioners because their perception and knowledge 'cannot be considered representational or theoretical', as Pyysiäinen argues, because their knowledge about God or any other supernatural being 'does not depend on our capacities for knowing, but on God's own self-revelation' (Pyysiäinen 2003: 229–30). Pyysiäinen therefore bases his argument on an understanding of revelation which is not shared in all of the examples presented above. For instance, though mediumship is based on belief in the existence of spirits, Spiritists regard it as having a secular, even scientific basis (though most scientists will disagree with this assessment of science). The main argument against

Pyysiäinen, however, is the idea that the validity of an explanation can be judged on the basis of evidence. I argue that an experience as complex as spirit possession cannot be reduced to material evidence. As Pyysiäinen argues elsewhere (2001), the materialist approach of, for instance, Pascal Boyer, lacks the acknowledgment of the 'reality of religious experience' as 'something vital – conscious experience and the emotional aspect of religion – is missing (2001: 71). Though Pyysiäinen rejects the importance of the subjective dimension of religious experience, he points towards the importance of the emotional side of religion. Referring to Whitehouse's doctrinal mode of religiosity and the imagistic mode (1995), Pyysiäinen challenges Whitehouse for ignoring the significance of the emotional and sensual stimulation for mainstream institution (Pyysiäinen 2001: 87–8). Pyysiäinen regards emotion as the basis of religious experience and religious belief – something, as I argue, highly subjective for the person experiencing it. Following this line, I have presented practitioners' explanations, which are embedded in distinct worldviews and even shaped by their own logic. While the interviewees undoubtedly have personal agendas, I see these as more politically motivated than religious. Even members of the priesthood did not want to convert me, but rather to explain the logic of their explanation so that I can educate others. Their aim is to combat the prejudices against their practice and increase the esteem for what they are doing. Though this goal could be perceived also as a religious agenda, I disagree with Pyysiäinen's rejection of their explanations just because of their religious agenda. As I have shown in this chapter, each tradition has its own interpretation of the experience, following its own logic, which cannot be judged from an outsider's perspective, whether religious or secular.

4

Agency, Cognition and Embodiment: Paradigms in the Body/Mind Debate

Introduction

On 19 March 2010, I attended an Umbanda ceremony for the spiritual entities called *preto velho* in Campinas, São Paulo State. I was given a lift from São Paulo by two *filhas de santo*, young women who belonged to the Umbanda community I was about to visit. My transport was arranged by the *mãe de santo*, the priestess and founder of this community, whom I had already met a few times in São Paulo. Upon arrival I was introduced to the other members and then was asked to sit down and wait with other clients in a dedicated area, just outside of the sacred circle. While I waited for the ceremony to begin, I noticed small stools and very short walking sticks situated around the room. The priestess was a tall woman, as were most of the other members, so I had no idea who might use them, or for what. However, at the end of the ceremony, after I had observed (and consulted) several mediums incorporating *preto velho* entities, I suddenly realized that the stools no longer looked too small and that the canes were the right size because the mediums suddenly resembled very old, bent people who could hardly walk.

Something similar happened in a Spiritist centre. I visited the centre for the first time on 30 March 2010 and was able to observe a healing session (*cura espiritual*). When I came back on 17 April to observe another *terapêutica espiritual*, this time a so-called *desobsessão*, I was also able to interview the woman who had worked as the main medium during my earlier visit.

Standing next to her, I suddenly realized that she was shorter than I. When I had observed her during my earlier visit, treating patients while incorporating her spirit guide, I had thought that she was quite a tall person, definitely taller than I. But in her 'normal' state I realized that my perception was wrong.

These are only a few personal impressions during ceremonies that are heavily charged emotionally, not the least for myself. I did not measure the mediums and cannot prove anything. Nonetheless, my impressions are in agreement with the mediums' reports about their feelings of how the possession experience affected them physically. But do these impressions enable me to understand the physical effects of the possession experience better? I am no closer to recognizing whether or not it is the spirit of a medical doctor who treats the patients in a Spiritist centre; whether it is an *orixá* or the medium who conveys his or her pleasure about the presence of so many clients; or whether it is a *caboclo* or a priest who criticizes me for an incorrect movement. I do not understand how a woman with a disfigured foot can dance for hours without pain; why a man wakes up from his trance feeling immensely sad about the loss of his *orixá*; or why someone who has consumed an enormous amount of alcohol exhibits no effects.

As Peter Fenwick (2001) points out, it is difficult, probably impossible, to scientifically evaluate and explain subjective experience. Fiona Bowie promotes a methodology that she describes as 'cognitive, empathetic engagement', involving 'mind and body, intellectual knowing and embodied engagement' (2013: 700, 713). Bowie bases her argumentation on Johannes Fabian (2001) and his explorations of ethnographic objectivity. 'Knowledge is not an object, but an intersubjective process of creative engagement between individuals'; however, as Bowie summarizes Fabian, knowledge 'is a time-bound, material element – we co-exist in time and space in our communicative embodiment' (Bowie 2013: 703). Instead of retreating into abstraction as a cognitive approach often does, Bowie urges the researcher to look at the data on its own terms. The methodology requires that research be conducted dialogically, which, as Bowie insists, can even be transformative for the researcher (2013: 723). Scientists following a biological approach usually dismiss this kind of methodology as subjective and even speculative. But while Bowie herself acknowledges that her data and the way she presents it are not necessarily objective, she nevertheless does not dismiss that they might be. She argues that her approach of cognitive, empathetic engagement 'does not presuppose any particular belief system or standpoint, but neither does it preclude them. It recognizes the dialogical position of the observer in the process of acquitting knowledge, while retaining a focus of attention on the other. Its purpose is to elucidate the object of study rather than become an exercise in self-reflection' (2013: 702–3). Yet it is not the question of objectivity or subjectivity that is on her agenda but rather the interpretation of the data: in her case, the perspective of the afterlife derived from trance séances. Bowie insists that 'resulting ethnographies allow the reader to experience something of these worlds vicariously through the lens of the ethnographer's first-hand account, and to engage with these worlds through an encounter with the other." Rather than stressing the distance between "their false" and "our correct" beliefs, the reader is given the opportunity to enter into other worlds and encounter their inhabitants as equals' (2013: 717).

Scholars following a biological approach – such as the new branch of cognitive scholars,[1] neuroscientists and other scientists who usually reject the empathetic methodology – insist that it is possible to study religious experience objectively, based on hard facts alone. They argue that religious experience derives from the brain and that it is physical rather than spiritual. But I question whether the fact that we can measure types of brain activity during spiritual experiences proves without any doubt that the brain is generating the experience. In a recent study by Julio Fernando Peres and others (2012), the authors examined ten Brazilian mediums during psychography (engaged in automatic writing, or, as Peres et al. write, 'while in a dissociative trance state', 2012: 2). They measured the brain activity with so-called neuroimaging and concluded that areas of the brain that are usually associated with writing were underactivated during the time the mediums were in a dissociative state, when compared with the brains of people not in a trance state. The authors do not offer an explanation for their findings, but they insist that studies based on neuroimaging techniques are replicable and therefore that it is possible to study mediumistic phenomena scientifically (Peres et al. 2012). But is a sample of just ten cases really enough to make wider generalizations? One is reminded at once of the study of fifteen Carmelite nuns (Beauregard and Paquette 2006) who were examined during a 'mystical condition'. However,

Mario Beauregard and Valerie Paquette acknowledged that the nuns told them that 'God can't be summoned at will' and that they had to revise the experiment in the light that the nuns were just asked to remember prior mystical experiences (2006: 187). From an anthropological point of view, one has to ask whether the environment, the cultural and historical context in which the experience happens, also influences the experience. Perhaps one should look at it in the other direction and ask whether the experience might cause the brain to make these changes.

These questions point to the main debate in this chapter, which deals with the mind/body dichotomy, also called Cartesian dualism after the French philosopher René Descartes (1596–1650). Descartes's *La description du corps humain* (1647) was, perhaps wrongly, understood as describing the body as a machine with material properties and the mind as purely non-material. Though some philosophers challenge this reading of Descartes by highlighting that Descartes also insisted on a bond between body and mind and the existence of elements that are not purely material nor non-material (e.g. Perler 2002, Zittel 2009), what is called 'Cartesian' philosophy sets the parameters of the body/mind dualism that influenced the way we think about the human body but also immaterial aspects. The main argument is that, though both parts interact with each other, in the end the mind controls the body. This approach to the body can be traced back even to the Greek philosopher Plato (429–347 BCE), who saw the body as an empty material vessel. The soul, however, was perceived as full of ideas and immortal. Any abnormal state, including madness, was therefore perceived by Plato as a 'disease of the body caused by bodily conditions'; however, he insisted that we can understand its meaning only in its everyday context. He wrote, for instance, that 'we only achieve [prophecy] when the power of our understanding is inhibited by sleep or when we are in an abnormal condition owing to disease or divine inspiration . . . It is not the business of any man so long as he is in an irrational state to interpret his own visions and say what good or ill they portend' (Littlewood 1993: 17, referring to Plato 1965: 47). Consequently religious experiences are often regarded as products of cognition, something that happens in the mind alone. Going back to the personal impressions I described at the beginning, this would mean that my perception of the physical changes originated in my mind. However, this interpretation limits our ability to understand the dynamics at play. Instead of allocating the experience to the mind alone, as is often done, I argue for the inclusion of a material dimension that brings the possession experience out of the area of 'pure belief' and into the area of human practice. As Saler writes, '[P]eople do not just "have" beliefs. They frequently *use* or deploy them in social interactions, in keeping with desires and interests, and there is a meaning in that use' (2001:66, emphasis in the original). While Saler prefers the cognitive approach, however, I favour the embodiment paradigm because it challenges dualistic thinking.

Concepts such as spirits, souls, gods or demons cause a dilemma because they are perceived as opposing our expectations 'about how things work in the real world' (Tremlin 2006: 87). Usually the adjective 'real' is attached to things that we can touch and measure, that have a physical quality. However, I failed to measure the mediums and their body dimensions. 'Real' experiences are experiences that can be repeated, preferably under scientific conditions in a laboratory. But why is it only 'real' when we can measure it scientifically? Morton Klass challenges our need for dichotomies such as real and unreal, natural and supernatural and so on to structure our thoughts and models. He insists that 'the dichotomizing of natural as against supernatural remains invincibly ethnocentric and therefore unsuitable for anthropological analysis'. He urges us therefore 'to give up, once and for all the effort to maintain this dubious dichotomy' (Klass 1995: 32). However, as the case of spirit possession demonstrates, dichotomies can be quite seductive and it can become difficult not to fall back into the kind of thinking that divides 'real' and 'belief', 'natural' and 'supernatural', or body and mind. Nevertheless, as my examples at the beginning already indicate, I have problems with the materialistic stance towards immaterial aspects of human cognition. I doubt whether the meticulousness of natural science and its established methods of proof can be applied to the humanities. Neuroscience still has to progress further before it can fulfil its promises for a better understanding of religious experiences and human behaviour. Though the new cognitive and other biological approaches might offer radical developments, at the moment at least I find it impossible to apply them to my ethnographic observations successfully. While I present an overview of the increasingly popular cognitive and biological approaches and their attempts to explain religious experiences, my preferences are in other areas of the embodiment debate. I therefore start this

chapter with a section on the agency of mediums that opens up the mind/
body debate before reflecting on materialist approaches. In the last section
I focus on embodiment and show a way away from the materialist discourse.
Unlike the foregoing, this chapter includes fewer excerpts from interviews,
though my sounding board is still the ethnographic data from my research
in Brazil. The reason is that the discourse connected to 'Cartesian' dualism
is largely a Western problem. Brazilian practitioners follow a different logic.
Though I also heard statements to the effect that 'the mind controls the body'
(e.g. in an interview 15 April 2010), most interviewees expressed a more holistic approach and saw body and mind as one. In the case of Candomblé, practitioners highlighted the unity between the human body and the *orixás* (see
Chapter 3). My aim in this chapter is therefore to connect the Western discourse on agency, embodiment and cognition with the Brazilian understanding of spirit possession in order to gain further understanding of the latter.

The agency of mediums

The debate about agency lies at the heart of the complex field of possession
studies. While in Chapter 3 I discussed the agency of the possessing entities,
I focus here on the agency of the mediums, the possessed bodies. The mediums often give very precise information about who is in control, the spiritual
entities or the human bodies. The position towards agency is sometimes even
the dividing line between traditions or between houses, as became visible in
the case of *Pai* Z. (to whom I referred in Chapter 3, describing the Candomblé
position). He clearly positioned Candomblé in contrast to Umbanda because
only in the latter tradition will a spirit take complete control of the human
body. *Pai* Z.'s explanation echoes the description of an Umbanda priestess in
Rio de Janeiro quoted by Hayes: 'I don't have free choice, I don't have it. I don't
have my own life: I am a slave' (Hayes 2011: 13). As mentioned already in the
second chapter, Maria Nazaré de Souza Oliveira, the Umbanda priestess with
whom Hayes mainly worked, on the one hand distinguishes firmly between
her feelings and those of the spirits. But on the other hand she also regards
herself as helpless with regard to the demands of the spirits. Nonetheless,
she submits freely to the demands of the spirits because she regards it as her

obligation, to the spiritual as well to the human world as the incorporation of spiritual entities in Umbanda serves as a means of communication between the spiritual and the human worlds. By being a medium she enables this communication, though in the moment of possession the mediums are usually unaware of the interaction. Umbanda mediums enter, as Engler writes, 'an unconscious trance state and are more likely to require subsidiary rituals to free them from the spirit that has possessed them' (Engler 2009a: 486). The Umbanda priestess *Mãe* M., whom I interviewed at length, differentiates between three types of trance, depending on whether a medium is unconscious, conscious or semi-conscious. 'In Umbanda we believe all mediums are semi-conscious because we know what is happening, we just cannot control the body. We speak in a different voice and say things that we had not thought of before. New things come to mind, with a different body language and movement. Sometimes we see people who are ill or are old doing things that people would not do naturally'.[2] She also insisted that mediumship cannot be forced upon a medium. The spirit is received by intuition, by choice; hence, mediumship is regarded in Umbanda as a gift so that spiritual messages can pass on to others.

Mãe M. stated that in early times mediums were unaware of what happened during trance. She explained that most mediums were illiterate at that time. 'They could not write, had no knowledge. When the spirits came and brought new knowledge, they (the mediums) spoke with more conviction'.[3] But she insisted that over time it came to be seen as problematic that a medium was unconscious, because it exempted this person from any liability. Referring to the intentionality of the action, *Mãe* M. suggested that being unconscious would prevent a medium from enriching her or his own life. Because the message is passed on by the spiritual entities without the medium's being conscious, the medium does not know what happened. Despite having passed on guidance and words of wisdom from the spiritual entities to the clients, the medium had no own guidelines, 'no words of love, advice, kindness, or virtues, when going through the same situation'. She also warns that when mediums are exempted from liability, 'they could make any atrocity. People made jokes, even said lies, or spread rumours about people.'[4] These problems led to the development, according to *Mãe* M., that mediums became semi-conscious in Umbanda. Her version of Umbanda resembles a form that

Engler would probably locate at the 'white' end of the spectrum, in proximity to Kardecism, because of the attitude towards agency, which is, according to Engler, in Kardecism more similar to the North American and European view (2009a: 486).

Engler's distinction between Umbanda and Kardecism with regard to practitioners' attitudes towards agency during the possession rituals is largely based on ritual theory developed by Strawson and Bloch. In order to understand his argumentation I will shortly summarize the main points of their ritual theory before returning to the case study of Umbanda. Engler's starting point is Strawson's distinction between reactive and objective attitudes. A reactive attitude indicates that 'we judge the actions of the person who has benefited or harmed us to have been intentional, willed, self-directed, etc.', and an objective attitude refers to a situation in which 'we judge the person to have acted unknowingly, unintentionally, or in some other manner outside their conscious control' (Engler 2009a: 470). With regard to the debate on spirit possession, a reactive attitude would imply that the action is regarded as normal because it is voluntary and willed. An objective attitude, in contrast, implies that the action is involuntary and unwilled, hence abnormal in Strawson's argumentation. Religion, and in particular cases with an ASC, the general attitude can be usually described as objective because the action of the agent (the person) is regarded as non-intentional. Hence, the action of the person becomes 'unhooked' from intentionality due to ASC, and the attitude towards it shifts from reactive to objective. Applying Strawson's model to spirit possession, Engler states that 'in spirit possession it is appropriate to adopt an objective attitude towards the agency of the person who is possessed (though perhaps a reactive attitude to the spirit or other agent that is possessing the patient)' (Engler 2009a: 471).

However, Engler argues that various factors such as the type and degree of possession and the specific belief have to be taken into consideration. He refers in particular to normative constraint actions which are typical in a religious context. For instance, ritualized actions imply that a person acts according to certain constraints dictated by the belief system, even against one's will. It is therefore important, as Engler points out, 'to distinguish cases where participants see intentions linked "normally" to ritualized action and those where they do not' (2009a: 474). Interestingly, Engler locates the sacred in the transformation of the balance between the two attitudes towards human action because 'the postulated supernatural agents often serve as the objects of these displaced reactive attitudes' (2009a: 481). When we see, for instance, a case of spirit possession, we react naturally, but then we have to alter our reaction and adopt an objective attitude towards the ritual actor due to the ritualized nature of the action, because his or her actions are dictated by normative constraints. Our reactive attitudes towards the medium are displaced onto the supernatural agency, the possessing spirits.

At this point Bloch's concept of deference becomes important. Bloch defines deference as 'the reliance on the authority of others to guarantee the value of what is said or done' (Bloch 2006: 497); however, it is, according to Bloch, less clear or even indeterminable to whom the person is deferring:

> The secret to the problem of wanting to locate meaning without having normal originators of the meaning is to merge all the shadowy transparent figures into one phantasmagoric quasi-person who may be called something like 'tradition', 'the ancestors as a group', 'our way of doing things' our 'spirit', our 'religion', perhaps even 'God'. (Bloch 2006: 502)

While deference can be seen in all human activities, ritualized and non-ritualized, Bloch argues that rituals are distinctive because of their high degree of deference and that the ritual agents are conscious about it. Though he fails to distinguish between rituals and non-ritualized actions, as Engler criticizes, Engler acknowledges that Bloch's 'link between non-intentionality and the legitimation of authority are valuable additions' (Engler 2009a: 474).

Engler then connects Bloch's explanation of deference with the distinction between reactive and objective attitudes towards agency (based on Strawson 1976). Engler argues that it is important to understand whether participants see intentions linked to ritualized actions or not. Especially when scholars characterize actions as non-intentional – as is normally the case in ritualized actions – participants in the rituals might have a different perspective. Engler highlights here the importance of 'ritual dynamics, of improvisation and individual variation, of choices between alternative possible forms, of spontaneous invention, and of negotiation between ritual participants' (2009a: 475). By distinguishing between reactive and objective attitudes towards ritualized and non-ritualized actions, we can learn something about the social relations evoked or transformed within ritual, as Engler argues.

Returning now to the ritual differences between Umbanda and Kardecism, Engler states that 'Kardecist mediums remain conscious of and largely in control of the presence of the spirits they receive; Umbanda mediums enter an unconscious trance state and are more likely to require subsidiary rituals to free them from the spirit that has possessed them' (2009a: 486). Engler sees the ritual difference connected to the attitude towards agency, in particular the distinction between reactive and objective attitudes. The key element is the pervasive patron–client relationships that constitute Brazilian society (see da Matta 1991) and that are echoed and transformed in the possession rituals (Engler 2009a: 483). These relationships are crucial because they counteract the limitation of one's agency in the non-domestic sphere of society. Engler argues that as a result of the limitation, 'objective attitudes are more often appropriate' (2009a: 484); hence, actions of people are regarded as 'outside their control'. On the scope of non-intentionality, 'the point at which one is no longer responsible for what has happened' (2009a: 484), personal relations such as the patron–client relationship gain importance over public systems as they are regarded as ineffective or corrupt. This general feeling correlates to the widespread belief that spirits influence one's life. Engler points in particular to the belief in *encostos*, relatively harmful spirits 'that obstruct, distract, hinder, cause illnesses, etc.' (2009a: 485), and that are openly discussed in self-help programmes on Brazilian television. Consequently, a sense of not being responsible for one's actions increases. Engler concludes that 'in Brazil, it is easier and more "natural" to adopt an objective attitude towards a medium, displacing one's reactive attitude onto a postulated supernatural being' (2009a: 486). However, due to the different social stratification of Kardecists and Umbandists (see also Chapter 2), the practitioners of these two traditions 'are rehearsing and reorienting different tensions between reactive and objective attitudes towards agency, correlated with their ability to wield social capital' (2009a: 486). Hence, because Kardecists have better access to social and economic capital within Brazilian society, Engler argues that they are 'less likely to be accustomed to adopting an objective attitude towards their own agency' than are Umbanda mediums, who are more likely poor and have only restricted access to social capital (2009a: 486). Coming now back to the case of *Mãe* M. and her *terreiro*, it becomes evident that with her claim about the importance of semi-consciousness and the liability of mediums, she does not fit into Engler's broad classification of Umbanda. However, as he states in his article, there are many variations within Umbanda. Each Umbanda *terreiro* represents its own spectrum of doctrinal and ritual characteristics. Umbanda branca ('white' Umbanda) even resembles Kardecism, according to Engler (2009a: 464). While *Mãe M.*'s *terreiro* is definitely Umbanda and not Kardecism with its pantheon of spiritual entities (*preto velhos, caboclos* and so on) and rituals, it represents a different variation from the one to which Engler is referring in his analysis of agency. *Mãe M.* has a relatively large *terreiro* (at least large for São Paulo, since space is expensive in the city), and she is regularly engaged in public activities in order to increase public awareness of Umbanda. In 2010, for instance, she organized a march around her neighbourhood and managed to get priests from other *terreiros* to collaborate with her. Though she might not be as visible in São Paulo as some of the Candomblé priests I interviewed, *Mãe M.* is very politically active for her faith. She has, to use Engler's terms, more access to social capital than other Umbanda *terreiros*. However, this does not make her *terreiro* more special than other Umbanda *terreiros*. Umbanda is a highly diverse tradition, and because of this diversity it has become extremely important in Brazil, as many scholars have recognized. Peter Fry, for instance, describes Umbanda in the 1970s as being very important for the social and political structures of Brazilian society:

> Umbanda is plausible insofar as the personal relations established with the spirits, in hopes of obtaining favours, are homologous with the real relations established for people's benefit in the broader social system. . . . Umbanda . . . is a ritual dramatization of the principles that govern life in the large cities of Brazil. . . . Umbanda is a ritualized and dramatized metaphor that refers to Brazil's social and political reality. (Fry 1978: 45, 47)

This 'refraction of Brazilian social relations in Umbanda' makes Umbanda different from other Brazilian traditions including Kardecism, as Engler points out (2009: 466). And in this way *Mãe M.*'s *terreiro* represents Umbanda as other *terreiros*, too, despite her different attitude towards agency of the mediums. I would even say that it increases the importance of her *terreiro* for Umbanda in the twenty-first century. While many Candomblé *terreiros* have gone through a process of re-Africanization in recent decades and put a stronger emphasis on the African origin of their doctrines and rituals in order to increase their social capital, Umbanda went the other direction. Some Umbandists founded federations, organized national congresses, participated in conferences and even started teaching faculties – that is, they engaged in typical enterprises of the educated middle class. Though Kardecism still has the strongest emphasis on textuality – for example, each medium has to take classes before being allowed to work as medium in a Spiritist centre – some Umbanda leaders acknowledge the importance of teaching. *Mãe* M., for instance, offers weekly lectures during which she explains the Umbanda doctrines (see Figure 4.1 with a photo of her *terreiro* where she offers lectures as well as religious ceremonies). And she is not the only one. Francisco Rivas Neto (Yamunisiddha Arhapiagha) even founded a theological faculty of Umbanda (Faculdade de Teologia Umbandista, or FTU) in São Paulo, which offers theology degrees in Umbanda (though it is not [yet] officially accredited by the state).[5] Though FTU does not have the authority to impose any central norms on Umbanda *terreiros*, it can be seen as analogous to the Kardecist federation as it also represents an umbrella

Figure 4.1 Umbanda terreiro, São Paulo

organization without the absolute authority of a central hierarchical institution. Though many centres are members, no one has to join in order to be recognized as Spiritist. *Pai* Rivas's Umbanda represents another form of Umbanda. He emphasizes, for instance, the belief in karma, connects Umbanda with Tantric chakras and introduces mandalas in the Umbanda practice (Arhapiagha [Neto] 2003). Nonetheless, with his emphasis on education, teaching and self-improvement, he also resembles – similar to *Mãe* M. – an important development in Umbanda that affects attitudes towards agency, since the individual becomes more responsible for his or her life. Following Engler's argument that ritual agency reflects the tensions in society, it becomes evident that the attitude towards the agency of a medium in Umbanda is increasingly shifting from reactive to objective. The description of mediums in *Mãe* M.'s and other *terreiros* as semi-conscious represents therefore an important development in Umbanda that reflects changes in society, though not everyone agrees with her, as she acknowledges in this excerpt from my interview with her:

> The work of a medium can be described as someone watching a movie without interfering with its content. One can get carried away with the story but not interfere. But at any moment when something happens against one's moral values or goals, . . . then one can intervene and stop instead of just watching. But it is a big taboo, even for people who think it's a hoax or that the person is inventing things. I always mention then Chico Xavier. Nobody ever asked whether he was conscious or not because he gave evidence of things, so people never cared if he was seeing or perceiving them, or what he was doing. Umbanda has many prejudices as well, so it's a big taboo. Most do not want to speak about this subject, they do not talk about it and sometimes the mediums are also afraid to talk. . . . But actually I think it is very rare for a medium to be conscious today, most are semi-conscious. And be aware that the mediums do not need to go into a trance. They only need to be influenced but do not need to incorporate a spirit. Though this idea is still not very well developed in Umbanda.[6]

An even more radical position was expressed by another interviewee, who used the expression that the *encantados* (spiritual entities in his tradition) spoke 'through his mouth', despite describing his state as conscious. He insisted that he could not control the message: 'when I think of something, then the *encantado* talks about something entirely different'.[7] My interviewee, a postgraduate student at the University of São Paulo, even described the 'whole situation' as 'funny' because, as he explained, 'there is a separation between speech and thought'. Though his insistence on remaining consciousness contradicts other mediums, most mediums – whether they claim to have been conscious, semi-conscious or unconscious during the rituals – say that they had no control over their bodies, including their voices. When I asked him specifically about the difference between being conscious and semi-conscious, he referred to the control of the situation, explaining that a conscious medium 'does not control but can interfere in some way'. However, like other mediums he also mentioned the learning process and said that it takes a while before the voice of the *encantado* became clear. At the beginning, in the case of inexperienced mediums, it happens very fast. For instance, once he nearly fell and became dizzy, and when he returned to his normal state, people around him had to explain what just happened ('your *caboclo* caught you, you have to take care of him now'[8]).

These excerpts from some of my interviews highlight the changing position towards agency among Umbandistas and practitioners of other traditions. It shows, in particular in light of Engler's reflection on agency among Umbanda and Kardecist groups, the significance of connecting any discussion about cognition – whether the focus is on agency or embodiment – to the wider social and cultural context. In the following section, I discuss the contribution of an area of studies that argues in the opposite direction, promoting the development of universal answers by extracting the worldwide possession practice from any locally specific features.

Spirit possession and the human brain

When cognitive anthropology became established in the 1990s, it was defined as the study of the relation between human society and human thought (D'Andrade 1995: 1). Since then, however, it has become more and more focused on brain activity, supported by developments in neuroscience and related disciplines. Cognitive science is understood today, generally speaking, as the study of the cognitive processes of the brain which simultaneously takes the cultural context of the individual into consideration. The main idea is to investigate and understand how the brain works and how it reacts to various stimuli, external and internal. To a certain degree one can follow the approach back to Adolf Bastian (1826–1905), who – coming to anthropology as a ship surgeon – promoted the idea of a psychic unity of mankind. Like cognitive scientists today, Bastian wanted to find out universal traits (*Elementargedanken* in Bastian's terminology) that all people share. He wrote, for instance, in 1860:

> What a tremendous and exciting advance could be made if we could assemble an index, or statistic, of ideas which showed that the same number of psychological elements (like cells of a plant) is circulating in regular and uniform rotations in the heads of all people, and that this is so for all times and places. (quoted in Koepping 1983: 46)

His goal shows similarities to the work of Eugene d'Aquili and Andrew Newberg (1999), who describe their approach as 'neurotheology'. They argue that religious experiences from various religious and cultural contexts are similar because of our shared biological structures. Our brains produce the same types of cognitive and chemical activities, and consequently the religious experiences are also similar. D'Aquili and Newberg define the brain as a 'bodily organ that allows us to think, feel, and receive input from the external world', while the mind is a product of the functioning of the brain (1999: 21). Having mapped brain activity during meditative states, they argue that the brain generates the experience someone has during meditation or any other form of religious activity. For them 'religions and their theologies necessarily arise from the machinery of the human brain operating within a social context' (1999: 206). However, they also write – referring here to mystics – that 'the brain may have evolved in such a way that these experiences were possible' (1999: 206).

Mario Beauregard and Vincent Paquette (2006) use the term 'mediated' by the brain instead of 'generated'. However, their study of the brain activity of fifteen Carmelite nuns is highly controversial, as I have already mentioned. While they indicate that they have scanned the brains of the nuns 'in a state of union with God', the study clearly shows that they really only studied the memory of the experience. Because the nuns insisted that it is impossible to create a mystical experience on command, the researchers asked them only to close their eyes and remember the most intense mystical experience they ever felt in their lives as members of the Carmelite Order. However, the study is unclear about how exactly the mystical experience is different from the control condition (remembering the most intense state of union with another human) and the baseline condition (a normal restful state with closed eyes). Another criticism refers to the timeframe, since every MRI scan lasted five minutes. As one critic argues, it is 'difficult to know what is being modeled by the analysis' during this interval.[9] In which moment exactly did the nun think of her mystical experience and in which moment did she just think of the cup of tea she wanted to indulge herself after the scan?

Studies such as the one by Beauregard and Paquette follow a materialist approach. The brain is regarded as part of the body, and cognitive elements are allocated to the mind, where they can be ignored. As Pyysiäinen (2001) writes,

> The human brain, in this view, is like a digital computer carrying out computations on material symbols. And, because we do not have conscious access to these computations, the whole notion of consciousness seems irrelevant. Consciousness is merely a useless projection of some subset of elements of the computational mind. (2001: 71)

Pyysiäinen explains this materialist approach only to disagree with it, despite its long history. That approach can also be recognized in studies about certain forms of behaviour that is perceived to have originated in individuals' biology. I refer here in particular to the tendency to regard religious practices as the consequence of biological determinants, hence as mental illness that can be traced back to a dysfunction of the brain. Any irrational behaviour – and most types of religious experience are categorized as irrational or abnormal by outsiders – is ascribed to an experience of illness caused by a bodily disease. Littlewood writes that 'the development of psychiatry as a medical discipline in the nineteenth century, together with the establishment of public mental hospitals, deprived madness . . . of the possibility of even conventional meaning. It was merely the external symptom of an underlying bodily disease' (1993: 18). It should not surprise anyone, therefore, that leaders of millennial cults and other new religious movements were incarcerated in psychiatric hospitals (see Littlewood 1993: 16 for a list of cases). To speak about divine visions and revelations or even the possibility of communicating with spirits of the dead was seen as the outcome of a physical disturbance of the brain. It must be noted, though, that this was not the argument of all scholars of the nineteenth and early twentieth centuries. The above-mentioned Bastian, for instance, in some ways a forerunner of psychoanalysis, considered mystical experience as normal, not sick, even as part of a 'larger horizon' (1890: 20), as long as it occurred among the so-called primitive, and as a psychical (not physical) illness only if appearing in modern society.[10] In the twentieth century, even William James criticizes simple biological equations and urges us to establish the meaning of radical experience by its fruits instead of by its ground, though he also talks about 'nervous instability' and 'borderline insanity' in his discussion of the origins of religion (James 1958: 24, 36, in Littlewood 1993: 20). Nonetheless, his emphasis on assessing the experience within the wider context puts James in opposition to his contemporaries, who disregarded the cultural meaning of such behaviour and promoted the pathologization of whole institutions such as shamanism and other forms of religious experience. Littlewood argues that 'the Europeans' encounter with other societies was initially characterized by exotic description and the simple force of arms, then, confronted with the threat of approaching emancipation and independence, by theories of racial superiority and manifest biological destiny, and finally, in the twentieth century, by the imposition of psychiatric categories to characterize them as inadequate, co-opting them through an internalisation of their ascribed inadequacy' (1993: 25–6, referring to Littlewood and Lipsedge 1989: chapter 2). According to Littlewood, anthropologists today object to such an approach as 'an oversimplified unitary hypothesis . . . based on comparative data which assumes a unilinear mode of cultural evolution and hence an inherent racism, together with ignorance of the specific context' (1993: 28). Littlewood himself promotes a dialectical approach, taking biology and local representations into consideration. In his monograph about the Earth People in Trinidad, he uses the term 'psychopathological' in order to characterize the revelation of Mother Earth, arguing that the term psychopathology refers 'to both uncommon brain states as understood biologically and the changed affects, thoughts and actions immediately associated (for the psychiatrist, causally) with them: both social and biological facts and the relationship between them at a particular historical moment' (Littlewood 1993: 257, n.23). Littlewood acknowledges that the term 'pathology' has an inappropriate undertone, but he insists that these states are usually perceived locally as 'discrete and undesirable'. However, this is not always the case with the type of experience I study, spirit possession and mediumship. It is obviously not the case with shamanism either, which is highly appreciated today. In Siberia, for example, after discrimination against shamanist phenomena as psychic illness (e.g. 'arctic hysteria', at the beginning of the twentieth century) and as imposture or retrograde archaism during the Soviet period, Siberian shamanism (and its trance rituals) is returning as a way of finding cultural identity today. It is indeed the case that some people interpret it as undesirable and encourage those 'afflicted' by it to reverse the condition, hence to exorcize the spirits. But the majority of people experiencing it embrace the experience, after an initial resistance, freely and willingly. Littlewood's terminology (psychopathology) therefore fits only part of the local understanding of the experience.

The Brazilian anthropologist René Ribeiro, who challenges the interpretation of spirit possession as a merely psychological phenomenon, defines possession as a 'dissociative personality phenomenon', to be distinguished from other levels of dissociation including trance in other religions (1982: 167, 158). Despite using 'phenomenon' instead of 'syndrome', the categorization of the experience as dissociation is still problematic. The term 'dissociation' is, as Klass shows, a psychopathological condition that includes 'some degree of pathological *loss of consciousness* and *loss of identity*' (2003: 79, emphasis in the original). Though the term dissociation is frequently used to describe altered states of consciousness, in particular in medical literature, Klass insists that we have to ensure that *dissociation* does not imply *disorder*, a euphemism for mental illness. 'Just as sleep disorder is a malformation, or illness variant, of normal sleep, so, I would argue, the dissociative disorders studied and treated by psychopathologists are illness variants of a normal (that is, a *nondisorder*) capacity of humans to dissociate, by either external or internal suggestion' (Klass 2003: 115). And spirit possession and other forms of dissociation are not mental disorders, illnesses to be cured. In his argument Klass refers to the social setting and argues that when spirit possession is practiced within a community – that is, when the behaviour is supported by the society – it is

not a disorder (2003: 109). Highlighting the positive function of spirit possession for the individual, he states that spirit possession reflects 'the construct-
ive capacity of the person in the context of the culture' (2003: 125).

Klass's argumentation is based on a distinction between biological organism and personhood, following Radcliffe-Brown's distinction between
individual and person (1940). Radcliffe-Brown describes an individual as a
biological organism, 'a collection of a vast number of molecules organized in
a complex structure, within which, as long as it persists, there occur physiological and psychological actions and reactions, processes and changes'
(Radcliffe-Brown 1952: 193–4). While this description can also be applied
to animals, a human being is – in distinction to an animal – also a person,
'a complex of social relationships': 'He is a citizen of England, a husband
and a father, a bricklayer, a member of a particular Methodist congregation
. . . and so on' (Radcliffe-Brown 1952: 193–4). During one's life the social
relationships change, the person changes as well, and the social personality
('personhood' for Klass) is dynamic, adaptable and even multidimensional.
Klass summarizes Radcliffe-Brown's definition of 'person' as follows: 'as
the position occupied by a human being in a social structure, the complex
formed by all his social relationships with others'. Thus while humans and
animals both exhibit individuality, only humans exhibit personhood (Klass
2003: 111). Personhood is consequently a cultural construct, something
human. While animals are conscious individuals, they lack 'the capacity to
abstract, or to formulate in any way the distinctions between "I" and "you"
(or between "you" and "thou"), between "us" and "them"' (Klass 2003: 113).
Personhood includes the capacity to position oneself in a social system, to
be a member of a particular social structure, hence personhood include a
degree of identity that animals lack.

Klass argues then that spirit possession is connected to this concept of personhood. He states, as I summarized elsewhere, that 'during the possession
an identity is present that is perceived as "real" as any other identity because
every identity is a cultural construct' (Schmidt 2010: 107). The crucial point
is therefore that the new or additional identities are recognizable and iden-
tifiable 'as part of the individual's (and the individual's community's) belief
system' (Klass 2003: 115). In the case of mental illness, however, the new identities would be unpredictable.

In order to distinguish between mental illness and a culturally patterned phenomenon such as spirit possession, Klass proposes a new set of categories, integrating approaches from psychology and anthropology. He labels the overarching heading 'Human Dissociative Phenomenon' (HDP) and differentiates three subsets: 'Dissociative Consciousness Phenomenon', 'Dissociative Identity Phenomenon' and 'Imposed Dissociative Phenomena'. Spirit possession falls into the second category, Dissociative Identity Phenomenon. However, Klass distinguishes further between 'Dissociative Identity Disorder' and 'Patterned Dissociative Identity' and argues that only the first one is a mental illness. Spirit possession, which Klass allocates into the second category (Patterned Dissociative Identity [PDI]), is not a disorder, not an illness, despite exhibiting similar behaviour. 'Individuals exhibiting PDI present alters deriving from and recognizable as entities of their society's belief system (variously, spirits, demons, divinities, ancestors, and so forth) who speak and act in known, predictable, and recognizable ways' (Klass 2003: 119). Even when the entities are perceived as threatening or evil to the individual or the community, Klass still rejects the pathologization of the behaviour and argues that as long as the behaviour is 'patterned', it should not be viewed as mental illness. In both cases an identity is present that is perceived by the individual as 'real', similar to any other identities. But only during spirit possession (and related phenomena) are the identities culturally patterned and accessible, and therefore not pathological.[11]

While Klass's aim is to bridge anthropology with psychology, Harvey Whitehouse and Emma Cohen, both anthropologists like Klass, go in a different direction. Their contribution to possession studies marks the new field of cognitive science of religion, which argues that, when studying a universal trait such as spirit possession, it is possible to discover which aspects of it are biological and which are cultural. Whitehouse writes that the challenge in the cognitive science of religion is 'to show that significant features of the content, organization, and spread of religious phenomena can be explained in terms of the ways in which panhuman, evolved psychological mechanisms are activated' (Whitehouse 2005: 207). Instead of looking at religious phenomena as culturally and historically distinct, cognitive scientists such as Whitehouse see religion as less variable than most anthropologists think. The collected data points, as Whitehouse writes, 'to a massive amount of cross-cultural recurrence' which relates not only to the forms of religious systems but also to aspects of doctrinal content (2005: 207). According to Whitehouse, the main discovery of cognitive science is that these universal cognitive mechanisms can be initiated in various ways, which supports the argument that 'human minds develop in fundamentally similar ways the world over, even though cultural settings differ widely' (Whitehouse 2008: 19).

The work of Cohen is of particular interest for this study as she also focuses on spirit possession in Brazil, though in a different area (Belém) and with a different agenda. In line with Whitehouse and other scholars in cognitive studies, Cohen argues that, despite the various cultural interpretations of spirit possession, it is potentially explicable by generalizable psychological factors – at least in part. Using the cognitive approach of Whitehouse, her study aimed at explaining the higher number of female participants in possession rituals in what she calls *culto afro*, a combination of different Afro–Brazilian traditions. Following Whitehouse, Cohen argues that the spread of and the gender difference in spirit possession can be explained by universal mechanisms of cognition that generate predispositions and tendencies towards certain patterns of thinking and behaviour (Cohen 2007: 181). She states, for instance, that 'our minds are constrained to process and represent divine beings in certain ways. The resemblance, therefore, fundamentally operates in the reverse direction. Our intuitive notions about agency are so bound up with our expectations about human psychological properties that we are predisposed automatically and easily to make gods in our own image' (Cohen 2007: 122). Hence, our minds are used to represent divine beings in specific, mainly human forms, and with specific, usually human, characteristics. As human resemblances they are recognizable by the observers, who can identify the possessing spirits and can even comment on the ability of the host medium to express the spirit.

Looking at ethnographic survey data of spirit possession belief (e.g. Bourguignon 1968), Cohen identifies certain environmental factors that contribute to the spread of the belief in the existence of spirit possession. Referring to psychological studies, Cohen points out that in uncontrollable situations – for instance, in the case of terminal illness or natural disasters such as hurricanes or earthquakes – individuals maintain a sense of control by using certain strategies, including religious practices and beliefs. Hence,

Cohen argues that the involvement in spirit possession rituals can provide individuals with a sense of control in uncontrollable situations: 'Lack of perceived control and the desire to regain control are precipitating factors in leading people to embrace religious and magical and superstitious ideas and practices.'[12]

Though knowledge about these ideas and practices already has to be present in the society, Cohen argues that under certain conditions, ideas such as belief in spirits may become more compelling in a person's mind. However, in order to successfully transmit cultural and religious knowledge – that is, in order to have cognitively intuitive concepts in one's mind – Whitehouse points to the pre-existence of certain characteristics which he describes as two contrasting modes of religiosity, the doctrinal and the imagistic. The two modes of religiosity are not two distinct types of religion but 'organizing principles for religious experience and action', which can even be present in the same religious tradition, as Whitehouse (2002) argues (though with different effects). Nonetheless, both modes have an impact on the transmission of religious knowledge, according to Whitehouse. The doctrinal mode is, for instance, more likely to establish centralized ecclesiastic hierarchies that have an impact on the content and organization of authoritative religious knowledge (Whitehouse 2005: 211–12).

Interesting for my argument is Whitehouse's inclusion of the environment in his cognitive approach. Instead of limiting cognition to the brain, Whitehouse proposes an 'extended' approach by including a sense of cognitive environments. He explains that 'environments and sociocultural systems do not affect people's thoughts and actions unless they are somehow registered by their perceptual systems, resulting in responses generated by intricate and flexible processes of mentation' (2005: 221, referring in a footnote to Sperber 1996). Consequently, certain contexts may encourage the presence of spirit belief in one's mind or the inhibition of certain cognitive concepts. Whitehouse states, for instance, that in the authoritative presence of a standardized set of doctrines and rituals that excludes or even forbids spirit possession, it will be less likely that concepts about spirits are transmitted.[13] And even if the knowledge is successfully transmitted, not every member of the society will experience it in the same way. Looking at the variety of spirit possession in Brazil, as outlined in Chapter 1, Whitehouse's argument explains not only the range of beliefs but also why even in neo-Pentecostal churches, whose doctrines forbid spirit possession, there is observable continuity with possession rituals, though with a reverse agenda. Hence, the doctrinal mode within neo-Pentecostalism does not totally suppress the imagistic mode and cannot prevent the fact that ideas of spirits maintain importance among members of neo-Pentecostal churches. Though the presence of belief in spirits is not directly encouraged, the fight against it – performed in elaborate exorcism rituals – does not cause the inhibition of these cognitive concepts but a reversed interpretation.

Nonetheless, Whitehouse's elaboration does not explain sufficiently why some people are more involved in spirit possession practice than others. Cohen therefore connects his ideas with the idea of a Hypersensitive Agency Detection Device (HADD), developed by Justin Barrett (2004). She argues that HADD 'may be instrumental in explaining apparent variations among people and across population in attributions of supernatural agency to events and happenings in their lives' (Cohen 2007: 190). The HADD is a mental mechanism that connects events to a possible agency. When no human or animal can be detected as responsible for an event, the person may detect another kind of agent. For instance, when someone fails to detect a human agent in a startling and frightening event, another possibility would be a supernatural agent such as a spirit. Cohen states that a HADD in a human being is 'always on the lookout for agency'; however, certain situations such as situations under stress 'put it onto "high alert"' (Cohen 2007: 193). Cohen defines stress as 'a psychological and physical response to a situation of pressure', what she calls a 'stressor' (2007: 193). Cohen highlights that, though the stressor is experienced and therefore measurable at an individual level, its effect can also be experienced on a collective level. For instance, in the case of a natural disaster that affects the harvest, the stressor, the situation of pressure, is experienced population-wide. In particular, in high-stress situations the invocation of supernatural-agent causation can increase, and Cohen concludes therefore that HADDs can be seen as a possible explanation for the correlation between stress/oppression/uncontrollability and the high incidence of spirit phenomena and other paranormal beliefs in these situations.

Though I agree to a certain degree with the logic of her conclusion, it cannot explain the development I outlined above, in particular the expansion of spirit possession rituals through the wider sections of Brazilian society. The increasing popularity of Candomblé, for instance, among middle-class Brazilians – who are university-educated professionals – and the ongoing presence of Spiritist mediumship among all sectors of society contradicts her picture of spirit possession as a predominately lower-class phenomenon. One should also not ignore the fact that not everyone is attracted to spirit possession and that different means are often chosen. Other factors must intervene to increase the sensitivity of individuals towards this practice, as also Cohen acknowledges. Justin Barrett, for instance, points to individual background and dispositions: 'People who believe in ghosts are more likely to see ghosts than non-believers. Being a believer – or merely open to believing – in a god makes one more sensitive to detecting the god's action or presence' (Barrett 2004: 39). But he also acknowledges that the situation of the incident affects the agent's sensitivity to this kind of detection. According to Barrett, belief in spirits and other agents is more prevalent in more traditional societies, an assumption that can be challenged by the Brazilian data since spirit possession is a highly urbanized practice in Brazil, hence part of the modern (or even postmodern) Brazilian culture. Cohen, who disagrees with Barrett on this point, supports Barrett's other points and confirms the causal association between HADDs and environmental contextual conditions such as survival and urgency concerns. She states that 'the incidence of phenomena that invoke the special powers of supernatural agents for explaining and predicting events increases under environmental pressures that threaten immediate survival and control' (Cohen 2007: 194). She even regards the tendency to invoke intentional agency as panhuman. But because stress and uncontrollability increase the emergence of beliefs in spirits or other supernatural agents, Cohen predicts that one can find a 'higher level of institutionalized forms among individuals and populations in situations that contribute to such stress (e.g., lower-class, marginalized/unemployable/oppressed sectors of society)' (Cohen 2007: 194–5).

As I have outlined elsewhere (Schmidt 2010: 109–10), Cohen turns at this point to the Theory of Mind (ToM) to explain the predominance of women in spirit-possession practices. Her argumentation is mainly based on Simon Baron-Cohen's work (e.g. Baron-Cohen 2003). ToM refers to the mental ability to reflect on the content of one's own and others' minds. It is connected to our mental capacities to feel, imagine, believe and so on (see Baron-Cohen 2000: 3). Human beings have developed ideas about people, relationships, groups and more, as well as a way to organize these ideas. Some people are better at handling an array of conceptions than others which, according to Baron-Cohen, points to a more highly developed ToM capacity. Baron-Cohen proposes that the ToM capacity is connected to brain types linked to specific cognitive activities, in particular systematizing and empathizing. Individuals with a brain of Type S have a higher score in systematizing, while individuals with a brain of Type E a higher score in empathizing. However, it is important to highlight that these two brain types have to be seen as opposite poles of a continuous spectrum. Most people will score somewhere in the middle range between these two poles, and Baron-Cohen characterizes individuals with a brain of Type B as those who score high in both dimensions. To be located on one of the two ends of the spectrum would even indicate a deficit such as autism, one of Baron-Cohen's main fields of research.

Empathizing is important for any religious practice because it supports the ability to analyse the social world and to understand the behaviour of other people. In particular, spirit possession requires a high score on empathizing and ToM capacity as it involves, as Whitehouse writes, 'keeping track of at least two mental entities (the possessing spirit and the host) at the same time, and typically a number of such entities' (2008: 22). This applies not only to the medium but also to the other participants in the ceremony because they, too, have to 'keep track' of many things at the same time.

At this point the argumentation turns to another of Baron-Cohen's observations that has an implication for the discussion about the spread of spirit possession to certain groups. Baron-Cohen found out that women score higher on empathy measures than men and that men score higher on systemizing measures. His result does not indicate that women have a Type E brain and men, Type S. As I mentioned above, most people score in the middle range. Hence, it is important not to see this observation as indicating an essentialist difference between men and women. Rather, his observation is used by cognitive studies scholars to explain why spirit possession can be seen as a 'domain of religious activities that will tend to involve higher levels of participation from women than from men' (Whitehouse 2008: 22). Cohen, for instance, explains the higher number of women than men involved in

spirit possession ceremonies in her fieldwork with the higher score in empathizing among women. She argues that the ToM difference between men and
women, which points to their different ability to understand and predict the
behaviours of others, is 'a causal factor in the high incidence of female sensitivity to the actions and intentions of supernatural agents' (2007: 202). People
with a higher score in empathizing (hence, Type E individuals) are better at
detecting and decoding social communication, which is important for a spirit
medium as well as the other participants. Cohen states that Type E individuals are more likely to be more sensitive 'to the perspectives, motivations,
beliefs, and desires of the spirits that possess others as well as of the spirits
that they themselves are host to' (2007: 203). And, as women score higher in
empathizing, women dominate possession activities.

Her observation from the Belém area in Northern Brazil is not confirmed
in my research in the mega metropolis São Paulo, as I explained in Chapter 2.
Despite early reports of a predominance of women in possession rituals, the
social and political changes of Brazil have had a radical impact on the gender stratification of the communities practising spirit possession. The predominance of women is declining, not because women are stepping back but
because nowadays an increasing number of men are involved in the practice.
However, this tendency does not contradict the relevance of Baron-Cohen's
observation, because one could also argue that Brazilians of both genders
have higher-developed ToM capacities and score higher on empathizing. Or,
as Matory writes, 'the male possession priest displays the selected feminine
qualities that enable a man or woman to be "fertile" in this sexual and political order that enables him or her to embody the power of the royal god'
(Matory 1993: 76). Unfortunately, I do not have the data to back up this rather
weak hypothesis. It is, nonetheless, remarkable that religious activities in
urban Brazil in the twenty-first century seem to be less confined to the female
sector of society than in the early decades of the twentieth century. While
Afro–Brazilian religious communities used to regard femininity as convey-
ing privileged status in the allocation of religious authority, changes in society as well as the revised gender socialization of children have influenced
the gender stratification of these communities as well as the way the practice is perceived. This observation supports Whitehouse's inclusion of 'a sense
of cognitive environment' in his approach. The environment and its many

contextual changes affect the way spirit possession is perceived, which again has an impact on the practice itself. While Cohen's cognitive science approach can be useful to explain choices we make, it is crucial not to ignore the other aspects that influence any religious practice. Also arguing from a cognitive perspective (but a less materialist one), Pyysiäinen defines religion as 'a concept that identifies the personalistic counter-intuitive representations and the related practices, institutions, etc. that are widely spread, literally believed, and actively used by a group of people in their attempt to understand, explain and control those aspects of life, and reality as a whole, that escape common sense and, more recently, scientific explanation' (2003: 227). In addition to cognitive concepts Pyysiäinen's definition embraces other elements that have an impact on the way religious practices are performed and adapted. This strand of cognitive studies sees religion, as this definition by Armin Geertz and Jeppe Sinding Jensen shows, as 'an expression of cognitive mechanisms that are both biological and social and which reveal themselves through culture' (2011: 1). Instead of limiting the cognitive approach to human brains and brain activities, they put cognition in relation to culture and the social world. As Geertz writes, 'any theory of human cognition must deal with the power, formative impact and constitutive role that culture plays' (Geertz 2010: 317). Consequently, he defines cognition as 'anchored in brain and body (embrained and embodied), deeply dependent on culture (enculturated) and extended and distributed beyond the borders of individual brains' (Geertz 2010: 304, see also Jensen 2011: 35). In order to emphasize that humans are biological and cultural creatures, Geertz introduced the term 'biocultural'. However, as he continues, 'the term [biocultural] does not mean that cultural features are biological or that biological features are cultural. . . . I use the term simply to mean that we are hybrid creatures uniquely situated in biological and cultural systems on more or less equal terms' (2010: 306).

A result of this 'cultural turn' in cognitive studies is the acceptance of locally specific features, visible, for instance, in the investigation of the connection between cognition, religion and culture through the study of religious narratives – from religious texts to personal narratives. These narratives, as Geertz writes, 'draw on and stimulate our neurochemistry and make optimal use of the brain's map-making capacities' (2011: 23). Geertz locates this mapping process at all levels of human existence, hence biological, psychological, social and cultural (2011: 11). Referring to Firth (2007), Geertz writes that 'we do not experience the world itself, rather we experience our brain's map of the world' (Geertz 2011: 11). And narratives are at the heart of it, because they are 'at the centre of a matrix of relations between individuals, groups, cultural repertoires and social institutions' (Geertz 2011: 23). Geertz, Jensen, Pyysiäinen and other members of the Scandinavian school therefore present a way to overcome the limitations of cognitive science that has highlighted the materialist approach and overlooked the wider cultural and social context. Environment is, as Jensen outlines, more than physical surroundings, and cognition cannot be limited to the perception of the physical environment alone. The human environment includes – in addition to the physical – as Jensen states, 'the mental, social, symbolic, and linguistic aspects' (2011: 35), and cognitive activities have to be studied in relation to other social activities as well as symbolic information.

The significance of an all-embracing perspective can also be seen in my research data, both observations and interviews. From a cognitive scientific perspective, it is evident that each medium handles more than one consciousness during the possession incident, and hence – using Cohen's language – has a significantly high ToM capacity. However, while the emotions are described relatively similarly, the presence of another consciousness is perceived in different ways. Candomblé mediums in general do not account for anything that has happened during the incident because mediums in Candomblé are thought to be unconscious; thus, their consciousness can only be described as like being asleep. Consequently, a woman who danced with the *orixás* one night, despite a slightly handicapped foot, could not remember anything the next morning and wondered loudly why she was so tired. Other mediums were physically exhausted, with sweat all over their clothes and bodies. Nonetheless, despite being unable to remember anything from the event, the emotions involved in it have a strong resonance. A medium, for instance, told me how sad he felt about the lost connection, just moments after he came out of a trance. Other mediums mentioned their feeling of joy, though they could not remember what had just happened. Umbanda mediums, in contrast, usually remain aware of what is going on, though the spiritual entity is perceived as being stronger, more powerful than the consciousness of the medium. The medium has to handle two kinds of consciousness at the same time, the dormant one of the medium and the dominant one of the spirit. However, while in both cases, Candomblé and Umbanda, the consciousness of the medium is suppressed, Candomblé mediums do not regard the *orixás* as limited entities with a specific consciousness but as divine forces of nature (see Chapter 3). Spiritist mediums also point to a state of semi-consciousness or even full consciousness in the moment when a spirit uses the body of the medium, or a part of the body such as a hand and an arm, to communicate its message to the world of the living. As with the other mediums, Spiritist mediums also have to handle more than one consciousness and therefore need a high level of ToM. However, mediumship ability is perceived as a combination of intuition and learnt technique. All mediums have to undergo a series of classes before they are regarded as full mediums. But as one interviewee told me, passing the classes does not lead automatically to being accepted as a medium, and though the technique can be learnt, ability has to be ratified on a supernatural level.[14]

In the fourth case, the neo-Pentecostal churches, the spirits are blamed for their negative influence on human beings who are regarded as being not aware – initially – about the negative influence of these spirits. Here one sees the conflict between doctrinal and imagery modes of religiosity elaborately performed during the exorcism rituals. Only during these rituals of disobsession do the afflicted become aware of them; hence, only in the moment of exorcism do the spirits reveal, according to neo-Pentecostal doctrine, their true identity. In this case, therefore, an afflicted person does not handle a multitude of consciousnesses apart from the moment of exorcism. Hence, there is no need for a high level of ToM. The afflicted individuals experience an unusually high level of stress, in line with Cohen's elaborations. Some neo-Pentecostal churches that offer spiritual healing through exorcism recruit a large part of their followers from socially problematic environments, which put much pressure on women in particular, who are often the main carer for their children. This observation also confirms why in other Pentecostal churches, which focus more on healing via the Holy Ghost instead of exorcism, the social stratification of the communities is quite different. The shift from such experiences to Bible reading usually supports a higher recruitment of educated individuals, who are often middle class or people who aspire to become middle class. It is nonetheless important to remember that this shift from experience to literacy only reflects the situation within Pentecostalism. As explained above, some Afro–Brazilian religions have developed in the other direction, and recruit increasingly successfully among people missing the physical dimension of the divine in mainstream Christian churches.

These reflections on the Brazilian situation demonstrate the importance of understanding spirit possession not only as a cognitive concept but also within the wider social and cultural environment in line with Geertz's bio-cultural theory of religion (Geertz 2010: 314). While Geertz does not present any application of his theory of religion since his intention in this article was to present his theory, his challenge to cognitive scientists for ignoring the powerful impact of culture on our minds presents an interesting addition to the debate.

The embodiment paradigm and the possessed body

Theorists on spirit possession have long ignored, as Stoller criticizes, the 'centrality of the sentient body in possession' (Stoller 1994: 637), despite the fact that people practising possession rituals highlight its importance. In all my interviews with mediums, the possession experience is always described as an embodied practice (to use Stoller's terminology). The mediums feel strong emotions when encountering spiritual entities and express these experiences physically, with their bodies (see also Lambek 1996: 239). This experience has encouraged the development of highly sophisticated concepts about the body, not only among Candomblé practitioners (as presented in Chapter 3) but also among devotees of the other traditions. My interview data reflect an important change in possession studies since Stoller's critique. Recent decades have seen a 'corporeal turn' in anthropology and other disciplines (see e.g. Sheets-Jonstone 2009), which has also enriched possession studies. One feature of this turn is the rich debate on embodiment that is firmly connected to Thomas Csordas (e.g. Csordas 1990, 1994).

Csordas regards the body not as an object to be studied in relation to culture, but as a subject of culture. For Csordas, the embodiment paradigm is a method foremost, or, in his words, a 'methodological perspective that encourages reanalyses of existing data and suggests new questions for empirical research' (1990: 5). Consequently, he argues that 'when the body is recognized for what it is in experiential terms, not as an object but as a subject, the mind-body distinction becomes much more uncertain' (1990: 36). Csordas work is focused on Charismatic Christianity in the United States, and in particular on charismatic healing and deliverance. Criticizing former – mostly physiological – explanations of speaking in tongues and trance, he argues that they 'do not take us very far unless we are willing to accept trance and catharsis as ends in themselves rather than as modus operandi for the work of culture' (1990: 32). His main critique focuses on the dualism of mind and body, which he challenges in favour of a 'phenomenology of perception and self-perception that can pose the question of what is religious about religious experience without falling prey to the fallacies of either empiricism or intellectualism' (1990: 33).

It is evident that Csordas's embodiment paradigm is heavily influenced by the phenomenologist Maurice Merleau-Ponty (1908–1961) and his ideas of embodiment, in which he connects the object with the experience of the body. Merleau-Ponty argues that 'it is as false to place ourselves in society as an object among other objects, as it is to place society within ourselves as an object of thought, and in both cases the mistake lies in treating the social as an object. We must return to the social with which we are in contact by the mere fact of existing, and which we carry about inseparably with us before any objectification' (Merleau-Ponty 1962: 362). Merleau-Ponty regards the body consequently as 'a certain setting in relation to the world' (1962: 303), or, as Voss summarizes,

> due to its being-in-the-world, Merleau-Ponty indicates an indissoluble enmeshment of the perceiving body and the world. The body is oriented towards the world and involved in a dynamic process of constructing the world, which at the same time exists as an entity which always confronts a subject. In such a conception oppositions such as subject and object, inner and outer or ownness and foreignness entangle themselves in a process of mutual references which makes it impossible to get a clear analytical distinction between them. (Voss 2011: 170)

Csordas takes a slightly different turn when he connects Merleau-Ponty with Pierre Bourdieu and his concept of habitus, with which Bourdieu promotes the idea of a 'groundedness in the body'. Connecting cognitive and evaluative structures he states that

> this principle is nothing other than the *socially informed body*, with its tastes and distastes, its compulsions and repulsions, with, in a word, all its senses, that is to say, not only the traditional five senses – which never escape the structuring action of social determinisms – but also the sense of necessity and the sense of duty, the sense of direction and the sense of reality, the sense of balance and the sense of beauty, common sense and the sense of the sacred, tactical sense and the sense of responsibility, business sense and the sense of propriety, the sense of humour and the sense of absurdity, moral sense and the sense of practicality, and so on. (Bourdieu 1977: 124, emphasis in the original)

Following in these steps, Csordas regards 'the lived body is an irreducible principle, the existential ground of culture and the sacred' (1990: 23). He states that his approach to embodiment 'begins from the methodological postulate that the body is not an object to be studied in relation to culture, but is to be considered as the subject of culture, or in other words as the existential ground of culture' (Csordas 1990: 5). Referring to speaking in tongues in Charismatic Christianity, Csordas interprets Pentecostal glossolalia as asserting unity of body and mind, establishing a shared human world and expressing transcendence (1990: 31). Two examples shed a light on his way of thinking:

> When a thought or embodied image comes into consciousness suddenly, the Charismatic does not say 'I had an insight', but 'That wasn't from me, how could I have thought of that. It must be from the Lord'. . . . When a bad habit becomes a compulsion, when one can no longer control one's chronically bad temper, the Charismatic does not say 'My personality is flawed', but 'This is not me, I am under attack by an evil spirit'. The demon does not cause the bad habit or the anger but is constituted by the lack of control over these things. (Csordas 1990: 34)

Csordas concludes that 'the sui generis nature of the sacred is defined not by the capacity to have such experiences, but by the human propensity to thematize them as radically other'(1990: 34). Hence the crucial point, for Csordas, is the identification of otherness as a modality of human experience instead of just describing the experience as God inhabiting the 'socially informed body'.

Though Bowie refers explicitly and positively to embodiment when she writes that 'anthropological methodology offers the possibility of personal, embodied encounters with the other – with living as well as written texts, and challenged the ethnographer to include embodied experiences as part of the theoretical and analytical matrix of interpretation' (Bowie 2002: 19), she nonetheless argues in a recent paper that Csordas's embodiment paradigm does not solve the methodological problem for possession studies:

> When we consider trance mediumship we are not talking about the body as a social metaphor (Lewis 1989), nor as the seat of social and political resistance (Comaroff 1985). It is not just a symbol (Sutherland 1977) or a complex collection of firing neurons within a specific genome (Dennett, 1991). We are not even talking about more sophisticated views of the body as 'embodied culture' (Csordas 1994) or as 'mindful' (Lock and Scheper-Hughes 1987), insightful and useful as each of these paradigms might be. For the trance medium the body is matter controlled by spirit, not spirit conceived as something abstract or spiritual, but as energy within our physical world, interpenetrating and interacting with it. (Bowie 2012: 14)

Her approach seems to promote a religious reading of the situation despite her insistence that 'we are not in the realm of mystical visions or the contemplation of Divine Love' (Bowie 2012: 14). She argues, for instance, that the 'inescapable ontological materiality' of the seances she attended 'challenges notions of conscious intentionality as coterminous with the temporal and spatial boundary of the individual physical body' (Bowie 2012: 15). For Bowie, the basic aspect of the seances is 'the notion of a separable self that is able to transfer consciousness from one body to another, from an incarnate physical body to a discarnate immaterial one and vice versa, and then back again' (Bowie 2012: 14). Hence, while Csordas sees the otherness as a modality of human experience, it seems to exist as an independent entity for Bowie. She writes that her approach does not necessarily indicate that what she reports is 'objectively the case' (Bowie 2012: 2); however, she does not dismiss the possibility that it could be. And despite her explanation that 'readers can make up their own minds as to the veracity of the phenomena described' (Bowie 2012: 2), she promotes her approach very clearly when she writes that 'communication with spirits provides data in much the same way as conversations with the living' (Bowie 2012: 2). In the end, therefore, she seems to echo Keller's theological position, presented at the beginning of the third chapter of this book, which makes it difficult for scholars following a less engaged approach to spirit possession and similar practices to agree with her approach.

While I support Bowie's argument that in a seance every participant, including the observing anthropologist, is actively involved and that 'the intentions, energy and emotions of each person present form part of the collective experience of the séance' (Bowie 2012: 15), the feelings of the mediums have to be different from my own. As I described at the beginning of this chapter, my own impression of the bodies of the mediums was affected by my emotions during the rituals. I cannot objectively determine whether the bodies indeed became taller or shorter. I also did not measure them. Nonetheless, my perception echoes an important point that the mediums made in the interviews, when they spoke about their feelings of how the possession experience affected them. In particular, the experience of the approach as well as the departure of the spiritual entity is described in nearly every interview in very similar terms, highlighting the physical dimension of it. The mediums mentioned how it tickled in the arm or hand; how they sensed something coming; how they felt their body responding to the approach; and how the possessing agency then took over from one moment to another. Afterwards they usually felt a strong emotion, and often they were tired and did not know why. They felt a resonance of joy or satisfaction, but also sadness and a sense of loss when the possessing agency had left. One interviewee described the experience eloquently as vibration: 'you feel a vibration when the entity approaches, . . . [and] the longer one works with those entities, one can notice the subtle approach, even before the trance'.[15] The interviewee, an Umbanda priestess, described the approach of the entities as receiving pictures in one's mind, in particular for experienced mediums: 'in time one will focus. [It is as if] a fluid comes in one's mind, the image of an awareness about the entity that is there next to you. And each one gives a kind of a shock in one part of your body. Some take over the mind, others take over the chest, gives an irradiation, or vibration to stomach, back, legs'.[16] The *mãe de santo* insisted that 'the feeling is different, you feel for one this way and for another in that way. And after a while . . . it gives a kind of shock which comes from the energy . . . which gives you that shock which your body feels different'.[17] Consequently, the behaviour expressed in trance would be always very distinct:

> the accent is different, the voice type, some are more cheerful, others more withdrawn, angry, some slower, some more agile, the dance movement [is different], the type of dance and the costumes, [whether they] smoke a cigar, cigarette, or a pipe, some drink beer, some liquor, others water. Each has its features and its manner of speaking, singing, dancing, rhythm, customs and paraphernalia such as a hat, some sticks, a garment or the colour of clothing. So each one has a whole way of being, a complete profile with all those characteristics. . . . Each has their way of expressing them-selves, both in gestures and in movement as in the speech, drink, the type of smoke, each has his/her own way.[18]

Her emphasis on physical features such as body movement and feeling was also evident in other interviews; all interviewees pointed to specific features of each entity that would be visible during the possession rituals.

As this point I move on to Sidney Greenfield's work about religious healing in Brazil as he offers an interesting addition to the embodiment debate from a different perspective. Greenfield argues that in the case of the Brazilian religious healers, one can discover 'a new imagery for the healing sciences' (2008: 167) that challenges the mind/body divide. His argument, however, goes in a different direction to those of other oppo-nents of the mind/body controversy. While Bowie and others seem to argue (more or less indirectly) against the existence of a mind/body divide and highlight the material aspect of spirits (and vice versa the immaterial aspect of the physical body), Greenfield does not want to dismantle but to revise it. He argues that it would prevent the academic enterprise of translating local belief systems into a wider academic debate if we abolish Cartesian dualism. He proposes therefore that we should reconceptual-ize Cartesian dualism by bringing the oppositional dualism of body/mind, natural/supernatural together. His approach, which is firmly embedded in his rich ethnographic material about Brazilian healers, offers an interest-ing solution.

Similar to other contributions, Greenfield begins with the Cartesian dualism of *res extensa* and *res cogitans* because he traces the problem of embracing the spiritual explanations of the Brazilian healers back 'to the beginnings of science and its effort to separate itself from religion' (2008: 157). He argues that science in the tradition of Descartes is based on the acceptance of two different realms of study, the supernatural and the natural, though only the latter one, the natural realm, was perceived as the place for science. Consequently, 'Cartesian science excluded whatever was placed in the category supernatural from scientific examination' (2008: 159). Brazilian healers, however, accept without any doubt that the supernatural intervenes regularly in the (natural) universe, from the creation of the universe to humans suffering from illnesses, all prominent features of the natural realm. The (current) Cartesian dualism therefore undermines the understanding of the perspectives of Brazilian healers and others who lack such an ideal. Voss criticizes Cartesian dualism for leading to a scientific ideal of objectivity that 'does not correspond with the reality of research because it does not seem to be possible to make a clear distinction between subject and object (as well as similar oppositions) as it is claimed against the background of such an ideal' (2011: 169). Voss argues that it is not enough just to criticize Cartesian dualism. More needs to be done because 'reflecting on alternatives means reflecting not only on categories such as body and soul/mind or ownness and foreignness, but also on experience and the Self as well as the relationship between the Self and the Other' (Voss 2011: 169). Greenfield, however, disagrees and argues that dualism remains important, in particular when translating the local beliefs of, for instance, Brazilian healers into the academic debate on medicine.

Inspired by Thomas Kuhn's idea of scientific revolutions (1970), Greenfield wants to incorporate social and cultural aspects into 'a reformulation of science and its applications in healing' (2008: 162). The starting point is his understanding of science as a cultural process in which two groups are participating: scientists and scholars on the one side and the people they study on the other (Greenfield and Droogers 2003: 32). Greenfield argues that each side is interested in understanding the world and has developed a social group with a shared language and a shared image of the world. 'The consensus its members hold enables them to ask similar questions, the answers to which expand their collective understanding of their field or subject of interest' (Greenfield 2008: 164, referring to Kuhn's work *The Structure of Scientific Revolutions*). However, the consensus can be shattered when people encounter anomalies they cannot explain. Greenfield argues that 'if the anomalies are of a sufficient magnitude, they may bring the utility of the paradigm itself into question' (2008: 165). The result is that an alternative image of the world may be proposed which incorporates former knowledge but makes also space for the anomalies.

Turning now to the body/mind paradigm, Greenfield promotes a new paradigm which he calls 'culturalbiology', in which he combines the embodiment concept with neuropsychology, in particular the work of psychologist Ernest Rossi. Greenfield argues that embodiment is predominately discussed by medical anthropologists and describes, in his own words, 'a model of symbolic transformation where in response to a flow of information at the cultural level, usually while participating in a social ritual, an afflicted individual undergoes a transformation that results in the abatement of disappearance of debilitating symptoms' (2008: 167). Applied to healing, this suggests that some individuals will feel better due to information provided in a therapeutic ritual. But, as Greenfield declares, so far no one has successfully explained how it works. And here is where Greenfield turns to neuroscience and its insights about the flow of information inside the body.

To a large extent Greenfield relies on Rossi's work *The Psychobiology of Mind-Body Healing* (1986) in which he promotes the idea that 'information may flow between different systems within a complex organism, or separate systems at different levels' (Greenfield 2008: 169). In short, Rossi suggests that pathways of brain activity are involved in memory, learning and behaviour. Contrary to contemporary genetics, Rossi argues that a combination of information from genes and sources external to genes and even the organism itself act together to influence the behaviour of the organism. In answer to the question of how information presented in a ritual can affect the body, Greenfield turns to the anthropological concept of culture, which is a cornerstone of his 'culturalbiology' paradigm. Greenfield argues that 'each social group over time has developed its own symbolic categories, patterns of normative cultural conduct, and the symbolic means for representing and understanding them' (2008: 173). Referring now to the idea that the human organism has the ability to absorb information flow and that certain classes of genes are 'mediators between learned behaviour from the psychocultural domain and all other genes' (2008: 174), Greenfield connects culture with the biological organism. He argues that 'cultures . . . contain views of the cosmos that include understandings as to what exists and what has causal efficacy with respect to the life of the individual'. However, as he continues,

> These beliefs are more than superstition. By focusing on the information they contain and how it may be transduced, via the brain of someone who accepts them, to the other bodily systems – to the level of the cell and genes – we may discover that cultural beliefs are part of the communication system that instruct the T cells and killer cells of the immune system, for example, to attack the pathogens that cause somatic illness. (Greenfield 2008: 177–8)

Applied to the case of religious healers, Greenfield states that during a healing ritual (see for instance Figure 4.2 with a photo taken during a healing ceremony), whether it is in Candomblé, Spiritism, Pentecostalism or any other tradition, 'the cultural images in the universe believed to be able to heal him or her, often conceptualized as spirits and other supernatural beings, are brought forth from the person's implicit memory and, as information, transduced, first into psychological codes and then into biophysiological codes, and communicated through the body' (2008: 180). Greenfield therefore argues that we have information stored in our memory but that we might not be aware of the information until a ritual triggers it. The outcome is that the information is then transduced via the brain to 'codes of bodily systems' that consequently initiate the healing process. In Greenfield's words,

> healing and other benefits to suffering occur when information at the cultural level, held as beliefs (that interrupt habitual patterns of association) as to what in the universe has the ability to cause and cure illness or resolve other problems, such as spirits, saints, orixas, and the Holy Ghost (in their specific cosmological settings), is transduced via the psyche of the participants of a religious ritual. (2008: 190)

Greenfield argues that even suffering participants of a healing ritual who do not share the beliefs of the group can enter into an ASC – 'during which the belief that spirits or another form of the supernatural could cure them would become part of the expanding view of therapy and healing' (2008: 201).

Figure 4.2 Xango ceremony, Recife

Greenfield does not argue that the spiritual entities such as Dr Fritz in Spiritism, St Francis in the charismatic movement of the Roman Catholic Church, Pomba Gira in Umbanda, the Holy Ghost in Pentecostalism or Oxala in Candomblé actually cure. He states instead that the belief in any of them 'and their ability to relieve pain and suffering, may cure when it is placed as information in the working memory of a participant in a religious ritual', and during the possession ritual, 'that information may be transduced, via the brain, to become part of the communication flow. This in turn may release the body's own painkillers (endorphins) and activate the immune and other systems, analogous to the way suggestions in hypnotically facilitated therapy work' (Greenfield 2008: 201). And if the healing remains unsuccessful, the individual will continue his or her search on the growing religious market in Brazil.

Greenfield's culturalbiology shows some similarities with the biocultural theory of Arnim Geertz presented above, though Geertz clearly locates his theory in the area of cognitive studies more than Greenfield. However, while Geertz presents a theoretical framework, Greenfield furthers our understanding of different types of religious healing in Brazil. Though Greenfield cannot explain why some people experience possession trance and others not, or why people are cured once but not other times, he shows the interrelationship of the different types of healing with Brazilian culture. Even in the healing sessions of the Pentecostal churches, such as the IURD, include similar elements as the Afro–Brazilian rituals such as drumming, singing, chanting and dancing. These rhythmic, auditory and other stimulations are sufficient to induce ASCs, as Greenfield states, even among newcomers who do not share the epistemology and worldview of the community. The result is that bodies begin to heal naturally, as Greenfield writes, though not the bodies of everyone (2008: 199). Greenfield sees the ASC as the core element in healing which, to a certain degree, confirms Felicitas Goodman's study of the neurobiology of ecstasy. However, despite some remarkable results about the changes in blood serum, betaendorphin and more (see Goodman 1988:10), the sample of people was too small to draw any wider conclusions. Nonetheless, the problem with Greenfield's interpretation is the case of Spiritist healing. As I explained previously, though Spiritists practise a type of ASC under the label mediumship, it is always the medium who goes into trance and enters an ASC, not the patients. The aim of the trance is to receive the spiritual guides who help with healing. While this distinction was visible in my interviews with Spiritists, Greenfield states that he also saw some of the patients enter an ASC during the preliminary part of the rituals. He therefore challenges the Spiritist account and explains Spiritist healers' reluctance to acknowledge their patients' trance state with the Western model of medicine and theatre, which regard patients as part of the audience. Consequently only the healers themselves, separated from the audience, should go into trance. However, he writes that he was convinced that while not every patient went into trance, a few did, and that 'those who did enter ASC had sufficient information about the other reality to transduce it and activate their bodily systems' (2008: 197).

***

This chapter has highlighted an important feature of my argumentation, the bricolage of ideas. From Engler's agency theory to Geertz's biocultural theory of religion to Csordas's embodiment paradigm and Greenfield's cul-turalbiology – each of these contributions to the body/mind debate promotes a different way of studying possession rituals scientifically. Though Engler and his discussion of agency seem out of place in this group, I decided to include him nonetheless because he also writes about an objective approach to such a subjective phenomenon. While I am still not convinced of the need to apply scientific methodology to the humanities, in particular to the study of immaterial ideas, during my journey through the growing field of scien-tific studies of religion I discovered a rising awareness of two elements: first, the rejection of examinations of cognition which do not take the environ-ment into consideration, and second, the shift to studies of the body with all its features, including the brain and body language, dance and voice. Though I mentioned at the beginning of this chapter that Brazilian practitioners have little interest in the Western debate about Cartesian dualism, these two aspects are also visible in the ethnographic data I presented throughout the chapter. After interpreting possession practices in terms of their social func-tion (Chapter 2) and religious connotation (Chapter 3), this chapter has dem-onstrated the significance of a third level that brings culture, environment and cognition together.

Conclusion: Spirit Possession as a Deictic Concept

One of the many friends who guided me through the world of Brazilian ecstatic religions, a student at the University of São Paulo, not only introduced me to his *pai de santo* and the *terreiro* he attended in São Paulo but also spoke to me about his own experiences with the Holy Ghost during his time as an *evangélico* and with the *encantados* in Afro–Brazilian rituals later on. The first ceremony we attended together took place in a remote part of São Paulo I had never visited before. Since we changed from the metro to a bus and then to another bus, I felt quite lost when we arrived at the small *terreiro*. It was an impressive ceremony and I enjoyed every moment of it – until suddenly the body of my companion was possessed. After a while I got worried, not so much because of the ceremony but – very selfishly – because I could not remember how to get back to the metro. One of the elders of the *terreiro* seemed to have noticed my unease and asked whether everything was alright. I told her carefully that it might be a good time for me to leave the *terreiro* and that I would try to find a cab at the main road. But she just said not to worry and a short while afterwards – most of the other participants had already left – my companion came out of his state. After eating dinner ravenously – his body seemed to have forgotten the previous meal just an hour earlier – he told me that it was time to say goodbye and to make our way back to the city. While I learnt a lot about spirit possession and Brazil from the conversations I had with him before and afterwards, this evening in the small *terreiro* in São Paulo helped me realize and confront some of my personal difficulties with spirit possession. I began this research with conflicting feelings. On the one hand, I had been fascinated by possession rituals for many years, after attending numerous Afro–Caribbean rituals for hours after hours in New York City. I never felt fear, only fascination. On the other hand, I failed to comprehend the depth of what was going on. I was fascinated by the music, the movements and the whole atmosphere, but because I did not share the beliefs in spirits and deities, I could not accept the presence of these entities during the ceremonies I attended. Years later, having arrived in Brazil in order to get to grips with this problem, I still felt stuck in the middle of this dilemma between my anthropological distance towards the situation and the reading of it made by participants. In New York, I encountered many people struggling with the same problem, despite regularly attending ceremonies and sometimes even being initiated. But Brazil was different. As I explained in the introduction, I encountered a very open-minded attitude towards paranormal phenomena throughout all social, racial and ethnic groups of society. How the phenomenon was experienced and interpreted sometimes differed radically, but the acceptance was widespread. Though Afro–Brazilian communities as well as Spiritists were generally tolerant and did not force their understanding of the world onto others, I felt that I should try to find a way to communicate their understanding to a wider public, outside Brazil. Nonetheless, reflecting on my feelings during the ceremony described above – my concern about my safety and feeling of abandonment – made me realize that I have to confront my own position.

My dilemma lies in the core of anthropology. Anthropology has been and will always be a secular discipline, as is often highlighted (e.g. Lambek 2008). 'Palimpsests and erasures, phenomenological bracketing and positionality, objectifications and embodiments, identities and dialectics, romanticizations and reductions' (2008: 122) – these are the great difficulties of anthropology, as Lambek outlines, but also its attraction, since they force us to reconsider our position again and again. The outcome leads us to the core of academic discourse, not only in anthropology but beyond. 'The questions are not only can the subaltern speak or whether the intellectual should speak sometimes for or above the subaltern, but whether both intellectuals and subalterns can speak for themselves with a vocabulary that both is and is not theirs, about a subject and about experience that both is and is not theirs' (Lambek 2008: 122). Applied to my research on ecstatic religions in Brazil, Lambek's comments show me a way how to speak about the experience, though I did not experience it, but also to present the interpretations of the experiencers, though I am not one of them. Lambek urges us to overcome a binary logic of either/or in favour of both/and, referring at this point to Dipesh Chakrabarty:

> We cannot subscribe exclusively to European meta-narratives or analytic stances they presuppose or generate, but we cannot do without them either. What I want to provincialize is not all aspects of the Abrahamic religious traditions but rather their dedication precisely not to such a pluralistic logic of both/and but rather to a binary logic of either/or. Indeed, it is this binary logic of mutual exclusion that also poses the alternative of secularism: either belief in, and invocation of, religion – or not. In a cultural universe characterized by both/and, scepticism and rationalism are simply part of a larger repertoires of attitudes and positions, invoked according to shifting practical considerations, rather than a matter for strict adjudication. (Lambek 2008: 123)

Lambek's challenge of binary logic echoes to a certain degree Roberto da Matta's characterization of the Brazilian culture (see da Matta 1991, 1995). Put in this framework my dilemma loses its power. My scepticism as well as my fascination are equal parts of the repertoire of positions, alongside the religious position of the practitioners. Lambek sees a connection between the Western idea of Religion, which is centred on the idea of the Abrahamic tradition that 'belief in God requires rejecting alternatives', and secularism because, as he writes, 'the secular is by definition a perspective that imagines it can look at religion from the outside. If Abrahamic religion has often denigrated the practices it locates outside its borders, secularism turns that partly around in order to claim that the external space offers a privileged vantage point from which to view what lies within' (2008: 124–5).

Lambek's solution is provincializing God or, in other words, embracing locally specific features of God. In support of his argument, Lambek looks at Edward Evan Evans-Pritchard's work about the Nuer, in particular his book *The Nuer* (1940), together with his book on the Azande witchcraft, one of the core monographs in anthropology. In *The Nuer*, Evans-Pritchard demonstrates the significance of cultural translation, which is the heart of anthropology. However, though Evans-Pritchard makes a good case for the cultural sensitivity of this task, he overlooks, as Lambek argues, the depth of the problem for such a task. Lambek refers here to deixis – that is, the problem that the meaning of certain words depends on a given context. As Evans-Pritchard has successfully demonstrated in his work, the Nuer language is highly deictic. However, his translation of the term *kwoth* with God neglects, as Lambek argues, that the meaning of *kwoth* also depends on the situation, hence that it is also a deictic form of speech. This misreading relates to other misinterpretations which are visible, according to Lambek, in debates such as whether the Nuer religion is monotheistic or polytheistic.

In the past, encounters with other religious practices have led to many misinterpretations due to a misreading of deictic terms, and not only in the wider context of African religion. Lambek urges us therefore to move in the opposite direction and 'to consider the possibility of deictic deity', which would give way to provincializing God. Lambek argues further that 'a deictic word is one that is open and inclusive, characterized by a both/and rather than an either/or logic', and continues that 'attention to deixis implies putting practice ahead of belief; it thus supports a turn away from "neo-Tylorean" perspectives in religion, which emphasizes explanation and rationality, toward Foucauldian accounts of discipline and neo-Aristotelian cultivations of the virtues' (Lambek 2008: 137). His critique reminds me Sol Montoya Bonilla's evaluation of the representation of cultures in a museum. Like Lambek, she highlights anthropology's need to create 'coherent images in order to domesticate cultures'. Instead of a standardized 'antropología de bronce', Montoya advocates the fusion of contradictory attitudes, as visible in the representation of the Amazonia spirit Curupira, whose feet are turned in one direction, while his face glances in the opposite direction (2003: 108).

Lambek's anthropological contribution to the debate on religion offers the perfect framework for my Brazilian research. I want to highlight the significance of two points which reinforce the overall argument of this book. First, in applying Lambek's account of *kwoth* among the Nuer to spirit possession, I argue for an understanding of spirit possession – despite its being an academic concept – as a deictic form of speech. As I have demonstrated throughout this book, the wider meaning of spirit possession always depends on the situation, on the context. While Lambek argues for a provincialization of God, I stress that we also need to increase the provincialization of the experience itself. Instead of establishing theories of spirit possession, which remain superficial and limited since they originate against the background of the Western idea of religion (see Johnson 2011), we need to embrace the locally specific features of religious experiences. The Brazilian Spiritist idea of mediumship will always remain different from the Candomblé idea of merging the realm of the *orixás* with the human realm in the moment of possession trance, or the Umbanda idea of incorporation will always differ from the Pentecostal idea of demonic possession and divine experience with the Holy Ghost. The differences between these ideas do not make one of them less valuable than the other, nor are they incoherent; rather, every one of these ideas makes an equal contribution to a wide range of positions.

The same approach can be applied to the wider discourse about spirit possession. Possession studies tend to mirror, as Lewis writes, 'the current fashions of anthropological theory', and he warns further that 'if we are not careful, the voices of those we seek to report are in danger of being silenced as we pursue our own ethnocentric preoccupations' (2003: xii). However, as I have demonstrated, the sometimes opposing readings of spirit possession and mediumship in Brazil also contribute to furthering our understanding of the experience – if we understand them as always depending on the context. Because Brazilian society changed dramatically during the twentieth century, the meaning of the experience has changed for people involved in the rituals and so has the discourse about it. The impact of the changes for the practitioners is nowhere more visible than in Chapter 2 of the book, in which I discussed the social dimension. Comparing the studies from the first part of the twentieth century with my own research, I highlighted, for instance, the changed gender distribution among participants and the priesthood and the growing racial diversification of these religions' membership. But, as I argued above, I see the different interpretations of Landes and others not as opposing views but as contextdependent, in this case dependent on a different historical context. In addition, one can see a further impact of social changes on academic discourse in Chapter four of the book, which focused on a relatively new paradigm in possession studies. While gender has been a constant in possession literature over several decades now, cognitive studies and embodiment represent new trends. But, to a certain degree, their growth can also be linked to the changes in Brazil since they reflect the highly sophisticated debate among practitioners. The growing social diversification of the communities supports an impressive intellectualization of the membership. Not only do numerous practitioners pursue further training (e.g. in the Faculdade de Teologia Umbandista in São Paulo) and higher education degrees, but also the number of publications, conference papers and lectures by members of the priesthood and other members in Brazil outnumber those in any other country. The application of Jungian archetypes to the *orixás* is long established, not only among Umbandistas, and it should not be a surprise therefore that attention has now shifted to cognition. Provincializing the experience on a conceptual level allows, as I argue here, the co-existence of these and more discourses as equally relevant contributions to the debate.

Second, Lambek's argument that attention to deixis will help us appreciate the importance of practice over belief supports the final departure from a neo-Tylorean perspective in religion, which is the other case I have sought to make in this book. The shift from belief to practice makes the debate about whether spirit possession belongs to the range of religious experiences irrelevant. The outcome is the acknowledgement of the specific Brazilian situation I described in the introduction, in which it does not matter whether someone self-identifies as agnostic, Christian or atheist – only their practice is important. Even the rise of secularism, which is transforming Brazilian society, will have little impact on the continuity of possession rituals since their main function for individuals (and society) lies outside the religious arena. It may sound strange that it is not necessary to believe in the *orixás* exclusively when inducing the possession trance, but as Greenfield demonstrates for the power of religious healing (see Chapter 4), it is not always necessary to believe to be cured. By moving away from belief towards practice, the study of possession rituals avoids the conceptual trap of studying something that is not 'real', a purely 'religious' experience, something irrational – hence it moves away from the Western focus on rationality which has affected possession studies since its beginning, as Johnson writes:

> Discourses and legal actions naming and constraining 'spirit possession' over the past four centuries helped to create the dual notions of the rational individual and the civil subject of modern states. The silhouette of the propertied citizen and free individual took form between the idea of the automaton – a machine-body without will – and the threat of the primitive or

animal, bodies overwhelmed by instincts and passions (or the two merged, as in Descartes' 'nature's automata', animals-*as*-machines (2003: 24, 29, 66).

The balance between the lack of will and its unchecked excess has been considered through the prism of the dangers of spirits in relation to persons and objects at least since the mid-seventeenth century. (Johnson 2011: 396)

Moving away from Tylor's definition of religion as belief in spirits that will be overcome by science in the future collapses the dichotomy between Western rational civil religion on the one side and the irrational other on the other side. Instead of struggling with the challenge of how not to offend practitioners when one does not share their beliefs, the focus shifts to what they do and not what they believe. To a certain degree we come back here to Evans-Pritchard, as this statement shows: 'there is no possibility of [the anthropologist] . . . *knowing* whether the spiritual beings of primitive religions or of any others have any existence or not, and since that is the case he cannot take the question into consideration' (quoted in Bowie 2006: 6). As Evans-Pritchard explained in the context of his research about Azande witchcraft, the meaning of the phrase 'to believe' is very different from the Western idea of belief. As Byron Good (1994) elaborates, while for Geoffrey Chaucer 'to believe' meant 'to pledge loyalty' and 'to believe in God' was more a promise to live in the service of God, the meaning changed, and by the end of the seventeenth century 'belief' included a notion of choice between two options, one 'correct' and the other 'false', for instance, the choice to believe in God's existence or to believe that God was a human creation. Among the Azande, however, belief in witchcraft was very different and reflects more of a pre-Enlightenment idea, as Bowie summarizes: 'for the Azande, there was a single, hegemonic worldview. The possibility that witches might not exist was not part of Zande "collective representations"' (Bowie 2006: 20). Without the notion of a 'correct belief', questions about whether one believes in the spirits or in the *orixás* become irrelevant. In her work among the Karo Batak in North Sumatra, Indonesia, Mary Steedly (1993) related that she mistranslated a question people asked her frequently and which she struggled to answer. While she thought they asked her whether she believed in the spirit, she realized after a while that they were asking her whether she trusted the spirits. The belief in the spirits' existence was presupposed since no alternative could be imagined, but her loyalty to them was questioned. Robert Horton (1994) categorizes this kind of thinking as 'closed' because of the availability of just one belief system, in contrast to the 'open' worldview in the West. Hurton, however, also points to the dangers of the Western choice between alternative systems because it can create uncertainty and fear, to which some people respond with fanatical missionary activity to promote their own belief (the only 'true' one) or by even demanding authoritarian control of dogma (Hurton 1994: 256–7). As Bowie highlights, 'traditional peoples rarely try to convince others of the rightness of their worldview. It is self-evident. Once choice is introduced, so is uncertainty' (2006: 23). It is, however, not the case of either/or, either Western or traditional, either open or closed. As Paul Gifford explains, 'In Africa most Christians operate from a background little affected by the European Enlightenment: for most Africans, witchcraft, spirits and ancestors, spells and charms, are primary and immediate and natural categories of interpretation. . . . Most Africans have an "enchanted" worldview' (Gifford 1998: 327–8). A similar observation can be made in Latin America. While mainstream Christian churches in Africa as well as Latin America promote Enlightenment thinking, most lay people hold on to what Bowie describes as, 'a much more "traditional", supernaturalistic view of the world, one common in Europe prior to the Enlightenment' (Bowie 2006: 22). However, when we look at the fastest-growing churches on both continents, which preach a prosperity Gospel, Bowie notices that, though they reject traditional culture vehemently, they also promote a quite 'traditional vision of reality with a discourse between God and the Devil, with miraculous interventions, and with an instrumental understanding of religion' (2006: 22). This apparent contradiction shows that different worldviews can co-exist, even within one society and even within one person. For Bowie, the existence of apparently incompatible worldviews draws the conclusion that it is possible to be a scientist and a believer, an anthropologist and a witch: it all depends on the society and the individual, as Evans-Pritchard has already shown us in his book on Azande witchcraft:

> In my own culture, in the climate of thought I was born into and brought up in and have been conditioned by, I rejected, and reject, Zande notions of witchcraft. In their culture, in the set of ideas I then lived in, I accepted

them; in a kind of way I believed them . . . If one must act as though one believed, one ends in believing, or half-believing as one acts. (Evans-Pritchard 1976: 244)

Whether the spirits, the *orixás* or God exists is not the question, but rather how the relationship between human and non-human beings is maintained. In my research I have treated corporeal experience during possession rituals or other sessions as the key aspect of the maintenance of this relationship. This shift in thinking moves me away from a focus on ontological differences between the range of experiences I portrayed in my book and from any attempt to define the differences between spirit possession, mediumship, and other types, because, as Lambek points out, the meaning of all these different types depends on the situation. I can therefore continue to use the term 'spirit possession' despite its ambivalent, sometimes even contradictory, usage by characterizing it as a deictic concept, without essentialist meaning. By focusing on the way people relate to their supernatural entities, I avoid the trap of well-defined (and limited) categories and can concentrate on what people do – their practices – and how they interpret their experience. And this is what I did in the second and third chapters of the book (after the introduction). First, I looked at the gender roles associated with the practice and showed how those roles have adapted alongside changes in society in the last hundred years. I also discussed the racial stratification of the communities and outsiders' perception of it and highlighted how the latter influenced the relationship between the communities. The focus of the second chapter was therefore firmly on the social features of possession practice in order to demonstrate the need to understand the practice within its social frame. The third chapter of the book shifted then to the way people interpret their practice. As it is the core feature of maintaining the relationship with supernatural entities, the focus of the chapter was on the possessing agencies. The aim was to demonstrate that the various interpretations of this practice depend on the ontology of the possessing agencies and the human relationship to them. Both chapters together therefore showed the complexity of the practice and how its meaning depends on the social and historical situation in which it is located.

The fourth chapter changed the line of argumentation, being centred on the Western discourse of mind/body dualism. I approached it in three different ways, focusing on agency of the mediums, cognition and embodiment. Though these areas go beyond the practice itself, they nonetheless confirm the significance of discussing possession within a wider framework that embraces physical elements as well as cultural ones. Whether it is called culturalbiology (Greenfield) or bioculture (Geertz), the important step is not to limit our view to one aspect alone (cognition, deprivation, gender and so on) but to look at all features together. And this includes the corporeal feature because possession practice cannot be understood, as this book has shown, without taking the body into account. The body, however, is not only the brain or blood components but the whole body and, to use Mauss's terminology, its body techniques such as dancing and speaking. Roberto Motta defines Candomblé and the other Afro–Brazilian traditions consequently as 'religion of the body and the image' and writes that these religions 'encourage the display of the body with all its drives and tendencies' (2005: 301, 299).[1]

Both dance and speech are common means of communication between human beings and supernatural entities, the spirits and *orixás*, but they are performed in distinct ways depending on the tradition, the community, the situation (time and place) and function. Even body trance, to use Motta's term, does not transform mediums into helpless victims, but is vital for the relationship between humans and non-humans. Mark Münzel compares the dance during trance, for instance, with the performance of a dressage horse guided by the rider through elegant and difficult figures (1997: 153). Without the rider the horse would not accomplish its complex task as well and, vice versa, without the horse the rider could not carry on. However, we cannot see, touch or communicate with the 'rider' (the spirit or *orixá*) without the 'horse' (the medium). Objectively we are unable to confirm its existence with scientific measures, though subjectively we can feel and observe the impact. But the main point here is to highlight the importance of the corporal features of the practice that goes far beyond the aesthetic appreciation of the dance. As Alcide writes about a similar practice in Haitian Vodou: 'No doubt that the primary function of Voodoo rituals is religious, but it should be pointed out that within that context emerge elements of entertainment. . . . Religious, surely. Recreational, carnal, without a doubt' (1988: 184, 186). The embodiment of possession practice demonstrates the interrelation – and interdependence – of body and mind, which have to be regarded as a unity.

I conclude with an excerpt from another interview in which the interviewee describes his journey from being born into a family of Jehovah's Witnesses to the search for a different spirituality, his call to become involved in Candomblé, his first possession experience and the meaning of the religion for him today. It highlights the physical dimension of the experience but also the cognitive one, and illustrates how fulfilling the practice can be.

Everyone in my family is Jehovah's Witness. And when I was a child I was forced into it by my family because as a minor, under the law, I had to follow their religious principles. But it was a religion to which I felt no motivation, no pleasure in being a member of that religion. I practised because of my obligation towards my parents. When I turned eighteen, I talked to my mom and told her that from that moment I wanted no part in that religion. They were very sad, but it was a decision I had to make for myself . . . And I stopped attending any kind of religion. But about two years later I felt the need to seek some spiritual guidance but did not know how. A friend who knows Pai Z. said 'Why do you not ask the shells [i.e. a form of oracle reading]? It can help you. You are passing through a very difficult phase of your life, and I think it might do you good'. I said "Oh no, I do not believe in those things. I learned [as a child] that these things were wrong. I want to learn, not to play [shells]." But one day I decided that I would do it, I would ask the shells, and was surprised when he [Pai Z.] told me that the shells told him about me, about my private life, my past, how I was raised, and other things that only I know, no one else knew. And it really confused me when he told me that I had to do spiritual work. 'Look, you have to do spiritual work, this is it'. But I was like, 'I do not do it . . . I do not know if I do it . . .'. But in that week, while I was at my house, *Egum* took me. I was at home, normal, lying in my bed, and suddenly I felt as if something jumped on top of me and started to shake me. I got stiff, fell to the ground, I opened my bedroom door and when my friend who lived in the same house saw me, I was all red-purple, choked. When I came to, I asked him to call Pai Z. Pai Z. came at once and told 'No, you have to go to the *terreiro*, you have to do your stuff'. This was when I did my first *ebó* [sacrifice], my first spiritual works, and since then, since that time, twenty years ago, I never let go of Candomblé. I started attending, I attended the first Candomblé ceremony, I was watching others, I was attending, I was participating, and after four years . . . there are some things I could not see, there were certain things you can do and cannot do, then I had already taken *bori* [the first step to initiation], and I could enter the holy room. And then my father [Pai

Z.] asked me to take some fruit to Xango and that was the first time I was possessed. . . .

And so it was love at first sight, you know, it made me complete. And I had serious problems with possession, because I did not believe in it. I thought it was all a lie, did not think anything would happen. Because I did not feel anything at ceremonies, I thought it was a thing of the imagination. Until it happened to me the first time. . . .

It totally changed my life. But I believe now that my first spiritual manifestation, my first trance happened when I was seven years old. But I had no idea then what I know today – Candomblé gave me the insight to see. I was seven years old when I lost consciousness, and my parents thought I had a seizure but in fact it happened only once in my life, when I was seven years. And I did tests, CT scans, electro, a lot of tests and they never found anything. . . . I believe that it was the first manifestation of the *orixá* when I was seven years old and without the knowledge of my family – without anyone knowing, not even myself, because no one knew, my family did not practice it. Because a boy of seven years old suddenly faints one morning and ends up in the hospital and doctors say, 'Look, there is nothing, he has nothing . . . '. They did tests but did not find anything. I consider this my first spiritual manifestation. . . . And the feeling I had when I fainted was the same feeling when I started, the loss of consciousness, the same feeling. . . . And when I started [with Candomblé], which got me Xango, I could no longer practise anything else, I had not no desire to go to another religion. It is a complete world within Candomblé; to me it is very important. It changed my character, my personality, my social life, my patience, understanding of what is religion, understanding the limits of other people. I do not want to prove to people that my religion is better than others. I think you show that you have a good character through actions, and behind this is the religious principle, in a certain way.

The fact is, you help us preparing clothes and when you see the *orixá* out, fully dressed, you will say 'Wow, . . . the *orixá* is happy, dancing, people feel pretty.' I mean, look at all this, I think it's a form of a God who manifests, I think it is a message from the *orixá*. Just imagine a religion in which God, the gods come dancing with you and manifest in you, it is unique, it is very unique.[2]

Notes

Chapter 1

1 Interview with Zacharias in São Paulo on 15 April 2010.
2 Instituto Brasileiro de Geografia e Estatística. Censo Demográfico 2010: Características gerais da população, religião e pessoas com deficiência. (no date). Retrieved from: http://www.ibge.gov.br/home/estatistica/populacao/censo2010/caracteristicas_religiao_deficiencia/default_caracteristicas_religiao_deficiencia.shtm, accessed on 24 August 2012.
3 Office of National Statistics. Census 2011. (no date). Retrieved from: http://www.ons.gov.uk, accessed on 31 December 2012.
4 In 2010 all questionnaires with more than one religious affiliation ticked were disregarded as invalid.
5 I use the term 'narrative' or 'informal narrative' based on the definition of Armin Geertz (2011: 23) in which he highlights, among other things, the collaborative effort of narrator and listener. He writes that 'narratives assume cultural values and implications thereby serving fundamental cognitive and social functions for participants. Narrative is essential to constructing selves and monitoring social relationships' (2011: 23).
6 For instance, Rouget uses mediumship as a subset of trance as opposed to ecstasy (see Rouget 1985; Donovan 2000).
7 The Haitian religion Vodou is often labelled in US literature as 'Voodoo' despite the fact that the latter term is widely rejected by Haitians and most scholars. In 2012 the Library of Congress finally decided to change its label to Vodou, which will hopefully have an impact on the wider usage of 'Voodoo'.
8 See also Lambek's idea of 'provincializing God' (2008) Lambek challenges the Western idea that Abrahamic religions are 'tokens of a universal or natural type in which distinct religions are bounded entities constituted by belief in God or gods' (2008: 120).
9 Johnson is referring here to Fabian 2002 and Keller 2002: 5–7.
10 Engler disagrees with Strawson slightly, as I elaborate later.
11 The term 'abnormal' does not necessary indicate that one has to categorize the experience as pathological. According to Cardeña and Krippner, abnormal is defined as irregular or uncommon (quoted in Machado 2009, 5).

12 It would be interesting to run a similar trial in Puerto Rico. The belief in the existence of spirits of the ancestors is part of Puerto Rican culture and identity (Schmidt 2009); however, the island is linked to the United States, and due to the over one hundred years of US domination, is influenced by the Calvinistic rejection of extrasensual experiences.

13 Instituto Brasileiro de Geografia e Estatística. *Censo Demográfico 2010: Características gerais da população, religião e pessoas com deficiência.* (no date). Retrieved from: http://www.ibge.gov.br/home/estatistica/populacao/ censo2010/caracteristicas_religiao_deficiencia/default_caracteristicas_religiao_ deficiencia.shtm, accessed on 24 August 2012.

14 The term 'cultural religion' is adapted from Day 2011: 187, who refers to Demerath 2000: 127.

15 Instituto Brasileiro de Geografia e Estatística. *Censo Demográfico 2010. Resultados do Universo do Censo Demográfico 2010. Tabela 1–4*, (no date). Retrieved from: ftp://ftp.ibge.gov.br/Censos/Censo_Demografico_2010/ Caracteristicas_Gerais_Religiao_Deficiencia/tab1_4.pdf, accessed on 24 August 2010.

16 'População que se declara branca diminui, diz IBGE'. *FatimaNews* on 1 May 2011 http://www.fatimanews.com.br/noticias/populacao-que-se-declara- branca-diminui-diz-ibge_116224/, accessed on 6 February 2012.

17 *O Alabama*, 29 September 1868, quoted in English in Sansi 2007: 1.

18 See Parés 2006 for the history of the formation of Candomblé.

19 As Selka correctly states, residents of Salvador refer to the rural town of Cachoeira as the standard for Candomblé and not Bahia, the capital of Salvador (Selka 2009: 22).

20 See Richard Price in his foreword to the new edition of Bastide 2007: xi.

21 See also Motta de Oliveira (2007) for the relationship between Umbanda and the so-called *Estado Novo*, the authoritarian regime under President Getúlio Vargas (1882–1954).

22 For the growing reception of Bantu as a term of reference in the African Diaspora, see *Muntu*, by Janheinz Jahn (1958 in German, 1961 in English), which presents quite a broad overview of African culture as expressed in art, religion and more. It became influential as an important source for African identity among African Americans.

23 At the same time, Kardec's teachings also made an impact in the Spanish colonies in the Caribbean, particularly Puerto Rico (see Schmidt 2009, for a discussion of the meaning of Puerto Rican Spiritism).

24 For a history of Spiritism in Brazil, see also Hess 1991.

25 While in the beginning, newspaper articles speculated that this murder was a religiously motivated hate crime, the police did not find any evidence of this and arrested a mentally disturbed friend of the victim.

26 See Csordas 1997 (chapter 1) for an overview of the Catholic Charismatic Renewal in the United States and how it spread internationally.

27 The first Lutheran colonies were established in Brazil in 1808, though French Huguenots had already settled in 1557 and Dutch Calvinists in 1624 in areas that would become Brazilian soil (though without leaving any permanent marks due to the short time between settlement and their repulse).

Chapter 2

1 For an overview of studies on spirit possession see, e.g. Boddy 1994.

2 Later, however, after spreading my research to the United States, I noticed a predominance of women in the Caribbean religions, though never exclusiveness. I came to the impression that these religions with possession rituals enabled women (but not only women) to express themselves in a hostile environment such as the United States (Schmidt 2000, 2002).

3 Recent developments after the earthquake indicate that the rejection of Vodou by the establishment is enforced by the growing influence of Evangelical missionary churches, which might even have had an impact on a change in the constitution in 2012 that affects the position of the Vodou priesthood.

4 Since then the situation has changed again, in particular due to the increasing influence of fundamental Islamism that led to a switch from *saar* to *sitaat*, which is regarded as more appropriate for Muslims than *saar* possession rituals (see Tiilikainen 2010).

5 Summarized by Hayes 2010: 121, with reference to Sered 1994.

6 Sorafim da Silva 1998: 69, on the basis of a leaflet prepared and handed out by the IURD.

7 Interview with R. in São Paulo on 14 April 2010.

8 Chesnut 1997: 69, referring to the research by Leacock and Leacock in Belem.

9 Interview with *Mãe* I. in São Paulo on 16 March 2010. For another *mãe de santo* in Umbanda, Mãe M., it is also a question of space. Her *terreiro* is much larger than the one of the Mãe I. (about one hundred in comparison to thirty-six), and though the majority are also women, she has also several male members. (interview with Mãe M. in São Paulo on 22 March 2010).

10 Hayes 2006: 160; for a longer presentation of Nazaré's testimony, see Hayes 2011.

11 Interview with P. in São Paulo on 13 May 2010.

12 Bush's research focuses on the role of female slaves, though mainly in the Caribbean (e.g. Bush 1990).

13 See e.g. Carneiro 1940: 272 for a list of the founding 'mothers' of Candomblé terreiros in Bahia in the 1830s.

14 Interview with *Pai* R. in São Paulo on 14 April 2010.

15 *Pai* R. is not an exception with his vast knowledge of the literature about the Afro–Brazilian religions. In particular, the priesthood is very familiar with the literature, at least the one published in Portuguese. Some have even published their own monographs about the tradition performed in their *terreiro* or encouraged members of their *terreiros* to do so.

16 An exclusively male ritual position that links this group of priests to the *ifá* divination ritual.

17 Clark blames early researchers, who were predominately men and would have preferred to interview male practitioners instead of female. However, Rosalind Shaw points towards the influence of Christian missionaries who had characterized the Yoruba *babalawos* as high priests because they have favoured *ifá* diviners due to assumed similarities between *ifá* and Christianity (quoted by Clark 2005: 65).

18 Iyakemi Ribeiro highlights in her paper that the *ifá* initiations performed in Brazil are not initiations of new babalowos; hence, the rituals performed in Brazil do not confer the status of a babalawo on the new initiate.

19 Originally King was the tutor for the Yoruba language at the Centro de Estudos Africanos at the University of São Paulo (USP), but according to my information he no longer offers these classes at the USP, but rather only at his centre. Nonetheless, many anthropologists currently working on Candomblé and other Afro–Brazilian religions learned Yoruba under King at the USP.

20 I noticed during my visits a growing dissatisfaction with the *babalorixá* due to his many journeys and his unavailability to look after the members of the temple. The position of a leader of a *terreiro* involves being contactable night and day, available to help and support the members constantly. His overseas activities make this impossible.

21 I saw only in her *terreiro* a woman taking over a drum during a ceremony, though several women can play all the rhythms and do so outside a public ceremony.

22 Interview with *Mãe* I. in São Paulo on 16 March 2010.

23 Engler sees a correlation between the social stratification and the attitude towards agency as I explain below.

Chapter 3

1 Interview with Zacharias in São Paulo on 15 April 2010.
2 In the literature one can find other examples of non-verbal communication such as non-verbal sounds that require translation (e.g. Palmisano 2003, about the Zar cult in Ethiopia).
3 Interview with *Pai* Z. on 23 April 2010.
4 Interview with *Pai* Z. on 23 April 2010.
5 Interview with *Pai* Z. on 23 April 2010.
6 Interview with *Pai* Z. on 23 April 2010.
7 Interview with *Pai* F. in São Paulo on 21 May 2010.
8 Interview with *Pai* F. in São Paulo on 21 May 2010.
9 Interview with *Pai* Z. on 23 April 2010.
10 Interview with *Pai* Z. on 23 April 2010.
11 Interview with *Mãe* I. in São Paulo on 16 March 2010.
12 Interview with *Mãe* M. on 22 March 2010.
13 Interview with C. in São Paulo on 17 April 2010.
14 Interview with C. in São Paulo on 17 April 2010.
15 Interview with J. in Florianopolis on 5 May 2010.
16 Interview with J. in Florianopolis on 5 May 2010.

Chapter 4

1 Not to be confounded with cognitive anthropologists in general who are looking for cultural systems as mental representations more than for nature (see d'Andrade 1995).
2 Interview with *Mãe* M. in São Paulo on 22 March 2010.
3 Interview with *Mãe* M. in São Paulo on 22 March2010.
4 Interview with *Mãe* M. in São Paulo on 22 March 2010.
5 See 'Faculdade de Teologia com ênfase em Religiões Afro-brasileiras', by Faculdade de Teologia. (no date). http://www.ftu.edu.br/ftu/, accessed on 22 August 2012.
6 Interview with *Mãe* M. in São Paulo on 22 March 2010.
7 Interview with F. in São Paulo on 13 May 2010.
8 Interview with F. in São Paulo on 13 May 2010.
9 http://brainethics.wordpress.com/2006/08/04/spiritual-neuroscience, accessed on 19 October 2012.
10 I want to express my gratitude to Mark Münzel for clarifying Bastian's position.

11   To a certain degree Klass here comes back to Émile Durkheim's argument that divinities are expressions of community unity.

12   Cohen 2007: 189, with reference to James and Wells 2003, Keinan 1994 and other studies.

13   Cohen 2007: 220, n.4, summarizing Whitehouse 1995, 2000 and 2004.

14   In her case, she failed the final 'examination' and the spirits rejected her as medium. As this outcome surprised her teachers – she was regarded as a good student with advanced mediumship faculties – they allowed her another attempt, but the spirits rejected her request to be recognized as a medium a second time. This experience was explained later on by the migration of her family from Brazil to the United States. Though she was not aware of any plans to leave Brazil at this stage, the rejection by the spirits was regarded as evidence that the spirits already knew that she would eventually leave the country.

15   From an interview with *Mãe* M. on 22 March 2010, in São Paulo.

16   From an interview with *Mãe* M. on 22 March 2010, in São Paulo.

17   From an interview with *Mãe* M. on 22 March 2010, in São Paulo.

18   From an interview with *Mãe* M. on 22 March 2010, in São Paulo.

Chapter 5

1   While Motta distinguishes between religions of the body and religions of the book (referring here to the French historian Victor Tapié [1972]), he uses the term 'trance' for a wide range of experiences, including Kardecism and Pentecostal glossolalia, distinguishing them only as body trance and word trance.

2   Excerpt from an interview with M. on 23 April 2010.

Glossary

ASC	altered state of consciousness
Ashe [Engl. spelling], *axé* [Port. spelling]	spiritual force or energy that is in all living beings
Babalaõ [Port. spelling], babalawo [Span. spelling]	priest of the ifá divination
Babalorixá	see pai de santo
baianos	spirits of people from Bahia
Batuque	Afro–Brazilian tradition developed in the area of Rio Grande do Sul, similar to Candomblé
Boiadeiros	spirits of cowboys from the north-eastern hinterland of Brazil
Caboclo	rural settler in Northern Brazil; in the religions here described: spiritual entity that represents Brazilian indigenous people
Candomblé Angola	variation of Candomblé with a preference for Bantu influences
Candomblé Jeje	variation of Candomblé, developed in Bahia
Ciganos	spirits of gypsies
crianças	spirits of deceased children
Ebó	sacrifice
Egum	spirit of the dead
Encantados	spiritual entities
encostos	disturbances connected to the spirits of the dead
evangélico	evangelical Christian
Exu	male messenger between *orixás* and humans with ambivalent reputation, partly due to a link to Satan inflicted on the figure by Christian missionaries
filha de santo [female] / filho de santo [male]	a person initiated into an Afro–Brazilian religion
guia	guide, spiritual entity regarded as a spiritual protector
ialorixá	see mãe de santo
Iemaná [Yemanya]	female deity of African origin, usually regarded as mother of the *orixás*, also seen as goddess of the ocean

Ifá	Yoruba divination ritual
jogo de búzios	divination technique of African origin during which a priest or priestess uses shells to determine the destiny of a person
Macumba	Afro–Brazilian tradition, developed in Rio de Janeiro, similar to Umbanda
mãe de santo	priestess in an Afro–Brazilian religion
marinheiros	spirits of sailors and fishermen
obrigação	ritual offering to the deities or other types of spiritual entities
obsessão	spiritual disturbance
ogã	position of someone who does not experience any form of possession or trance but nonetheless occupies a relatively high position within the community and assists the priest or priestess
Ogum	male deity of African origin, usually regarded as the *orixá* of war and fire
orixás	divine entities of Afro–Brazilian religions
Oxum	female deity of African origin, usually regarded in Brazil as the goddess of sweet water (such as rivers and lakes)
pai de santo	priest in an Afro–Brazilian religion
Pombagira [also written pomba gira]	female equivalent to Exu
preto velho	spirits of old black slaves and runaways
Tambor de Mina	Afro–Brazilian tradition, developed in the area of Maranhão and Pará, the term 'mina' refers to a fortress in West Africa (São Jorge da Mina) from which enslaved Africans were shipped to Brazil during the trans-Atlantic slave trade
terreiro	location of an Afro–Brazilian tradition where ceremonies are performed, used often as synonym for the community
Xambá	Afro–Brazilian tradition, developed in Pernambuco, similar to Candomblé but with a stronger preference for Bantu influences
Xangô	1) deity of African origin, derived from the figure of the king of Oyó, a West African Yoruba kingdom; 2) Afro–Brazilian tradition, developed in Pernambuco, similar to Candomblé
Yalorixa	see mãe de santo

Bibliography

Alcide, M.-J. (1988). 'Theatrical and Dramatic Elements of Haitian Voodoo', PhD thesis, City University of New York.

Alencar, G. (2005). *Protestantismo Tupiniquium: Hipóteses sobre a (não) contribuição ão evangélica à cultura brasileira*. São Paulo: Arte Editoral.

Alexander, B. C. (1989). 'Pentecostal Ritual Reconsidered: Anti-structural Dimensions of Possession', *Journal of Ritual Studies* 3 (1): 109–28.

Almeida, R. de. (2003). 'A Guerra dos Possessões', in A. P. Oro, A. Corten and J.-P. Dozon (eds), *Igreja Universal do Reino de Deus: Os Novos Conquestadores da Fé*. São Paulo: Paulinas, 321–42.

Arhapiagha, Y. [Neto, F. Rivas]. (2003). *Sacerdote, Mago e Médico: Cura e Autocura Umbandista; Terapia da Alma*. São Paulo: Icone.

Asad, T. (1993). *Genealogies of Religion: Discipline and Reasons of Power in Christianity and Islam*. Baltimore: Johns Hopkins University Press.

Baron-Cohen, S. (2000). 'Theory of Mind and Autism: A Fifteen Year Review', in S. Baron-Cohen, H. Tager-Flusberg and D. J. Cohen (eds), *Understanding Other Minds: Perspectives from Developmental Cognitive Neuroscience*. Oxford: Oxford University Press, 3–20.

Baron-Cohen, S. (2003). *The Essential Difference: The Truth about the Male and Female Brain*. New York: Basic Books.

Barrett, J. (2004). *Why Would Anyone Believe in God?* Walnut Creek: Alta Mira Press.

Barros, J. F. P. de and M. L. L. Teixeira. (2004). 'O Código do Corpo: Inscrições e Marcos dos Orixás', in Carlos Eugênio Marcondes de Moura (ed.), *Candomblé: Religião do Corpo e da Alma: Tipos psicológicos nas religiões afro-brasileiros*. Rio de Janeiro: Pallos, 103–38.

Bastide, R. (1975). 'La Rencontre des Diex Africanins et des Spirits Indiens', in R. Bastide, *Le Sacré Sauvage, et Autres Essays*. Paris: Payot.

Bastide, R. (1978 [1960]). *The African Religions of Brazil: Toward a Sociology of the Interpretation of Civilizations*. Baltimore: Johns Hopkins University Press.

Bastide, R. (2007 [1960]). *The African Religions of Brazil: Toward a Sociology of the Interpretation of Civilizations (supplemented with a biographical foreword by Richard Price and a thematic introduction by Brazilian sociologist Duglas*

T. Monteiro). Baltimore: Johns Hopkins University Press. Bateson, G. (2000 [1972]). *Steps towards an Ecology of Mind*. Chicago: University of Chicago Press.

Beauregard, M. and V. Paquette. (2006). 'Neural Correlates of a Mystical Experience in Carmelite Nuns', *Neuroscience Letters* 405: 186–90.

Berkenbrock, V. J. (1998). *A experiência dos Orixás: um estudo sobrea experiência religiosa no Candomblé*. Petrópolis: Ed. Vozes.

Birman, P. (1995). *Fazer estilo criando géneros: possessão e diferenças de género em terreiros de Umbanda e Candomblé no Rio de Janeiro*. Rio de Janeiro: Relume Dumaná.

Birman, P. (1996). 'Cultos de possessão e pentecostalismo no Brasil: passagens', *Religião e Sociedade* 17 (1–2): 90–109.

Birman, P. and D. Lehmann. (1999). 'Religion and the Media in a Battle for Ideological Hegemony: The Universal Church of the Kingdom of God and TV Globo in Brazil', *Bulletin Latin American Research* 18 (2): 145–64.

Bloch, M. (2006). 'Deference', in J. Kreinath, J. Snoek and M. Stausberg (eds), *Theorizing Rituals: Issues, Topics, Approaches, Concepts*. Leiden and Boston: Brill, 495–506.

Boddy, J. (1989). *Wombs and their Spirits: Women, Men and the Zar Cult in Northern Sudan*. Madison: University of Wisconsin Press.

Boddy, J. (1994). 'Spirit Possession Revisited: Beyond Instrumentality', *Annual Review of Anthropology* 23: 407–34.

Bourdieu, P. (1977). *Outline of a Theory of Practice*. London: Cambridge University Press.

Bourguignon, E. (1968). *A Cross-Cultural Study of Dissociational States*. Columbus: Research Foundation.

Bourguignon, E. (1973). 'An Assessment of Some Comparisons and Implications', in E. Bourguignon (ed.), *Religion, Altered States of Consciousness, and Social Change*. Columbus: Ohio University Press, 321–39.

Bourguignon, E. (1976). *Possession*. San Francisco: Chandler & Sharp.

Bourguignon, E. (2004). 'Suffering and Healing, Subordination and Power: Women and Possession Practice', *Ethos* 32 (4): 557–74.

Bourguignon, E., A. Bellisari and S. McCabe. (1983). 'Women, Possession Trance Cults, and the Extended Nutrient-Deficiency Hypothesis', *American Anthropologist* 85 (2): 413–14.

Bowie, F. (2002). *Belief or Experience? The Anthropologists' Dilemma*. (2nd Series Occasional Paper 33). Lampeter: RERC.

Bowie, F. (2006). *The Anthropology of Religion: An Introduction*. 2nd ed. Oxford: Blackwell.

Bowie, F. (2012). 'Material and Immaterial Bodies: Ethnographic Reflections on a Trance Séance' (unpublished paper), Available online: https://kcl.academia.edu/FionaBowie/Papers (accessed on 11 December 2012).

Bowie, F. (2013). 'Building Bridges, Dissolving Boundaries: Towards a Methodology for the Ethnographic Study of the Afterlife, Mediumship, and Spiritual Beings', *Journal of the American Academy of Religion* 81 (3): 698–733.

Brown, D. (1986). *Umbanda: Religion and Politics in Urban Brazil*. Ann Arbor: UMI Research Press.

Brown, D. D. G. and M. Bick. (1987). 'Religion, Class, and Context: Continuities and Discontinuities in Brazilian Umbanda', *American Ethnologist* 14 (1): 73–93.

Brown, K. M. (1987). 'Alourdes: A Case Study of Moral Leadership in Haitian Vodou', in J. S. Hawley (ed.), *Saints and Virtues*. Berkeley: University of California, 144–67.

Brown, K. M. (2001). *Mama Lola: A Vodou Priestess in Brooklyn*. Updated and expanded edition. Berkeley: University of California Press.

Bush, B. (1990). *Slave Women in Caribbean Society, 1650–1838*. Bloomington: Indiana University Press.

Bush-Slimani, B. (1993). 'Hard Labour: Women, Childbirth and Resistance in British Caribbean Slave Societies', *History Workshop* 36: 83–99.

Cabrera, L. (1954). *El Monte*. Miami: Ediciones Universal.

Camara, E. (1997). *The Cultural One or the Racial Many: Religion, Culture and the Interethnic Experience*. Aldershot: Ashgate.

Camara, E. M. (1988). 'Afro-American Religious Syncretism in Brazil and the United States: A Weberian Perspective', *Sociological Analysis* 48 (4): 299–318.

Camargo, C. P. (1973). *Católicos, Protestantes, Espíritas*. Petrópolis: Editora Vozes.

Capone, S. (1999). *La Quête de l'Afrique dans le Candomblé: Pouvoir et Tradition au Brésil*. Paris: Editions Karthala.

Capone, S. (2010). *Searching for Africa in Brazil: Power and Tradition in Candomblé*. Durham and London: Duke University Press.

Carneiro, E. (1940). 'The Structure of African Cults in Bahia', *Journal of American Folklore* 53: 271–78.

Carneiro, E. (1964). *Ladinos e Crioulos: Estudos Sôbre o Negro no Brasil*. Rio de Janeiro: Editôra Civilização Brasileira.

Carvalho, G. O. (2000). 'The Politics of Indigenous Land Rights in Brazil', *Bulletin of Latin American Research* 19 (4): 461–78.

Cavalcanti, M. L. Viveiros de Castro. (1983). *O Mundo Invisível: cosmologia sistema ritual e noção da pessoa no Espiritismo*. Rio de Janeiro: Zahar.

Cavalcanti, M. L. Viveiros de Castro. (2006). 'Life and Death in Kardecist Spiritism', *Religion and Society* 1. (translated from *Religião e Sociedad* 24 (1) 2004: 168–73).

Chesnut, A. R. (1997). *Born Again in Brazil: The Pentecostal Boom and the Pathogens of Poverty.* New Brunswick: Rutgers University Press.

Chesnut, A. R. (2003). *Competitive Spirits: Latin America's New Religious Economy.* Oxford: Oxford University Press.

Clark, M. A. (2005). *Where Men are Wives and Mothers Rule.* Gainesville: University Press of Florida.

Clarke, P. B. (1998). 'Accounting for Recent Anti-Syncretist Trends in Candomblé-Catholic Relations', in P. B. Clarke (ed.), *New Trends and Developments in African Religions.* Westport: Greenwood Press, 17–36.

Cohen, E. (2007). *The Mind Possessed: The Cognition of Spirit Possession in an Afro-Brazilian Religious Tradition.* Oxford: Oxford University Press.

Concone, M. H. Villas Boas and L. Negrão. (1985). 'Umbanda: da Representação à Cooptação. O Envolvimento Político Partidário da Umbanda Paulista', in D. Brown et al. (eds), *Umbanda e Política.* Rio de Janeiro: Ed. Marco Zao, 43–79.

Corten, A., J.-P. Dozer and A. P. Oro. (2003). 'Introdução', in A. P. Oro, A. Corten and J.-P. Dozer (eds), *Igreja Universal do Reino de Deus: Os novos conquestadores da fé.* São Paulo: Paulinas, 13–45.

Crapanzano, V. (2005). 'Spirit Possession: An Overview', in L. Jones (ed.), *Encyclopedia of Religion.* 2nd ed. Detroit: Macmillan Reference USA, 8687–94.

Csordas, T. J. (1990). 'Embodiment as a Paradigm of Anthropology', *Ethos* 18 (1): 5–47.

Csordas, T. J. (1997). *The Sacred Self: A Cultural Phenomenology of Charismatic Healing.* Berkeley: University of California Press.

Da Matta, R. (1991). *Carnivals, Rogues, and Heroes: An Interpretation of the Brazilian Dilemma.* Notre Dame: University of Notre Dame Press.

Da Matta, R. (1995). 'For an Anthropology of the Brazilian Tradition; or "A virtude está no Meio"', in D. Hess and R. Da Matta (eds), *The Brazilian Puzzle: Culture on the Borderlands of the Western World.* New York: Columbia University Press, 270–91.

Dawson, A. (2007). *New Era – New Religions: Religious Transformation in Contemporary Brazil.* Aldershot: Ashgate.

Dawson, A. (2010). 'Taking Possession of Santo Daime: The Growth of Umbanda within a Brazilian New Religion', in B. E. Schmidt and L. Huskinson (eds), *Spirit Possession and Trance: New Interdisciplinary Perspectives.* London: Continuum, 134–50.

Day, A. (2011). *Believing in Belonging: Belief and Social Identity in the Modern World.* Oxford: Oxford University Press.

Demerath, N. J. (2000). 'The Rise of "Cultural Religion" in European Christianity: Learning from Poland, Northern Ireland, and Sweden', *Social Compass* 47 (1): 127–39.

d'Andrade, R. G. (1995). *The Development of Cognitive Anthropology.* Cambridge: Cambridge University Press.

d'Aquili, E. and A. Newberg. (1999). *The Mystical Mind: Probing the Biology of Religious Experience.* Minneapolis: Fortress Press.

de Vries, H. (ed.) (2008). *Religion: Beyond a Concept.* New York: Fordham University Press.

Descartes, R. (1974 [1647]). 'La description du corps humain', in C. Adam and P. Tannery (eds), *Oeuvres de Descartes.* Paris: Vrin.

Dickie, M. A. S. (2007). *Religious Experience and Culture – Testing Possibilities* (Antropologia em Primeira Mão, 1). Florianópolis: Universidade Federal de Santa Catarina.

Donovan, J. M. (2000). 'A Brazilian Challenge to Lewis's Explanation of Cult Mediumship', *Journal of Contemporary Religion* 15 (3): 361–77.

Droogers, A. (1987). 'A Religiosidade Minima Brasileira', *Religião e Sociodade* 14 (2): 62–86.

Eliade, M. (1989 [1964]) *Shamanism: Archaic Techniques of Ecstasy.* London: Penguin Books.

Engler, S. (2009a). 'Ritual Theory and Attitudes to Agency in Brazilian Spirit Possession', *Method and Theory in the Study of Religions* 21: 460–92.

Engler, S. (2009b). 'Umbanda and Hybridity', *Numen* 56: 545–77.

Engler, S. (2011). 'Other Religions as Social Problem: The Universal Church of the Kingdom of God and Afro-Brazilian Traditions', in T. Hjelm (ed.), *Religion and Social Problems.* New York: Routledge, 213–24.

Evans-Pritchard, E. E. (1976 [1937]). *Witchcraft, Oracles and Magic among the Azande.* Abridged edition. Oxford: Clarendon Press.

Evans-Pritchard, E. E. (1940). *The Nuer.* Oxford: Oxford University Press.

Fabian, J. (2001). *Anthropology with an Attitude: Critical Essays.* Stanford, CA: Stanford University Press.

Fabian, J. (2002). *Time and the Other: How Anthropology Makes Its Object.* 2nd ed. New York: Columbia University Press.

Fales, E. (1996). 'Scientific Explanations of Mystical Experiences. Part 1: The Case of St. Teresa', *Religious Studies* 32: 143–63.

Fenwick, P. (2001). 'The Neurophysiology of Religious Experience', in I. Clarke (ed.), *Psychosis and Spirituality.* London: Whurr, 15–26.

Ferretti, M. (1998). 'Non-African Spiritual Entities in Afro-Brazilian Religion and African Amerindian Syncretism', in P. B. Clarke (ed.), *New Trends and Developments in African Religions*. Westport: Greenwood Press, 37–44.

Firth, C. (2007). *Making up the Mind: How the Brain Creates Our Mental World*. Oxford: Blackwell.

Firth, R. (1959). 'Problem and Assumption in an Anthropological Study of Religion', *The Journal of the Royal Anthropological Institute of Great Britain and Ireland* 89 (2): 129–48.

Fitzgerald, T. (2010). '"Experiences Deemed Religious": Radical Critique or Temporary Fix? Strategic Ambiguity in Ann Taves' *Religious Experience Reconsidered*', *Religion* 40 (4): 296–9.

Franks-Davis, C. (1989). *The Evidential Force of Religious Experience*. Oxford: Clarendon Press.

Freyre, G. (1956 [1933]). *The Masters and the Slaves (Casa-grande & Senzala): A Study in the Development of Brazilian Civilization*. New York: Knopf.

Fry, P. (1978). 'Manchester e Sao Paulo: industrializacao e religiosidade popular', *Religião e Sociedade* 3: 25–52. [English version published in J. D. Wirth and R. Jones (eds), *Manchester and São Paulo: Problems of Rapid Urban Growth*. Stanford: Stanford University Press, 1978].

Gebara, I. (1999). '*A Recusa do Sincretismo Como Afirmação da Liberdade*', in C. Martins and R. Lody (eds), *Faraimará – O Caçador traz Alegria: Mãe Stella, 60 Anos de Iniciação*. Rio de Janeiro: Pallas.

Geertz, A. W. (2010). 'Brain, Body and Culture: A Biocultural Theory of Religion', *Method and Theory in the Study of Religion* 22: 304–21.

Geertz, A. W. (2011). 'Religious Narrative, Cognition and Culture: Approaches and Defintions', in A. E. Geertz and J. S. Jensen (eds), *Religious Narrative, Cognition and Culture: Image and Word in the Mind of Narrative*. Sheffield: Equinox, 9–30.

Geertz, A. W. and J. S. Jensen. (2011). 'Introduction', in A. E. Geertz and J. S. Jensen (eds), *Religious Narrative, Cognition and Culture: Image and Word in the Mind of Narrative*. Sheffield: Equinox, 1–7.

Geertz, C. (1973). *The Interpretation of Cultures: Selected Essays*. New York: Basic Books.

Gifford, P. (1998). *African Christianity: Its Public Role*. London: Hurst.

Gold, A. G. (1988). 'Spirit Possession Perceived and Performed in Rural Rajasthan', *Contributions to Indian Sociology* 22 (1): 35–63.

Goldman, M. (1985). 'A construção ritual da pessoa: a possessão no Candomblé', *Religião e Sociedade* 12 (1): 22–55.

Goldman, M. (2007). 'How to Learn in an Afro-Brazilian Spirit Possession Religion: Ontology and Multiplicity in Candomblé', in D. Berliner and

R. Sarró (eds), *Learning Religion: Anthropological Approaches*. New York and Oxford: Berghahn Books, 103–19.

Goodman, F. D. (1988). *How about Demons? Possession and Exorcism in the Modern World*. Bloomington: Indiana University Press.

Greenfield, S. M. (2008). *Spirits with Scalpels: The Culturalbiology of Religious Healing in Brazil*. Walnut Creek: Left Coast Press.

Greenfield, S. M. and A. M. Calvacante. (2006). 'Pilgrimage and Patronage in Brazil: A Paradigm for Social Relations and Religious Diversity', *Luso-Brazilian Review* 43 (2): 63–89.

Greenfield, S. M. and A. Droogers. (2003). 'Synrectic Processes and the Definition of New Religions', *Journal of Contemporary Religion* 18 (1): 25–36.

Greenfield, S. M. and R. Prust. (1990). 'Popular Religion, Patronage, and Resource Distribution in Brazil: A Model of an Hypothesis for the Survival of the Economically Marginal', in M. E. Smith (ed.), *Perspectives on the Informal Economy*. Lanham: University Press of America, 123–46.

Halperin, D. (1996). 'From Guilt to Gaya Scienza', *Anthropology Newsletter* 37 (2): 4.

Harding, R. E. (2000). *A Refuge in Thunder: Candomblé and Alternative Spaces of Blackness*. Bloomington: Indiana University Press.

Harding, R. E. (2005). 'Afro-Brazilian Religions', in L. Jones (ed.), *Encyclopedia of Religion, vol. 1*. 2nd ed. Farmington Hills: Thomson Gale, 119–25.

Hardy, A. (1979). *The Spiritual Nature of Man*. Oxford: Clarendon.

Hay, D. (1982). *Exploring Inner Space: Scientists and Experience*. Harmondsworth: Penguin Books.

Hayes, K. E. (2006). 'Caught in the Cross Fire: Considering the Limits of Spirit Possession; A Brazilian Case Study', *Culture and Religion* 7 (2): 155–75.

Hayes, K. E. (2010). 'Serving the Spirits, Healing the Person: Women in Afro-Brazilian Religions', in L. Ashcraft-Eason, D. C. Martin and O. Olademo (eds), *Women and New and Africana Religions*. Santa Barbara: Greenwood, 101–22.

Hayes, K. E. (2011). *Holy Harlots: Femininity, Sexuality, and Black Magic in Brazil*. Berkeley: University of California Press.

Hemming, J. (2001). 'Foreword', in C. McEwan, C. Barretto and E. Neves (eds), *Unknown Amazon: Culture in Nature in Ancient Brazil*. London: British Museum Press.

Herskovits, M. (1948). 'Review of The City of Women', *American Anthropologist* 50: 123–5.

Hess, D. J. (1991). *Spirits and Scientists: Ideology, Spiritism, and Brazilian Culture*. University Park: Pennsylvania State University Press.

Hofbauer, A. (2006). *Uma história de branqueamento ou o negro em questao*. SP: Ed. Unesp.

Horton, R. (1994). *Pattern of Thoughts in Africa and the West.*
　　Cambridge: Cambridge University Press.

Huskinson, L. (2010). 'Analytical Psychology and Spirit Possession: Towards
　　a Non-Pathological Diagnosis of Spirit Possession', in B. E. Schmidt and
　　L. Huskinson (eds), *Spirit Possession and Trance: New Interdisciplinary*
　　Perspectives (Continuum Advances in Religious Studies series).
　　London: Continuum, 71–96.

Huskinson, L. and B. E. Schmidt. (2010). 'Introduction', in B. E. Schmidt and
　　L. Huskinson (eds), *Spirit Possession and Trance: New Interdisciplinary*
　　Perspectives (Continuum Advances in Religious Studies series).
　　London: Continuum, 1–15.

Jahn, J. (1961). *Muntu: African Culture and the Western World.* New York: Grove
　　Weidenfeld.

James, A. and A. Wells. (2003). 'Religion and Mental Health: Towards a Cognitive-
　　Behavioural Framework', *British Journal of Health Psychology* 8: 359–76.

James, W. (2008). *The Varieties of Religious Experience: A Study of Human Nature.*
　　(Reprint) Rockwill: Arc Manor.

James, W. and H. James. (2008). *The Letters of William James. Two Volumes*
　　Combined. (Reprint of the 1920 edition). New York: Cosimo.

Jensen, J. S. (2011). 'Framing Religious Narrative, Cognition and Culture
　　Theoretically', in A. E. Geertz and J. S. Jensen (eds), *Religious Narrative,*
　　Cognition and Culture: Image and Word in the Mind of Narrative.
　　Sheffield: Equinox, 31–50.

Jensen, T. G. (1999). 'Discourses on Afro-Brazilian Religion: From De-
　　Africanization to Re-Africanization', in C. Smith and Jo. Prokopy (eds), *Latin*
　　American Religion in Motion. New York: Routledge, 275–94.

Johnson, P. (2002). *Secrets, Gossip, and Gods: The Transformation of Brazilian*
　　Candomblé. Oxford: Oxford University Press.

Johnson, P. (2011). 'An Atlantic Genealogy of "Spirit Possession"', *Comparative*
　　Studies in Society and History 53 (2): 393–425.

Kardec, A. (1857). *Le Livre des Esprits.* Paris. [Various English translations available,
　　e.g., *The Spirits' Book.* New York: Cosimo, 2006].

Kay, W. (2005). 'Angelology in Pentecostalism', Tyndale Lecture at the Religion,
　　Culture and Communication Study Group, 11–13 July, 2005.

Keinan, G. (1994). 'Effects of Stress and Tolerance of Ambiguity on Magical
　　Thinking', *Journal of Personality and Social Psychology* 67: 48–55.

Keller, M. (2002). *The Hammer and the Flute: Women, Power, & Spirit Possession.*
　　Baltimore: John Hopkins University Press.

Keller, M. (2005). 'Spirit Possession: Women and Possession', in L. Jones (ed.), *Encyclopedia of Religion*. 2nd ed. Detroit: Macmillan Reference USA, 8694–9.

Klass, M. (1995). *Ordered Universes: Approaches to the Anthropology of Religion*. Boulder: Westview.

Klass, M. (2003). *Mind over Mind: The Anthropology and Psychology of Spirit Possession*. Lanham: Rowman & Littlefield.

Koepping, K.-P. (1983). *Adolf Bastian and the Psychic Unity of Mankind*. St Lucia: University of Queensland Press.

Kramer, E. W. (2005). 'Spectacle and the Staging of Power in Brazilian Neo-Pentecostalism', *Latin American Perspectives* 32 (1): 95–120.

Krippner, S. (1989). 'A Call to Heal: Entry Patterns in Brazilian Mediumship', in C. A. Ward (ed.), *Altered States of Consciousness and Mental Health: A Cross-Cultural Perspective*. Newbury Park, CA: Sage Publications, 186–206.

Kuhn, T. (1970). *The Structure of Scientific Revolution*. 2nd ed. Chicago: University of Chicago Press.

Kunin, S. (2003). *Religion: The Modern Theories*. Edinburgh: Edinburgh University Press.

Lambek, M. (1989). 'From Disease to Discourse: Remarks on the Conceptualization of Trance and Spirit Possession', in C. A. Ward (ed.), *Altered States of Consciousness and Mental Health*. Newbury Park: Sage Publication, 36–61.

Lambek, M. (1996). 'Afterward: Spirits and Their Histories', in J. M. Mageo and A. Howard (eds), *Spirits in Culture, History, and Mind*. New York: Routledge, 237–50.

Lambek, M. (2008). 'Provincializing God? Provocations from an Anthropology of Religion', in H. de Vries (ed.), *Religion: Beyond a Concept*. New York: Fordham University Press, 120–38.

Landes, R. (1947). *The City of Women*. New York: Macmillan.

Leacock, S. and R. Leacock. (1972). *Spirits of the Deep: A Study of an Afro-Brazilian Cult*. Garden City, NY: Doubleday Natural History Press.

Lehman, D. (2001). 'Charisma and Possession in Africa and Brazil', *Theory, Culture and Society* 18 (5): 45–74.

Lerch, P. (1982). 'An Explanation for the Predominance of Women in the Umbanda Cults of Porto Alegre, Brazil', *Urban Anthropology* 11 (2): 237–61.

Lewgoy, B. (2006). 'O sincretismo invisível: um olhar sobre as relações entre catolicismo e espiritismo no Brasil', in A. C. Isaia (ed.), *Orixás e Espíritos: o debate interdisciplinar na pequisa contemporânea*. Uberlândia: EDUFU, 209–24.

Lewis, I. M. (1966). 'Spirit Possession and Deprivation Cults', *Man* 1 (3): 307–29.

Lewis, I. M. (1967). 'Spirits and the Sex War', *Man* 2 (4): 626–8.

Lewis, I. M. (1971). *Ecstatic Religion: A Study of Shamanism and Spirit Possession.* London: Routledge.

Lewis, I. M. (1989 [1971]). *Ecstatic Religion: A Study of Shamanism and Spirit Possession.* London: Routledge.

Lewis, I. M. (2003 [1971]). *Ecstatic Religion: A Study of Shamanism and Spirit Possession.* 3rd ed. London: Routledge.

Lewis, I. M. (1983). 'Spirit Possession and Biological Reductionism', *American Anthropologist* 85: 412–13.

Lewis, I. M. (1991). 'Introduction: Zar in Context: The Past, the Present and the Future of an African Healing Cult', in I. M. Lewis, A. Al-Sa and S. Hurreiz (eds), *Women's Medicine: The Zar-Bori Cult in Africa and Beyond.* Edinburgh: Edinburgh University Press, 1–16.

Littlewood, R. (1993). *Pathology and Identity: The Work of Mother Earth in Trinidad.* Cambridge: Cambridge University Press.

Littlewood, R. and M. Lipsedge. (1989). *Aliens and Alienists: Ethnic Minorities and Psychiatry.* London: Unwin Hyman.

Long, C. (1986). *Significations.* Philadelphia: Fortress Press.

Macedo, E. (1996 [1988]). *Orixás, caboclos & guías: deuses ou demônios?* Rio de Janeiro: Ed. Universal.

Machado, F. R. (2009). 'Experiências Anômalas na Vida Cotidiana: Experiências extra-sensório-motoras e sua associação com crenças, attitudes e bem-estar subjetivo', PhD thesis, São Paulo: USP.

Maggie, Y. (1986). 'O medo do feitiço – verdades e mentiras sobre a repressão às religiões mediúnicas', *Religião e Sociedade* 13 (1): 72–86.

Malandrino, B. C. (2006). *Umbanda: Mudanças e Permanencies. Uma Análise Simbólica.* São Paulo: Ed. PUC-SP.

Mariano, R. (1995). 'Neo Pentecostalismo: os pentecostais estão mudando', MPhil thesis, São Paulo: USP [later published under the title *Neopentecostais: sociologia do novo pentecostalismo no Brasil.* São Paulo: Ed. Loyola, 1999].

Mariano, R. (2001). 'Análise sociológica do crescimento pentecostal no Brasil', PhD thesis, São Paulo: USP.

Mariz, C. L. (1994). *Coping with Poverty: Pentecostals and Christian Base Communities in Brazil.* Philadelphia: Temple University Press.

Martins, C. and R. Lody (eds) (1999). *Faraimará–O caçador traz alegria. Mãe Stella, 60 anos de iniciação.* Rio de Janeiro: Pallas.

Mason, M. A. (1994). '"I Bow My Head to the Ground": The Creation of Bodily Experience in a Cuban American Santería Initiation', *The Journal of American Folklore* 107 (423): 23–39.

Matory, J. L. (1993). 'Government by Seduction: History and the Tropes of "Mounting" in Oyo-Yoruba Religion', in J. Comaroff and J. Comaroff (eds), *Modernity and Its Malcontents*. Chicago: University of Chicago Press, 58–85.

Matory, J. L. (1999). '*The English Professors of Brazil: On the Diasporic Roots of the Yoruba Nation*', *Comparative Studies in Society and History* 41 (1): 72–103.

Matory, J. L. (2005). *Black Atlantic Religion: Tradition, Transnationalism, and Matriarchy in the Afro-Brazilian Candomblé*. Princeton: Princeton University Press.

McCutcheon, R. T. (1997). *Manufacturing Religion. The Discourse on Sui Generis Religion and the Politics of Nostalgia*. Oxford: Oxford University Press.

Merleau-Ponty, M. (1962). *The Phenomenology of Perception*. Evanston: Northwestern University Press.

Métraux, A. (1959). *Voodoo in Haiti*, translated by Hugh Charteris. New York: Oxford University Press.

Meyer, B. (1999). *Translating the Devil: Religion and Modernity among the Ewe in Ghana*. Edinburgh: Edinburgh University Press.

Michtom, M. (1980). 'Becoming a Medium: The Role of Trance in Puerto Rican Spiritism as an Avenue to Mazeway Resynthesis', PhD thesis, New York University.

Miller, A. S. and J. P. Hoffmann. (1995). 'Risk and Religion: An Explanation of Gender Differences in Religiosity', *Journal for the Scientific Study of Religion* 34 (1): 63–75.

Montoya, S. (2003). 'Disonancias Rituals: Curupira y la ambigüidad', *Indiana* 19/20: 99–109.

Motta, R. (1998). 'The Churchifying of Candomblé: Priests, Anthropologists, and the Canonization of the African Religious Memory in Brazil', in P. B. Clarke (ed.), *New Trends and Developments in African Religions*. Westport: Greenwood, 47–57.

Motta, R. (2005). 'Body Trance and Word Trance in Brazilian Religion', *Current Sociology* 53 (2): 293–308.

Münzel, M. (1994). 'The Researcher as Shaman: Field-work between Musty Mystification and True Enchantment', *Anthropology and Ethics* 3 (2): 133–53.

Münzel, M. (1997). 'Tanz als Verehrung der Götter oder Verhöhnung der Geister: Ein Vergleich afrobrasilianischer und amazonasindianischer Tänze', *Jahrbuch Tanzforschung* 8: 150–61.

Negrão, L. N. (1996). *Entre a Cruz e a Encruzilhada: Formação do Campo Umbandista em São Paulo*. São Paulo: Edusp.

Neto, N. L., Brooks, S. and R. Alves. (2009). 'From Eshu to Obatala: Animals Used in Sacrificial Rituals at Candomblé "terreiros" in Brazil', *Journal of Ethnobiology and Ethnomedicine* 5 (23). Available online: http://www.ethnobiomed.com/content/5/1/23 (accessed on 11 December 2012).

Nugent, S. (1993). *Amazonian Caboclo Society: An Essay on Invisibility and Peasant Economy.* Providence and Oxford: Berg.

Olajuba, O. (2005). 'Gender and Religion: Gender and African Religious Traditions', in L. Jones (ed.), *Encyclopedia of Religion.* 2nd ed. Detroit: Macmillan Reference USA, 3400–406.

Oliva, M. M. C. (1995). 'Ação Diabólica e Exorcismo: Na Igreja Universal do Reino de Deus', MPhil thesis, São Paulo: PUC.

Oliveira, I. X. de. (1998). 'Ação pastoral da Igreja Universal do Reino de Deus: Uma Evangelizacão inculturada?', MPhil thesis, São Paulo: PUC.

Oliveira, J. H. M. de. (2007). 'Entre a Macumba e o Espiritismo: uma análise comparativa das estratégias de legitimação da Umbanda durante o Estado Novo', MPhil thesis, Rio de Janeiro: Universidade Federal do Rio de Janeiro.

Oro, A. P. (2003). 'A política da Igreja Universal e seus reflexos nos campos religioso e político brasileiro', *Revista brasileira de Ciências Sociais* 18 (53): 53–69.

Oro, A. P. (2006a). 'The Sacrifice of Animals in Afro-Brazilian Religions: Analysis of a Recent Controversy in the Brazilian State of Rio Grande do Sul', *Religião e Sociedade* 1 no. se: 1–14 [original article in Portuguese published in *Religião e Sociedade* 25 (2), 2005].

Oro, A. P. (2006b). 'O neopentecostalismo "macumbeiro"', in A. C. Isaia (ed.), *Orixás e Espíritos: o debate interdisciplinar na pequisa contemporânea.* Uberlândia: EDUFU, 115–28.

Ortiz, F. (1906). *Los Negros Brujos.* Miami: Edicioned Universal.

Otto, R. (1936 [1917]) *The Idea of the Holy.* Oxford: Oxford University Press.

Oyêwùmí, O. (1997). *The Invention of Women: Making an African Sense of Western Gender Discourses.* Minneapolis: University of Minnesota Press.

Palmisano, A. L. (2003). 'Trance and Translation in the Zar Cult of Ethiopia', in T. Maranhão and B. Streck (eds), *Translation and Ethnography.* Tucson: University of Arizona Press, 135–51.

Pálsson, G. (1993). 'Introduction: Beyond Boundaries', in G. Pálsson (ed.), *Beyond Boundaries: Understanding, Translation and Anthropological Discourse.* Oxford: Berg, 1–40.

Parés, L. N. (2006). *A formação do Candomblé: História e ritual da nação jeje na Bahia.* Campinas, SP: Editora da UNICAMP.

Peres, J. F. et al. (2012). 'Neuroimaging during Trance State: A Contribution to the Study of Dissociation', *PLOS ONE* 7 (11): e49360. doi:10.1371/journal.pone.0049360.

Pérez García, M. (1988). 'Spiritism: Historical Development in France and Puerto Rico', *Revista/Review Interamericana* 16 (1–4): 67–76.

Perler, D. (2002). 'Descartes' Transformation des Personenbegriffs', in. K.-P. Köpping et al. (eds), *Die autonome Person – eine europäische Erfindung?* München: Fink, 141–61.

Pierucci, A. F. (2004). ' "Bye bye, Brasil" – O declínio das religiões tradicionais no Censo 2000', *Estudos Avançados* 18 (52): 17–28.

Pierucci, A. F. and R. Prandi. (1996). *A realidade social das religiões no Brasil: Religião, sociedade e política.* São Paulo: Ed. Hucitec.

Pierucci, A. F. and R. Prandi. (1998). 'Introdução: As religiões na Brasil contemporâneo', in R. Prandi, *Un sopro do Espírito: a renovação conservadora do Catclicisimo carismático.* São Paulo: edUSP, 13–26.

Pimentel, F. da Silva. (2005). 'Quando Psiquê se liberta de Demônio – um estudo sobre a relação entre exorcismo e cura psíquica em mulheres na Igreja Universal do Reino de Deus', MPhil thesis, São Paulo: PUC.

Platvoet, J. (2000). 'Rattray's Request: Spirit Possession among the Bono of West Africa', in G. Harvey (ed.), *Indigenous Religions: A Companion.* London: Cassell, 80–96.

Prandi, R. (1998). *Un sopro do Espírito: a renovação conservadora do Catclicisimo carismático.* São Paulo: edUSP.

Prandi, R. (2001). *Os Candomblés de São Paulo: A velha magia na metrópole nova.* São Paulo: Ed. Hucitec.

Prandi, R. (2005). *Segredos Guardados: Orixás na Alma Brasileira.* São Paulo: Companhia dass Letras.

Pressel, E. (1973). 'Umbanda in Sao Paulo: Religious Innovation in a Developing Society', in E. Bourguignon (ed.), *Religion, Altered States of Consciousness, and Social Change.* Columbus: Ohio State University Press, 264–318.

Pressel, E. (1977). 'Negative Spirit Possession in Experienced Brazilian Umbanda Spirit Mediums', in V. Crapanzano and V. Garrison (eds), *Case Studies in Spirit Possession.* New York: Wiley, 333–64.

Pressel, E. (1982). 'Umbanda Trance and Possession in São Paulo, Brazil', in F. Goodman, J. H. Henney and E. Pressel (eds), *Trance, Healing, and Hallucination: Three Field Studies in Religious Experience.* New York: John Wiley, 113–225.

Prokopy, J. and C. Smith. (1999). 'Introduction', in C. Smith and J. Prokopy (eds), *Latin American Religion in Motion.* New York: Routledge, 1–16.

Proudfoot, W. (1985). *Religious Experience.* Berkeley: University of California Press.

Pyysiäinen, I. (2001). 'Cognition, Emotion, and Religious Experience', in J. Andresen (ed.), *Religion in Mind: Cognitive Perspectives on Religious Belief, Ritual, and Experience.* Cambridge: Cambridge University Press, 70–93.

Pyysiäinen, I. (2003). *How Religion Works: Towards a New Cognitive Science of Religion.* Leiden: Brill.

Pyysiäinen, I. (2008). 'After Religion: Cognitive Science and the Study of Human Behaviour', *II International Online Conference on Religious Studies: Comparative Religion – From Subject to Problem, 1 Oktober 2008.* Moscwa.

Radcliffe-Brown, A. R. (1940). 'On Social Structure', *Journal of the Royal Anthropological Institute* 70 (1): 1–12.

Radcliffe-Brown, A. R. (1952). *Structure and Function in Primitive Society: Essays and Addresses.* Glencoe: Free Press, 188–204.

Ribeiro, R. (1982). *Antropologia da religião e outros estudos.* Recife: Ed. Massangana.

Ribeiro, R. I. (no date). 'Oduduwa Templo dos Orixás: Território de entrelaçamento de religiões brasileiras de matrix Africana', *X Simpósio da Associação Brasileiro de História das Religiões (ABHR): Migrações e Imigrações das Religiões.*

Robbins, J. (2004). 'The Globalization of Pentecostal and Charismatic Christianity', *Annual Review of Anthropology* 33: 117–43.

Rodrígues Vázquez, E. (1994). 'El espiritismo en Puerto Rico es una inmensa telefónica metafísica', *III. International Symposium Afroamérica y su Cultura Religiosa in Rio Piedras, Puerto Rico.*

Rossi, E. (1993). *The Psychobiology of Mind-Body Healing.* New York: Norton.

Rouget, G. (1985). *Music and Trance: A Theory of the Relations Between Music and Possession.* Chicago: University of Chicago Press.

Saler, B. (2001). 'On What We may Believe about Beliefs', in J. Andresen (ed.), *Religion in Mind: Cognitive Perspectives on Religious Belief, Ritual, and Experience.* Cambridge: Cambridge University Press, 47–69.

Sansi, R. (2007). *Fetishes and Monuments: Afro-Brazilian Art and Culture in the 20th Century.* London: Berghahn Books.

Schleiermacher, F. (1999). *On Religion: Speeches to Its Cultured Despisers.* Grand Rapids: CCEL.

Schmidt, B. E. (1995). *Von Geistern, Orichas und den Puertoricanern: zur Verbindung von Religion und Ethnizität.* Marburg: Curupira.

Schmidt, B. E. (2000). 'Religious Concepts in the Process of Migration: Puerto Rican Female Spiritists in the USA', in J. Knörr and B. Meier (eds), *Women and Migration: Anthropological Perspectives.* New York/Frankfurt: Campus/St. Martin, 119–32.

Schmidt, B. E. (2002). 'Mambos, Mothers and Madrinas in New York City: Religion as a Means of Empowerment for Women from the Caribbean', *Wadabagei: A Journal of the Caribbean and its Diaspora* 5 (1): 75–104.

Schmidt, B. E. (2008). *Caribbean Diaspora in USA: Diversity of Caribbean Religions in New York City.* Aldershot: Ashgate.

Schmidt, B. E. (2009). 'Meeting the Spirits: Espiritismo as Source for Identity, Healing and Creativity', *Fieldwork in Religion* 3 (2): 178–95.

Schmidt, B. E. (2010). 'Possessed Women in the African Diaspora: Gender Difference in Spirit Possession Rituals', in B. E. Schmidt and L. Huskinson (eds), *Spirit Possession and Trance: New Interdisciplinary Perspectives.* London: Continuum, 97–116.

Schmidt, B. E. (2012). '"When the gods give us the power of ashé" – Afro-Caribbean Religions as Source for Creative Energy', in C. M. Cusack and A. Norman (eds), *Handbook of New Religions and Cultural Production.* (Brill Handbooks on Contemporary Religion series) The Hague: Brill, 445–61.

Schmidt, B. E. (2013a). 'The Spirit White Feather in São Paulo: The Resilience of Indigenous Spirits in Brazil', in J. Cox (ed.), *Critical Reflections on Indigenous Religions.* (Vitality of Indigenous Religions series). London: Ashgate, 123–41.

Schmidt, B. E. (2013b). 'Animal Sacrifice as Symbol of the Paradigmatic Other in the 21st Century: Ebó, the Offerings to African Gods, in the Americas', in J. Zachhuber and J. Meszaros (eds), *Sacrifice and Modern Thought.* Oxford: Oxford University Press, 197–213.

Schmidt, B. E. (2014a). 'Mediumship in Brazil: The Holy War against Spirits and African Gods', in J. Hunter and D. Luke (eds), *Talking With the Spirits: Ethnographies from Between the Worlds.* Brisbane: Daily Grail, 209–39.

Schmidt, B. E. (2014b). 'The Discourse about "Africa" in Religious Communities in Brazil: How Africa becomes the Ultimate Source of Authenticity in Afro-Brazilian religions', in A. Adogame (ed.), *The Public Face of African New Religious Movements in Diaspora: Imagining the Religious 'Other'.* London: Ashgate, 29–44.

Seligman, R. (2005). 'Distress, Dissociation, and Embodied Experience: Reconsidering the Pathways to Mediumship and Mental Health', *Ethos* 33 (1): 71–99.

Selka, S. (2009). 'Rural Women and the Varieties of Black Politics in Bahia, Brazil', *Journal of Black Women, Gender and Families* 3 (1): 16–38.

Sered, S. S. (1994). *Priestess, Mothers, Sacred Sisters: Religions Dominated by Women.* New York: Oxford University Press.

Sharf, R. H. (1998). 'Experience', in M. Taylor (ed.), *Critical Terms for Religious Studies.* Chicago: Chicago University Press, 94–116.

Sharpe, E. (2003). *Comparative Religion: A History.* London: Duckworth.

Sheets-Johnstone, M. (2009). *The Corporeal Turn: An Interdisciplinary Reader.* Exeter: Imprint Academic.

Silva, J. S. da. (1998). 'Caçadores de Demônios: demonização e exorcismo com método de evangelização na neopentecostalismo', Mphil thesis, São Paulo: PUC.

Silva, R. M. da. (2006). 'Chico Xavier: um bem simbólico nacional? Uma análise sobre a construção de imaginário espirita uberabense', in A. C. Isaia (ed.), *Orixás e Espíritos: o debate interdisciplinar na pesquisa contemporânea.* Uberlândia: EDUFU, 241–61.

Silva, V. Gonçalves da. (1994). *Candomblé e Umbanda: Caminhos da devoção brasileira.* São Paulo: Ed. Ática.

Silva, V. Gonçalves da. (1995). *Orixás da Metrópole.* Petrópolis: Vozes.

Silva, V. Gonçalves da. (2005). *Candomblé e Umbanda: Caminos da Devoção Brasileira.* 2nd ed. São Paulo: Selo Negro.

Silva, V. Gonçalves da. (2007). 'Neopentecostalismo e Religiões Afro-Brasileiras: Significados do Ataque aos Símbolos da Herança Religiosa Africana no Brasil Contemporâneo', *Mana* 13 (1): 207–36.

Sjørslev, I. (1999). *Glaube und Besessenheit: Ein Bericht über die Candomblé-Religion in Brasilien.* Gifkendorf: Merlin Verlag.

Sperber, D. (1996). *Explaining Culture: A Naturalistic Approach.* Oxford: Blackwell.

Stark, R. (2002). 'Physiology and Faith: Addressing the "Universal" Gender Difference in Religious Commitment', *Journal for the Scientific Study of Religion* 41 (3): 495–507.

Steedly, M. M. (1993). *Hanging without a Rope: Narrative Experience in Colonial and Postcolonial Karoland.* Princeton: Princeton University Press.

Stoll, S. J. (2002). 'Religião, ciência ou auto-ajuda? Trajetos do Espiritismo no Brasil', *Revista de Antropologia* 45 (2): 361–401.

Stoll, S. J. (2006). 'O espiritsmo na encruzilhada: mediunidade com fins lucrativos', in A. C. Isaia (ed.), *Orixás e Espíritos: o debate interdisciplinar na pequisa contemporânea.* Uberlândia: EDUFU, 263–78.

Stoll, S. J. (2009). 'Encenando o invisível: A construção da pessoa em ritos mediúnicos e performance de "auto-ajuda"', *Religião e Sociedade* 29 (1): 13–29.

Stoller, P. (1994). 'Embodying Colonial Memories', *American Anthropologist* 96 (3): 634–48.

Strawson, P. F. (1976). *Freedom and Resentment, and Other Essays.* London: Methuen.

Strenski, I. (1993). *Religion in Relation: Method, Application and Moral Location.* Basingstoke: MacMillan Press.

Tapié, V. (1972). *Baroque et Classicisme.* Paris: Plon.

Taves, A. (1999). *Fits, Trances, & Visions: Experiencing Religion and Explaining Experience from Wesley to James.* Princeton: Princeton University Press.

Taves, A. (2005). 'Experience', *Rever: Revista de Estudos da Religião* 4: 43–52.

Taves, A. (2009). *Religious Experience Reconsidered.* Princeton: Princeton University Press.

Teles dos Santos, J. (1995). *O Dano da Terra: O Caboclo nos Candomblés da Bahia*. Salvador: SarahLetras.

Terborg-Penn, R. (1996). 'African Feminism: A Theoretical Approach to the History of Women in the African Diaspora', in R. Terborg-Penn and A. B. Rushing (eds), *Women in Africa and the African Diaspora*. Washington, DC: Howard University Press, 3–42.

Thrower, J. (1999). *Religion: The Classic Theories*. Edinburgh: Edinburgh University Press.

Tiilikainen, M. (2010). 'Somali Saar in the Era of Social and Religious Change', in B. E. Schmidt and L. Huskinson (eds), *Spirit Possession and Trance: New Interdisciplinary Perspectives*. London: Continuum: 117–33.

Tremlin, T. (2006). *Minds and Gods: The Cognitive Foundation of Religion*. Oxford: Oxford University Press.

Turner, E. (1994). 'A Visible Spirit Form in Zambia', in J. Guy-Goulet (ed.), *Being Changed by Cross-Cultural Encounters: The Anthropology of Extraordinary Experience*. Peterborough, Ontario: Broadview, 71–95.

Turner, H. and P. Mackenzie. (No date) *Commentary on "The Idea of the Holy"*. Aberdeen: Aberdeen People's Press.

Turner, V. (1986). 'Dewey, Dilthey, and Drama: An Essay in the Anthropology of Experience', in V. Turner and E. M. Bruner (eds), *The Anthropology of Experience*. Chicago: University of Illinois Press, 33–44.

Van de Port, M. (2005). 'Circling around the Really Real: Spirit Possession Ceremonies and the Search for Authenticity in Bahian Candomblé', *Ethos* 33 (2): 149–79.

Vatin, X. (2005). *Rites et Musique de Possession à Bahia*. Paris: L'Harmattan.

Viveiros de Castro, E. (2004). 'Exchanging Perspectives: The Transformation of Objects into Subjects in Amerindian Ontologies', *Common Knowledge* 10 (3): 463–84.

Voss, E. (2011). 'The Struggle for Sovereignty: The Interpretation of Bodily Experiences in Anthropology and among Mediumistic Healers in Germany', in A. Fedele and R. Llera Blanes (eds), *Encounters of Body and Soul in Contemporary Religious Practices: Anthropological Reflections*. London: Berghahn, 168–78.

Wafer, J. W. (1991). *The Taste of Blood: Spirit Possession in Brazilian Candomblé*. Philadelphia: University of Pennsylvania Press.

Whitehouse, H. (1995). *Inside the Cult: Religious Innovation and Transmission in Papua New Guinea*. Oxford: Oxford University Press.

Whitehouse, H. (2000). *Arguments and Icons: Divergent Modes of Religiosity*. Oxford: Oxford University Press.

Whitehouse, H. (2002). 'Modes or Religiosity: Towards a Cognitive Explanation of the Sociopolitical Dynamics of Religion', *Method and Theory in the Study of Religion* 14: 293–315.

Whitehouse, H. (2004). *Modes or Religiosity: A Cognitive Theory of Religious Transmission in Papua New Guinea*. Walnut Creek: Alta Mira Press.

Whitehouse, H. (2005). 'The Cognitive Foundations of Religiosity', in H. Whitehouse and R. N. McCauley (eds), *Mind and Religion*. Walnut Creek: Alta Mira, 207–32.

Whitehouse, H. (2008). 'Cognitive Evolution and Religion: Cognition and Religious Evolution', in J. Bulbulia et al. (eds), *The Evolution of Religion*. Santa Margarita: Collins Foundation Press, 19–29.

Wilson, D. G. (2010). 'Waking the Entranced: Reassessing Spiritualist Mediumship through a Comparison of Spiritualist and Shamanic Spirit Possession Practices', in B. E. Schmidt and L. Huskinson (eds), *Spirit Possession and Trance: New Interdisciplinary Perspectives*. London: Continuum, 186–204.

Winant, H. (1992). 'Rethinking Race in Brazil', *Journal of Latin American Studies* 24: 173–92.

Zacharias, J. J. de Morais. (1998). *Ori Axé: A dimensão arquetípica dos Orixás*. São Paulo: Vetor Editora.

Zinnbauer, B. J. and K. I. Pargament. (1998). 'Spiritual Conversion: A Study of Religious Change among College Students', *Journal for the Scientific Study of Religion* 37 (1): 161–79.

Zittel, C. (2008). 'Menschenbilder/Maschinenbilder. Ein Bilderstreit um Descartes' De l'homme', *Deutsche Zeitschrift für Philosophie*, 56 (5): 709–44.

Zittel, C. (2009). *Theatrum philosophicum: Descartes und die Rolle ästhetischer Formen in der Wissenschaft*. Berlin: Akademie Verlag.

Index